2-10

Patterns
Teachers' guide 3

Schools Council Integrated Science Project

The Schools Council Integrated Science Project was set up at Chelsea College, London, from 1969 to 1975. The project team have developed their materials in association with many teachers and have tested them in a wide range of schools.

Organisers
W. C. Hall
B. S. Mowl

Team members
J. I. Bausor
Mrs M. P. Jarman
R. C. Landbeck
Miss B. A. Lawes
M. R. Nice
D. Wimpenny

Northern Ireland coordinator
S. J. McGuffin

Patterns
Teachers' guide 3
Energy

Authors
John Bausor
William Hall
Brian Mowl

Contributors
Michael Bradshaw
Roger Landbeck

Published for the Schools Council
by Longman and Penguin Books

Acknowledgements

We are grateful to the following for permission to reproduce copyright material: Gerald Foley for his letter to *The Times*, 10.7.72; Her Majesty's Stationery Office for a table from 'Medical Research Council Special Report 297 – The Composition of Foods' by R. McCance and E. Widdowson from *H.M.S.O.* 1960; Journal of the Society of Engineers for an extract from 'An Appraisal of the use of Solar Energy' by Dr. H. Heywood DSc (Eng) PhD CEng. from *Journal*, No. 4, 1966; *La Stampa* for an article by Mario Salvatorelli entitled 'Energy in Europe' in *La Stampa*, 5.7.72; The Times Newspapers Limited for the articles "Gases: 'Solid' fuel found in Soviet Union" in *The Times*, 25.3.71 and the article, "Communication: Windmill drives telephones" also from *The Times*; The authors and American Association for the Advancement of Science for 'Mechanochemical Turbine: A New Power Cycle' by M. V. Sussman and A. Katchalsky in *Science*, Vol. 167, pp. 45–47, Fig. 1, 2.1.70; Earlham College Press for extracts from *Tests for Chemical Systems*/Chemical Bond Approach by L. E. Strong, published by McGraw-Hill Book Co. Brian Bracegirdle for the photograph on page 91 from Freeman and Bracegirdle *An Atlas of Histology* (Heinemann Educational Books).

Longman Group Limited, London
Penguin Books Limited, Harmondsworth, Middlesex
for the Schools Council

© Schools Council Publications 1974

First published 1974
ISBN 0 582 34003 9

Phototypeset by Oliver Burridge Filmsetting Limited, Crawley
Printed in Great Britain by Compton Printing Limited

Contents

Foreword

The surge of curriculum study in science which has been witnessed in this country moves forward on a further wave with the commencement of publication of this Schools Council Integrated Science Project, *Patterns*. The work is the natural evolution of all that has gone before. Older members of the teaching profession will recall the pressures which increasingly developed calling for a balance of study across all the sciences but which led only to programmes composed of separate sections of biology, chemistry and physics.

The breakthrough in curriculum study initiated principally by the Nuffield Foundation gelled thoughts in quite different directions. The success of the Nuffield Combined Science Project for the early years of secondary education followed by the most welcomed Nuffield Secondary Science programme based on a thematic approach showed clearly that a new atmosphere prevailed and that the time was ripe once more for a serious study of a truly integrated approach to Science for the O-level ability range. The Schools Council accepted the challenge and have generously supported the investigations undertaken by a team so ably led by William Hall and Brian Mowl.

A refreshing approach has been given to science education. Applications of science to technology and implications of science for society figure prominently in this work. Changes in attitudes are sought alongside the acquisition of knowledge and understanding of principles and this had led to a most impressive study of examinations and assessments to accompany this programme. For this we are particularly grateful to the Associated Examining Board whose generous help and support have made these studies possible.

In conclusion I would like to express my warm gratitude to the Schools Council, its officers, committees and publications department, to the local education authorities whose generous support to schools has made possible the trial of this material, to the teachers who have borne the brunt of the development and of course to William Hall and Brian Mowl and their team. These publications are but the beginning – the seedling will require careful nurture, but its strength will depend on its adaptability to the wide variety of teaching situations to which it must be able to respond. For this care we must turn to teachers, advisers and the Inspectorate, in-service programmes, teachers' centres, and initial training – indeed to all those from whom we have come to expect and from whom we have received the utmost help and assistance.

K. W. Keohane

Director, Centre for Science Education, Chelsea College

Preface

The Teachers' handbook is essential reading before using other *Patterns* texts. The sample scheme (as illustrated in the *Teachers' guides* and *Pupils' manuals*) merely shows one way of achieving the aims of the project. It is hoped that the scheme will be modified by teachers in the following ways:

a The teacher's own investigations and problems will be substituted for those in the *Pupils' manuals*.

b The teaching sequence will be changed, perhaps by mixing work from the three parts of *Patterns*.

c The learning model (recall → problem-solving) will be adapted to any particular pupil's requirements.

There are four fixed aspects of *Patterns*:

1 The project model, whereby pupils' thinking can be based on the fundamental concepts of building blocks, energy and interaction; and throughout the scheme pupils 'search for patterns' and 'use patterns to solve problems'.

2 The learning model, whereby pupils progress from recall, to concept, to pattern and then on to problem-solving.

3 The concepts and patterns listed in the *Teachers' handbook*.

4 The emphasis on social implications and technological applications of science.

The emphasis in *Patterns 1* was on building blocks and in *Patterns 2* on building blocks and interactions. *Patterns 3* is mainly concerned with energy.

It is this part of *Patterns* which has caused the greatest debate and which has undergone the most radical rewriting following trials. Because of this, some of the ideas are only just past the developmental stage, and so further teaching of the sample scheme will probably show the need for considerable adaptation.

In short, it is particularly important in *Patterns 3* to remember that what is being presented is a *sample* scheme.

Introduction: learning about energy

1 Concept and principle

The concept of energy is in a different category from many with which we want pupils to become familiar, in that it is in no sense an obvious idea, but very much a theoretical construction, an idea which is found extremely useful because of the way things are. This implies that they cannot really see its usefulness until they know quite a lot about the way things are. The reason that energy is an extremely useful concept is precisely because it is possible to do book-keeping operations with it. Energy lost from one body or 'account' always seems to appear in another. In the physicists' jargon it is a 'conserved quantity', which gives something of permanence round which to structure one's thinking. Perhaps one of the most important things for children to appreciate about energy is that it is an invented idea which, in a quantitative way, reflects the way the world is. Further, one might hope to convey to them an important characteristic of science, particularly physical science, is that it produces abstract concepts which are very powerful aids to thought, and that energy is the supreme example.

The obvious analogy for energy, as indicated above, is money (also an invented idea, although we usually ignore this). The analogy would be even closer if we could forget about our tokens (currency) and think merely of value. This is, unfortunately, probably too much to ask of children.

The close inter-relationship of the energy concept and energy conservation is one of the major problems associated with learning about energy. This is borne out historically by the tortuous process by which the concept was developed. We tend to forget that the conservation principle was formulated less than 125 years ago by Joule and Helmholtz, about 25 years after Carnot discovered the second law of thermodynamics.

A second major difficulty in this context is the apparently universal applicability of energy conservation. The generality which makes the principle so powerful is a positive handicap to the person just beginning to learn about it, at least by a method which has any significant proportion of discovery learning in it.

1

One possible teaching scheme emphasising receptive learning (i.e. learning by instruction) would start with the introduction of the concept and principle, backed up by appeals to common experience, and continue by showing that its application to new situations led to accurate predictions. This is probably appropriate at the adult level, where familiarity with generalisations and defined concepts can be assumed, along with the ability to recall selectively from a considerable variety of relevant experience. Another possibility is the introduction of experience designed to lead to a generalisation in a small area, followed by the extension of this generalisation to successive new areas. This seems the appropriate development at school, once the children have a fair ability to make generalisations, i.e. find patterns, and this is the approach followed in *Patterns*.

Traditional courses have usually done what is in effect a mixture of both approaches at once, and this may in part account for the difficulty many (most?) pupils have in understanding both the nature of energy and the status of energy conservation.

'The idea that energy is conserved is not one that is difficult to grasp. In fact, once heat and work were clearly defined and the notion of caloric was discarded, the law of conservation of energy seemed to follow rather naturally. It is an idea, one can argue, that has universal appeal. Henry Bent, an American chemist, described the broad-based appeal of the first law in the following way:

Mathematicians [believe the first law is true] because they believe it is a fact of observation; observers because they believe it is a theorem of mathematics; philosophers because they believe it is aesthetically satisfying, or because they believe new forms of energy can always be invented to make it true. A few neither believe nor disbelieve it; these people maintain that the First Law is a procedure for book-keeping energy changes, and about book-keeping procedures it should be asked, not are they true or false, but are they useful.'

(From *Order and chaos* by S. W. Angrist and L. G. Hepler, Basic Books, 1967)

2 Work

When the concept of energy is subjected to close scrutiny, the thing which is conserved is seen to be the ability to do tasks of a certain sort, hence the traditional definition 'the capacity to do work'. If the question is asked 'what sort of tasks?' one can easily land in a circular argument. There are plenty of tasks which do not require energy (e.g. getting a brick from the top to the bottom of a building or getting sodium hydroxide to dissolve in water), but how can we specify the ones which do?

A non-circular answer appropriate at an early stage has been suggested in the form 'those that would need fuel', assuming a certain familiarity with engines and fuels (Nuffield O-level Physics), and this seems worth adopting. The concept of a fuel is elucidated more fully later, when the energy changes in chemical reactions are investigated.

The next step is to establish a quantitative measure of the energy requirement for a task. Why is it that the product (force × distance) is used? The answer which can be given is that this product is (in certain stated circumstances) conserved, whereas other combinations of variables are not.

Implicit in the above is the use of the term work not for a form of energy but for the quantity of energy transferred from one body to another. In the money analogy it corresponds to the sum written on the cheque; it represents a transfer, not a quantity in one account or the other. This avoids the confusion often caused by the phrases 'work done on' and 'work done by'. These can be omitted, and one can speak of energy being transferred from object A to object B, the work involved being X. Again this usage follows Nuffield O-level Physics. It seems important in this context to put some stress on non-gravitational work, so that pupils do not make the mistake of always thinking of forces as weights.

3 Forms of energy

The habit has grown up of speaking about a number of different 'forms of energy', of making a list of these (which can be extended as necessary), and of referring to energy transfers as changes of form of energy ('transforming' energy – even if transformers don't actually transform it!). This is useful in emphasising the change aspect of energy transfer, but tends to make energy seem more concrete than it really is, as if it were almost a sort of 'stuff' which comes in allotropic forms.

In fact when we say 'this object has kinetic energy', what we are doing is using a sort of shorthand for the statement, 'this object can perform a fuel-needing task because it is moving'. There is no distinct sort of energy in moving bodies: the phrase kinetic energy is a recognition that any body which is moving represents a source of energy.

Similarly potential energy is an indication of an energy source because of position, whether forces of a gravitational, magnetic or some other sort are involved. This shows that potential energy is in reality an attribute of a system, not strictly of a body, an emphasis which is frequently omitted. Perhaps the easiest way for pupils to understand this is an 'object in a context'.

When the term gravitational potential energy is used, it indicates not only that a body is situated in a gravitational field, but also that a convenient mechanism exists for transferring energy from the body-Earth system to some other. Water at sea level has no potential energy, unless you happen to be in a coal mine under the sea! Similar statements could be made about every other situation where potential energy is involved. It is therefore suggested that the most helpful emphasis in teaching is not 'does this body (or even this system) have energy?' but 'is there a mechanism by which energy can be had from this system?' This should help pupils to think of energy as 'potentiality' rather than as a special sort of 'stuff'.

4 Electrical energy

In addition to the terms potential energy and kinetic energy, use is frequently made of the phrases electrical energy, chemical energy, strain energy and several others. The expression electrical energy is sometimes used to describe the energy stored in a capacitor when it is charged. This is energy available from the system because of the relative positions of the charges on the plates, i.e. it is similar to any other sort of potential energy. More commonly the phrase is referred to an electrical circuit with a current in it, and here the use is more doubtful. A flow of charge is a process, and as such can more naturally be regarded as a mechanism for transferring energy (from battery, capacitor etc.) than as a source of energy, which is what is implied in the usual use of the term 'electrical energy'. A generator, a pair of cables, and a motor could in principle be replaced by a suitable pulley system. But the temptation to refer in such a case to the strain energy of the string is not a strong one: we are content to speak of the pulley system as a mechanism by which the energy is transferred. It is suggested that similar language is appropriate to the electric circuit. Because the movement involved is a flow of charge (Q), potential difference (V) arises naturally as the energy transfer per unit charge, and it is found that electrical work is measured by $Q \times V$ rather than $F \times d$.

5 Chemical energy

The situation is similar here. It is said that a mixture of hydrogen and oxygen has chemical energy because, once started, energy is released with explosive violence. But the adjective chemical applies more naturally to the process or mechanism of energy release than to the original store of energy. Clearly we have here a form of potential energy, in that the relative positions of the atoms or ions are what change in the process. However, a relevant point is that the quantity of energy available by a chemical process within a system is frequently much greater than that obtained by a moderate change of position or speed of the whole system, so that as a first approximation the latter can be ignored. It is also true that chemical processes are frequently such that the energy transfer is within the system, so that the original potential energy is distributed among the particles of the system, causing a rise of teι..perature. (In other cases mechanical or electrical work occurs, i.e. a transfer of energy from the system to its surroundings.) So a stronger case can be made for chemical potential energy than for electrical energy. However, a better terminology is probably to introduce the word source which makes it possible to speak of a chemical source of energy (rather than a source of chemical energy). Once the particle picture of matter is established one can introduce the idea of particle potential energy, which forms a link with strain energy.

6 Strain energy

While the chemical processes which transfer energy involve interactions between the particles of which a system is composed, processes in which the strain (i.e. the deformation) of a body is relevant also involve interactions between the particles, but in a different way. On any sort of particle model of matter, deformation of a body must imply some change of the relative positions of the particles, and if a force exists between two particles then the normal work calculation (force × distance) will give the energy transfer to or from the body in respect of those particles. The sum of these terms for all the interacting particles will give the total energy transfer to or from the body. These forces between particles are closely related to chemical bonding, because both are concerned with the energy needed to alter the separation of the particles. The bond energy represents the energy required to separate the particles completely, so it can be thought of as the limiting case of strain energy, when the body is pulled apart into its component particles. It should be illuminating to pupils to realise this close relationship, particularly when the energy required to melt a solid or vaporise a liquid is also discussed.

7 Energy in biological systems

Energy is important at two levels here, within the organism, and in the community context; both require some degree of familiarity with energy transfer in chemical changes.

In the organism respiration is the term given to a complex and interlinked series of chemical reactions whose primary importance relates closely to energy considerations. Food (i.e. fuel) together with oxygen is the source of (potential) energy. The chemical processes lead to its redistribution so that part finishes as potential energy in new tissue, part is transferred to the surroundings by mechanical work, and part is transferred to the surroundings because the organism has a higher temperature. Maintaining a (nearly) constant temperature is an advantage to birds and mammals, and this is achieved by the control of the rate of loss of energy to the surroundings. The organism can also acquire potential energy and kinetic energy but this is temporary and the energy is eventually dissipated to the surroundings.

Various internal processes also occur which involve energy transfer, but the energy relationships are difficult to elucidate and explain. This is partly because they are not fully understood (e.g. the role of ATP is still a matter of vigorous debate) and partly because it is difficult to specify what is 'system' and what 'surroundings' (for example, in muscle action blood, which might be considered part of the surroundings, permeates the tissue of the muscle).

The origin of food involved in respiration is another organism (plant or animal), except for the primary producers (green plants). These utilise energy from the sun to make their food in a complex series of chemical reactions called photosynthesis. The fact that only some of the food energy can be used for producing new tissue explains why the mass of new tissue grown per annum in a population decreases from producers to herbivores to carnivores, i.e. the ecological pyramid.

Both these contexts can be regarded as straightforward applications of the ideas mentioned above, particularly energy conservation and (chemical) potential energy. There are also some 'second law' ideas implicit in this work (see later), in that an organism constantly spreads energy to its surroundings, and this in part explains the limit to the efficiency of building new tissue from food.

8 Heat

The word heat is, unfortunately, used in several different ways which are not consistent. The everyday use instead of temperature (the heat of the bath water) can rapidly be dismissed. Most children learn without too much difficulty that temperature is the appropriate word for this particular concept, and one might even hope that common usage would gradually improve.

The commonest meaning of the word heat is probably 'the energy in a hot body'. This derives from the older view that a hot body contained more of a substance (caloric) than the same body when cooler. This early view can take one quite a long way, explaining thermal expansion, conduction and convection, and enabling accurate calculations of temperature change to be made, involving specific heats. It can be extended, with some degree of mystery, to cover latent heats. It was the view of heat held by Carnot when he wrote his paper outlining what is now called the second law of thermodynamics (1824), and by most scientists when Joule was performing his long series of experiments on the relationship between work and heat (1839–1850).

When it had been established that the 'amount of heat' bore a direct and constant relationship to the work involved, no matter what process was involved, the way was open for heat to be regarded as a form of energy, implying that there is a distinction between this energy and the energy a body (system) has for other reasons. This is the commonly-held and commonly-taught point of view in schools at the moment.

With this approach it is natural to use different units for heat (the calorie) and for other 'forms' of energy and energy-transfer (the joule). Joule's experiments, or a school laboratory version, then represent the determination of the mechanical equivalent of heat. If (following the usage of the SI) the calorie is dropped, it is hard to find a satisfactory way to describe these experiments. If one asks whether the heat (in joules) corresponds to the work (in joules) there is a built-in presupposition that it will, and an explanation would be needed for any discrepancy.

What should certainly not be omitted from an integrated science course is some treatment of the correspondence between energy transfer (measured as work, including electrical work) and temperature rise. A useful way of doing this is to regard it as a further extension of the conservation of energy, and a rather special one at that. In all the instances where energy conservation appears not to work (and they are numerous) we can find a 'non-conservative force', such as friction or air resistance which always hinders motion, but unlike weight which hinders motion up but helps motion down. Energy (measured as work) seems to be lost and the important question is whether it is really lost. The discovery of the inevitable temperature rise gives the clue, and quantitative measurements can show the correspondence to the energy lost. The increase of energy of an object which gets warmer turns out to be ($m \times s \times \Delta T$), and this does not depend on the mechanism of transfer. The interpretation in terms of the particle model of matter follows naturally, and understanding that temperature rise is equivalent to increase of the average energy of a particle is a good foundation for more advanced work.

The third use of the word heat is confined to thermodynamicists, certain of whom have for some time been attempting
to get other people to use it in the same way. The meaning they
give to the word heat is the energy transfer from a hot body to a
cooler one. Heat then has a similar status to work (as used above),
and the first law of thermodynamics is expressed as

$$\frac{\text{increase of internal}}{\text{energy of a system}} = \frac{\text{work}}{\text{(transfer)}} + \frac{\text{heat}}{\text{(transfer)}}$$

$$\Delta U \quad = \quad \Delta W \quad + \quad \Delta Q$$

(using the convention that energy added to the system is positive).
This certainly gives a consistent usage, and one that is now firmly
established in this restricted field. Thermodynamicists criticise
the second use of the word heat (above) because it is impossible
to distinguish part of the energy of a system as due to its high
temperature. The appropriate concept, they would suggest, is
internal energy which is increased when the temperature increases. There is certainly substance in this criticism, and it is
clear that the thermodynamicists' use of the word is in conflict
with the traditional school use.

There is no doubt that it is confusing to find that a word is used
at a later stage in a way which conflicts with earlier usage. If the
earlier usage is also somewhat misleading in its implications, and
presents difficulties in the teaching/learning situation, there is a
good case for dropping it, and this is what is proposed. The
following is an extract from a draft document prepared at the
Centre for Science Education, Chelsea College, by members of
some of the Nuffield and Schools Council projects in science.

'Heat is a word in the ordinary language of pupils, but it has
three meanings – hotness, the energy in a hot thing, and energy
flow from hot to cold. If heat is given a precise scientific
meaning, it ought to be the last. But we think that to use a word
in common currency in a special sense, without being able to
explain simply why other senses are "wrong", will hinder
rather than help. We recommend that in elementary teaching,
heat is not given a role as a term at all. Pupils will use it, and
need not be reproved for doing so, but when they do, it will be
necessary to find out what they mean. Sometimes it will be
hotness, sometimes the energy inside things.

When the idea of internal energy (the energy in things, the
energy shared among the molecules) is introduced, one can
mention that this is what we mean sometimes in everyday
language when we speak of heat. But "heat" should not be

used by teachers as if it were the scientific name for internal energy.

By having special terms, none of them "heat", for the most needed usages (hotness and the energy in hot things), we think that students may more easily come to see that science has more than one distinct concept, where ordinary language has one conflation of ideas. "Heat" can be used from time to time, as what it is – a common, vague, useful word. It will be useful in cases where energy flows from hot to cold, and to use it then is perfectly correct.

The verb "to heat" means to make warmer or hotter, and occasionally needs to be translated into that form tactfully when pupils use it. But because heat is given no special meaning, phrases like "immersion heater" are perfectly acceptable.

The term "heat" in "heat of reaction", "latent heat" etc. can be replaced by "reaction energy change", "energy required for vaporisation" etc.'

9 The second law of thermodynamics

'A story (perhaps apocryphal) told about Arnold Sommerfeld, a great physicist noted for his clarity of exposition, throws some light on the nature of the study of thermodynamics. During the course of his lifetime, Sommerfeld wrote a series of books, each book covering a particular area: mechanics, optics, electrodynamics, etc. When asked why he had never written a book on thermodynamics, he is reported to have answered in the following way. "Thermodynamics is a funny subject. The first time you go through the subject, you don't understand it at all. The second time you go through it, you think you understand it, except for one or two small points. The third time you go through it, you know you don't understand it, but by that time you are so used to the subject, it doesn't bother you any more." When Sommerfeld was killed in an accident, he was in the midst of writing a book on thermodynamics.'

(From *Order and chaos* by S. W. Angrist and L. G. Hepler, Basic Books, 1967)

The conservation of energy is very nearly (but not quite) the same as the first law of thermodynamics. But a case can be made out that the second law is of even more importance, since it is a rule indicating the direction in which changes of various sorts take place. However, while subject to the same difficulties as the first law about universal applicability, it has considerable difficulties of its own about formulation. The fact that there exist several alternative statements of the law which are in fact equivalent, but not obviously so, illustrates this point. It is not clear at present how the law could be either formulated or taught in an O-level course, desirable as this may seem, so that probably it will be necessary to give pupils familiarity with a wide range of phenomena to which the second law is relevant (i.e. changes which are not directly reversible) and some hints towards an interpretation.

The important idea which probably can be appreciated by O-level pupils, and which is fairly near to the second law, is that things tend to become more mixed up (disorder increases). This has a much wider application than to energy consideration (shaking up layers of different coloured particles for example) but has a number of apparent exceptions which are hard to explain convincingly at this level (for example the formation of crystals from a solution). This statement can be related to energy if it is suggested that energy tends to become spread more evenly among a collection of particles. This, however, is not simple: we do not mean that every particle will eventually have exactly the same energy. But the transfer of energy from a hot to a cold body can be seen as evening-up the average energy of the particles in the two bodies, i.e. sharing of the total energy among all the particles.

Nuffield Physics refers to 'heat, the final form' as an expression of the second law applied to energy. Avoiding the word heat, this can be translated to something like 'energy tends to finish up spread among a large number of particles', and the examples of this can be multiplied almost indefinitely. This can be a valid generalisation (pattern), given the particle model of matter. So it seems that it is worth considering energy not merely in bulk terms (ability to do fuel-needing jobs), but also in molecular terms, from the earliest possible moment. Expressing the generalisation in terms of the energy being 'spread among a large number of particles', while longer than the traditional formulation, should be a positive aid to understanding. One way of bridging the gap between the behaviour of matter in bulk and the particle model is by experiments which show the tendency of energy to spread evenly among a collection of large particles such as frictionless pucks on an air table. This will also bring out the statistical nature of the statement: it is unlikely that one puck will have most of the energy. If (as is generally held) the large scale events described by the second law are a reflection of the probabilities of different states occurring at the atomic scale, then a sound appreciation of elementary probability and statistics may be the best foundation to lay for more advanced work. It is encouraging that the trend in mathematics teaching is towards including such topics much earlier than they have been treated hitherto, and useful opportunities for cooperation may present themselves. The following statement of the laws of thermodynamics is taken from the Nuffield Advanced Physics book *Change and chance.*

The laws of thermodynamics

There are four laws concerning the way things change. You can find other statements of them in text books. The statements here are not meant to be absolutely complete.

Law 0 (zeroth law): the law of equilibrium

If any two objects are each in thermal equilibrium with a third, they will be found to be in equilibrium with each other.

The first law: the law of energy conservation

If you add up all the energy changes occurring in a process, the total energy does not change. Or, the energy in a closed system is constant ("closed" means that no energy comes in or goes out; that is, that you have thought of all the energy transfers). An informal version runs, "you can't win, you can only break even".

The second law: the "which way?" law

Heat flow never occurs by itself from cold to hot, or, a closed system will always end up in that condition which can be realised in the greatest number of ways, or – more informally – "if you think things are mixed up now just wait". The informal version to follow that of law 1 runs: "you can only break even at absolute zero".'

The third law says, in effect, 'you cannot reach absolute zero'.

Summary

1 The concept of energy and the pattern of its conservation need to be built up together gradually, starting with simple mechanical situations and then including a wider range of stages.

2 The term work is conveniently used for the measure of energy transfer, not a form of energy. It can also be extended to include electrical work.

3 It is more useful to emphasise mechanisms by which energy is transferred from one system to another than different forms of energy, so that electrical conductors, chemical reactions, and pulley systems are all seen as energy-transfer mechanisms.

4 Energy in biological systems can be dealt with in a similar way, both at organism and at community level.

5 The use of the word heat to mean the energy in a hot body is confusing, and it is suggested that the word should not be used with a specific scientific meaning.

11

6 The ideas contained in the second law of thermodynamics are very difficult to convey to pupils at this level. Much can be done, however, by referring to the energy shared among the particles of a body from an early stage, and by dealing with ideas of chance and probability.

1 Transferring energy

Introduction

Ideas which are probably already familiar to pupils are extended and made more precise in this section. Energy transfer by machines is made the basis of experiences leading to the concept of work as a measure of energy transfer (rather than a form of energy). The non-conservation of work in many situations, associated with dissipative interactions like friction, leads on to efficiency and a first consideration of the tendency of energy to become less useful, but not less in quantity. The concept of machine is extended to cover hydraulic, pneumatic and electrical transfer of energy, and this leads to a consideration of other ways of transferring energy which do not involve the transfer of any building block (i.e. waves). Ripples, sound and earthquakes are considered in some detail (with microwaves as optional work), and patterns of reflection, refraction and interference are developed. These patterns are then applied to the major problem of whether light is a wave. The social implications of noise and earthquakes are considered, and there is optional work on image formation, perception, musical instruments, colour, and the electromagnetic spectrum.

Objectives
Skills

1 To recall and to understand the following concepts: system, energy transfer, lever, fluid, current, machine, force, distance, work, energy conservation, efficiency, friction, ▷viscosity, ▷electrical resistance, energy spread, wave (ripple, water, light, sound, ▷earthquake, ▷centimetre region radiation), wavelength, frequency, speed, reflection, interface, refraction, diffraction, interference, coherence, superposition, ▷oscillation, ▷vibration, ▷mirror, ▷lens, ▷image, ▷magnification, ▷object, ▷electromagnetic wave, ▷spectrum, frequency (1).
2 To recall and to understand the following patterns.
a Energy can be transferred from one system to another by various means such as levers (including the bones of the skeleton), strings, rotating shafts, flow of fluids, electrical currents, waves and chemical processes (2).

b Machines are generally either 'force multipliers' or 'distance multipliers' (2).

c (Force × distance) is called work, and can be a measure of energy transferred (2).

d For any machine the output work is less than or equal to the input work (2).

e Efficiency is defined as (energy transferred as desired ÷ total energy transferred) (2).

f As energy is transferred from one system to another, the amount available tends to decrease. This decrease accompanies such phenomena as friction, ▷ viscosity and ▷ electrical resistance (2).

g Waves of various sorts can transfer energy without the transfer of building blocks (2).

h Ripples, sound, ▷ earthquakes, ▷ centimetre region radiation, and light show wave patterns (2).

i for any sort of wave, speed = (frequency × wavelength) (2).

j Both waves and building blocks can show the phenomena of reflection and refraction. For waves (▷ and in some circumstances building blocks) the pattern of reflection is: angle of incidence = angle of reflection. For waves passing an interface there is a relation between the speed and the direction, leading to refraction. ▷ For building blocks there is different relation (2).

k Only waves show the phenomena of diffraction and interference. Waves from twin coherent sources form a characteristic pattern of interference, which can be explained in terms of super-position (2).

▷l All waves appear to be produced by, or associated with, some sort of vibration or oscillation (2).

▷m Light passing through lenses and/or reflected by mirrors can produce optical images, which in general differ in size from the object. The magnification and position of an image is determined by the refraction and/or reflection of light from the object. This pattern also applies to other sorts of wave (2).

▷n Electromagnetic waves form a continuous sequence of waves of different frequency with patterns of behaviour in common (2).

(These patterns are linked to patterns in the *Teachers' handbook* as follows: a with 31; b and c with 32; d with 32 and 36; e with 34; f with 36 and 37; g with 31; h with 64, 65, 66 and 67; i with 64; j with 65 and 66; k with 67; ▷l with 64; ▷m with ▷G; ▷n with ▷E.)

3 To make a critical appraisal of the results of experiments on energy transfer, leading to patterns 2b, d, and f (3).

4 To solve problems using the patterns listed above (4).

5 To make a reasoned judgment about the nature of light, based on experiments and patterns 2g, j, and k (4).

▷6 To write an essay about the science of musical instruments, making use of various sources of information (4, 5).

7 To understand something of the technical, social and economic importance of energy transfer and distribution in an industrialised country, and to realise that decisions about energy transfer and distribution involve both complex scientific questions and matters outside the scope of science (6).

8 To understand that an important technological aim is the increase of efficiency of various processes, by reducing the effects of friction and similar phenomena (6).

▷9 To understand the significance of wave patterns in extending human sense perception, and the importance of this to scientific and technical progress, including alleviating individual problems such as deafness and sight defects (6).

▷10 To understand the importance of optical instruments in extending the range and precision of observation (6).

11 To be accurate in reporting the possibly surprising results of experiments on interference (7).

12 To make suggestions for experiments to investigate whether light (▷and centimetre-region radiation) are wave phenomena (8).

▷13 To design and perform experiments to investigate the phenomena of colour mixing (8).

Attitudes

14 To be willing to work as part of a group on experiments concerned with machines, ripples and light (9).

▷15 To be sceptical about whether the wave model of light gives a completely adequate description of the relevant phenomena (10).

▷16 To be concerned about the application of scientific knowledge to give warning of, or prevent, major earthquakes (11).

17 To be concerned about the effects of noise on people (11).

Flow diagram

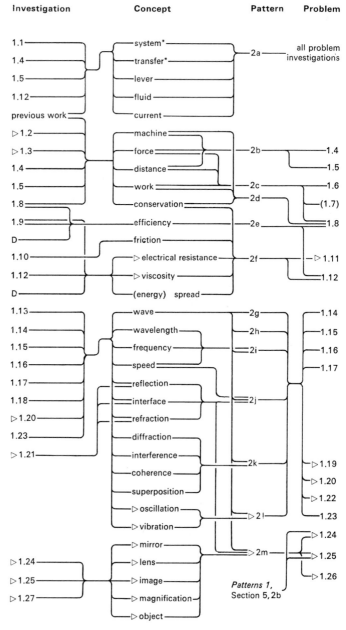

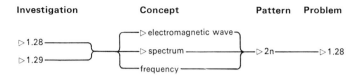

| Investigation | Concept | Pattern | Problem |

$\triangleright$ electromagnetic wave
$\triangleright$ 1.28
$\triangleright$ spectrum
$\triangleright$ 1.29
$\triangleright$ 2n
$\triangleright$ 1.28
frequency

*These concepts also apply to all the other investigations, patterns and problems of this section. They, and the concept of energy, have been omitted for simplicity.

Sample scheme

Time allocation for this section: $5\frac{1}{2}$ weeks (not including the large amount of optional work in this section).

	Description	Reference	Notes
1.1	Ways of transferring energy	NP Year II, expts 56–61 (selection) NSS Field 4.11	Variety of energy transfer experiments, can be arranged as a circus, or demonstrated
D	Forces and energy		
$\triangleright$ 1.2	Devising a way to measure forces		Design problem
$\triangleright$ 1.3	Measuring forces	NSS Field 4.21 NSS Field 6.22	Circus of pupil experiments
D	Machines		
B	*Machines and engines*	*Patterns* topic book	The first part is relevant at this stage
▶1.4	The lever: a simple machine		Individual experiment $(F \times d)$ conserved
D	Force multipliers and distance multipliers	NP Year III teachers' guide pp 24–27	
▶1.5	More machines	NSS Fields 4.27 and 6.22	Individual experiments using a variety of machines chosen so that $(F \times d)$ is approximately conserved, could be a circus

	Description	Reference	Notes
D	Introducing work	NP Year III teachers' guide pp. 37–39	$(F \times d)$ as a measure of energy transfer (not a form of energy)
▶ 1.6	Work and its measurement	NSS Field 4.23	Experiment and calculation. Emphasis on non-gravitational work
▶ 1.7	What is a person's work worth?		Relates everyday and scientific meanings to social questions, largely discussion
▷ T	*Energetically yours*	Film, Esso	Cartoon
▶ 1.8	Still more machines	NSS Field 4.27	Experiments and calculation using machines chosen so that $(F \times d)$ is not conserved
D	Is energy lost?	NP Year III teachers' guide pp 28–33	No definite answer provided at this stage, question arises of how one could tell
1.9	Perpetual motion machines	NP Year III teachers' guide pp 34–36	Paper and pencil work, optional projects possible
▷ T	*Perpetual motion*	Film available from NCAVAE	
1.10	Friction		Experiment or 'think' investigation
B	*Friction*	*Patterns* topic book	Part of this book presupposes work on energy conservation not yet covered
▷ T	*Frontiers of friction*	Film, Shell Mex and BP	

	Description	Reference	Notes
▷B	*Surfaces*	Deeson, Eric, Mills and Boon (with Griffin and George), 1971	Deals with friction and many other aspects of surfaces
▷T	*Vehicle wheel grip*	Project Technology, Project brief no 30	Investigational project
▷▶1.11	The efficiency of a machine	NSS Field 4.27, IV	Experiment, calculation, graph
▶1.12	Other ways of transferring energy	Link with Investigation 1.1	Largely paper and pencil investigation; distribution electrically, using fluids, transport of fuels
▷T	*Hydraulic turbine*	Project Technology, Project brief no 20	Constructional project
▷T	*Hydraulic transmission of power*	Film, Shell Mex and BP	
D	Other forms of work		Introduces ($p \times V$), electrical work (qualitatively)
1.13	Transferring energy without transferring building blocks	NP Year V expt 93	Brief demonstration of waves on liquids, strings, 'slinky' etc; sound; light; reference to sea waves and earthquakes
D	Is there any common feature?		Raises questions which need answering by experiment
▷T	*Waves and the ripple tank*	Film, Esso	Not suitable for pupils
▷T	*A wave machine*	Film loop, BBC/ Gateway PBB 634	Includes transverse waves, pulse/ continuous waves, energy transfer

19

	Description	Reference	Notes
▷T	*Non-recurrent wavefronts*	Film loop, Ealing ABO-2173/1	Super-8 only, shows pulses of some unusual sorts of wave
▷T	*Transverse waves*	Film loop, Macmillan PM 014	Shows working model
▷T	*Longitudinal waves*	Film loop, Macmillan PM 060	Shows working model
▶1.14	Is there a pattern in the way ripples are reflected?	NP Year III expts 4a to l	Pattern-finding experiment or demonstration
▷T	*Ripple tank reflection*	Film loop, Macmillan PM 023	Includes animation to show flow of energy
▶1.15	How does the behaviour of ripples depend on the depth of liquid?	NP Year III expt 4t	Pattern-finding, probably demonstration
▷T	*Refraction of waves*	Film loop, Ealing A80-2348/1	Super-8 only
▷T	*Ripple tank refraction*	Film loop, Macmillan PM 024	Includes animation to show flow of energy
▶1.16	Combining ripples	NP Year III expts 4n to s, 34, 35	Experiment or demonstration
▷T	Slides for projection showing concentric circles	Project Technology, Bulletin no 17, p 14	Shows twin-source patterns of interference
▷T	Prints of concentric circles		Suitable for making OHP transparencies to show twin-source patterns of interference
▷T	*Moiré Patterns 1 and 2*	Project Technology, Project briefs nos 27 and 28	Constructional and investigational projects

	Description	Reference	Notes
▷T	*Interference of waves*	Film loop, Ealing A80-2405/1	Super-8 only
▷T	*Interference*	Film loop, Macmillan PM 025	Includes animation to show flow of energy
▷T	*Single slit diffraction*	Film loop, Ealing A80-2421/1	Super-8 only
▷T	*Diffraction and scattering round obstacles*	Film loop, Ealing A80-2447/1	Super-8 only
▷T	*Diffraction*	Film loop, Macmillan PM 022	Includes animation to show flow of energy
▶1.17	Patterns of behaviour of sound	NSS Field 5.2; NP Year V expt 107a	Demonstration of various properties of sound
▷T	*Oscilloscopes and slow a.c.*	Film, Esso	Not suitable for pupils, the first part is relevant
▷T	The longitudinal nature of sound waves	Film loop, BBC/ Gateway PBB 636	
▷B	*Supersonic flight*	McKim, F. R., Longman Physics Topics book, 1971	Contains a short section on the sonic boom
1.18	Noise	NSS Field 5.26	Demonstration and discussion
B	*Science and decision-making*	*Patterns* topic book	
▷T	*Aircraft noise – enquiry*	Project Technology, Project brief no 12	Investigational project
▷▶1.19	Musical instruments	NSS Field 5.25	Cooperation possible with music department
B	*Sound : its uses and misuses*	*Patterns* topic book	

	Description	Reference	Notes
▷T	*Tuned percussion instruments*	Project Technology, Project brief no 42	Constructional project
▷►1.20	Earthquakes and energy		Paper and pencil investigation
▷B	*The elements rage*	Lane, Frank W., David and Charles, 1966	
▷1.21	Moving objects	NP Year III expts 6f, 30, 31	Demonstration or experiment
D	Waves		Identifies common features of ripples, sound, earthquakes
▷►1.22	Does a centimetre-radiation transmitter produce waves?	Including NP Year V expt 107b	Demonstrations to solve problems experimentally
▷T	*The use of centimetre waves in teaching optics*	Film, Esso	Not suitable for pupils
►1.23	Is light a wave?	NP Year III expts 26, 27a, 36; NSS Field 5.35	Major problem, experiment and demonstration
▷►1.24	Perceiving light	NP Year III expts 7, 14a, b, c, 22	Experiments and demonstrations
T	Model of eye	NSS Field 5.33	
▷►1.25	How does the eye focus on near and far objects?	NP Year III expt 23	Probably demonstration
▷►1.26	Improving perception	NP Year III expt 22b; NSS Field 5.33 X	Experiments and demonstration
▷T	*Solar telescope*	Project Technology, Project brief no 13	Constructional/ investigational project

	Description	Reference	Notes
▷ 1.27	Cameras and photography	NSS Field 5.31	Can be extended to science club activities
▷ T	*Miniature camera*	Project Technology, Project brief no 34	Constructional project
▷ T	*Photography*	Griffin Project no 14 (kit and booklet) S74–720	Contains simple camera, developing tank and accessories
▷ T	*Fundamentals of photography*	Kit from Kodak Ltd	Contains teachers' guide, slides, samples. Links science/technology/art
▷ B	*Pictures in silver*	NC background book	
▷ ▶ 1.28	Colour	NSS Field 5.34	Pupil experiments
▷ 1.29	Electromagnetic waves		Use of data
▷ T	The electromagnetic spectrum	Wallchart	To follow 1.29
B	*Electromagnetic radiation*	*Patterns* topic book	The first few pages deal with the electromagnetic spectrum

Teaching progression

The section starts with a reminder in Investigation 1.1 of the wide diversity of ways in which energy can be transferred, with the probable addition of some new ones, achieving part of objective 2a. The subsequent discussion is intended to bring out the common occurrence of forces in various energy transfer devices. Pupils may or may not realise that movement is always associated with such forces.

Optional work to reinforce ideas about forces (Investigations ▷ 1.2 and ▷ 1.3) is followed by an important series of investigations in which one aspect of energy, conservation, is explored and the significance of the concept of work established. The lever is treated in Investigation 1.4 as either a force-multiplier or a distance-multiplier (objective 2b). The question is then raised of whether anything remains constant. For some pupils this is the obvious thing to ask, having observed that forces increase when distances decrease and vice versa. Others may need help to see that the question is worth asking. Experimental results lead to the conservation of (force × distance), and in Investigation 1.5 a variety of machines is investigated, including a model of the arm, all of which approximately obey the same rule.

The pattern and thus the formal concept of work (objective 2c) can now be dealt with, starting from these experimental results. The point of view has been adopted throughout that work is not a 'form of energy' but a way (at this stage the only way) of measuring how much energy is transferred. Those not familiar with this approach are strongly recommended to read the references in Nuffield Physics Teachers' guide III. There are some pitfalls to be avoided here, particularly associated with the phrase 'doing work', which is often better replaced by 'transferring energy', with, if necessary, a separate statement about 'the work involved'. It may be best to reserve 'doing work' to describe the everyday human activity. Investigation 1.6 is an opportunity to see the value of the concept in an experiment and gain practice in using the pattern, while Investigation 1.7 deals with one aspect of objective 7 and reinforces the different meanings of work in science and in everyday life. These parallels also make it relatively easy in the ensuing investigations to include friction, ▷electrical resistance and ▷fluid viscosity in the same category of 'things which hinder' and tend to be associated with the decrease of useful energy (objective 2f). Discussion should give the opportunity to establish that the word 'work' could also be extended to the other forms of machine, leading to 'fluid work' and 'electrical work'. The latter is considered in Section 3, but a simple theoretical treatment of the former can be given here, showing the equivalence of (force × distance) and (pressure × change of volume) in a particular case. All the investigations up to this point, and particularly the associated discussions, contribute to achieving objective 3, and several up to this point help to achieve objective 8.

Machines are used in Investigation 1.8 for which (force × distance) is considerably less at the output than it is at the input. A degree of scepticism could be introduced here in discussion. It appears that energy is lost, although some pupils may be sufficiently sophisticated not to accept that, and refer at once to friction and temperature rise. What they are most unlikely to be aware of is that that 'story' (or explanation) is a good one only because *whenever* energy seems to be lost, there is a rise of temperature which is *quantitatively* equivalent, no matter what mechanism is involved.

This is the substance of the long historical development of ideas of energy ('heat and work'), which is dealt with in the next section. At this stage the intention is to raise the question so as to lead to the further question of how one could be sure whether energy was lost or not. Some pupils may be able to see at this point the need for a quantitative answer, but for most it will probably be an unresolved problem.

The same investigation (1.8) enables objective 2d to be formulated and efficiency defined (objective 2e). This leads directly to perpetual motion machines, and the reasons why they cannot be made (Investigation 1.9). This leads in turn to a consideration of friction (Investigation 1.10) which is reinforced by the topic book of the same name. If desired, ▷ Investigation 1.11 can be added to give practice in the use of the efficiency pattern in an experimental situation, and to find a minor pattern (efficiency increases with increasing load).

The concept of a machine is extended in Investigation 1.12 to include hydraulic machines, those using compressed air, and electrical machines. For the last it may be found helpful to suggest that the combination (generator-wires-motor) represents the machine, since this is what is equivalent to the mechanical device. This will emphasise that it represents the electrical transfer of energy in the same way as a water pipe or air line conveys energy: both a pump (or high reservoir) and a turbine are needed. Investigation 1.12 also contributes to objective 2a.

Investigation 1.13 acts as an introduction to a series of investigations dealing with means of transferring energy without the transfer of matter (building blocks). These cover patterns 2g to ▷ 2n, as well as other objectives. At the outset it is *not* suggested that these are all waves: some clearly are, but whether sound, microwaves and light are wave-like are real questions.

Objectives 2i and 2j are achieved in respect of ripples in Investigations 1.14 and 1.15 which also establish a number of the wave concepts, and the elementary techniques of using stroboscopes. Interference and diffraction of ripples (objectives 2k and ▷ 2l) are dealt with in Investigation 1.16.

The demonstrations (with class involvement) in Investigation 1.17 enable the similarities and differences between ripples and sound to be established, and sound to be firmly categorised as having wave character. This leads to consideration of the human aspects of noise and sound in Investigation 1.18 and ▷ 1.19 (achieving objectives ▷ 6 and 17).

▷ Investigation 1.20 identifies earthquakes as being caused by waves in the Earth, and uses this (with earlier patterns) to form a theoretical model of the interior of the Earth. The practical application to the dangerous situation of San Francisco is also considered (▷objective 16).

The extent to which building blocks may be similar to waves is briefly considered in ▷Investigation 1.21, which could be extended if desired.

The question whether the radiation emitted from an unfamiliar transmitter has wave character is the problem of ▷Investigation 1.22, which also achieves part of objective 12. This could be a relatively straightforward introduction to the next investigation.

The major problem of whether light is a wave is dealt with in Investigation 1.23, which has the advantage that whichever opinion pupils have to start with there is something to be said (eventually at least) on the other side. Those who 'know' from reading that light is a wave may be surprised by the end result. Objectives 5, 12, (part)14 and ▷15 are achieved here, and the fact that the crucial patterns are those concerning interference and diffraction is needed.

▷Objectives 9, 10 and 13 are achieved in a series of optional investigations (▷1.24, ▷1.25, ▷1.26 and ▷1.27) which establish and use ▷pattern 2m, and include work on the structure and function of the eye, image formation, correcting eye defects, and optical instruments and photography. This leads finally to consideration of colour (▷Investigation 1.28) which is extended to the electromagnetic spectrum (▷Investigation 1.29) achieving ▷objectives 2n and 13. The topic book *Electromagnetic radiation* is also useful here.

▷Objective 2l and the associated concepts of ▷oscillation and ▷resonance (vibration) may be achieved at various points if desired, particularly the work on ripples, sound and earthquakes.

Teaching notes

Investigation 1.1 Ways of transferring energy

There are several ways of arranging this investigation, and a very large number of transfer devices which might be used. The choice will differ from one school to another, and probably also from one teacher to another. (A selection of devices is given below.)

It is suggested that the experiments chosen should at least include examples of transfer by electrical means, and by fluid flow. The various ways in which systems can possess energy available for transfer should also be inherent in the examples chosen (although this is taken further in Section 5). These ways are associated with the following systems (not an exhaustive list): a mass at a height, a strained object (e.g. a spring), chemicals which can undergo suitable interaction (e.g. in a battery or a flame), an object at a temperature higher than that of the surroundings, an object in motion. It is not suggested that these should be memorised as 'forms of energy', but that pupils should understand that they can be used to obtain energy for transfer to another system, and to recognise the energy gain of that system. The table below gives examples of the sort of answer expected from pupils in this investigation. Some of the experiments lend themselves to a 'circus' treatment with pupils moving from one station to another; others may best be demonstrated. Some may be so familiar or so trivial as to be covered without actual experiment, although this is not true of most. Certainly many more than those listed can be included: these are merely to show the level of description intended. Further examples can be found in the Nuffield Secondary Science and Nuffield Physics references.

System from which energy is transferred	System to which energy is transferred	Way in which the transfer takes place
a *Steam engine driving generator linked to lamp bulbs*		
Fuel and oxygen	Hot gases	Combustion
Hot gases	Water/steam in boiler	Conduction
Steam	Piston/flywheel	Expansion of steam
Flywheel	Generator	Belt drive
Generator	Lamps	Electricity
Lamps	Air etc	Radiation, conduction
b *Pulley system using a falling mass to lift another mass*		
2.2 kg mass at height 1.0 m	4 kg mass lifted through 0.5 m	Cord moving over pulleys
c *Ions in a test tube*		
Sun (light)	Fresh silver chloride precipitate	Particle interaction
d *Pupil lifting brick on to a shelf*		
You	Brick lifted on to shelf	Muscles/bones (respiration)
e *Hammering a piece of lead*		
You	Lead (raised in temperature)	Muscles/bones/ hammer (respiration – see Section 2)
f *Swinging pendulum*		
Bob at top of swing	Bob in motion at bottom of swing	Forces due to cord and gravity

System from which energy is transferred	System to which energy is transferred	Way in which the transfer takes place
g *Battery used to light a lamp*		
Chemicals in battery	Lamp	Chemical interaction and electricity
h *Battery used to drive a motor to speed up a flywheel*		
Chemicals in battery	Motor	Chemical interaction and electricity
Motor	Rotating flywheel	Belt drive
i *Spring gun firing a pellet*		
Compressed spring	Moving pellet	Expansion and force of spring
j *Sodium hydroxide solution added to sulphuric acid solution*		
Sodium hydroxide and sulphuric acid	Particles of mixed solution (and container) as shown by temperature rise	Chemical interaction
k *Photographic exposure meter indicates light level*		
Sun or lamps (by reflection from other objects)	Photoelectric cell	Radiation
Photoelectric cell	Meter	Electricity
l *Striking a match*		
i You	Particles of match head (rise of temperature)	Muscles/bones (respiration)
ii Chemicals in match head	Hot gases	Combustion
Note: i initiates ii which is self-sustaining (for a short time)		

It should be noted that every example could, in principle, be continued until the energy is distributed to the surroundings by conduction, radiation etc. There is no need to do this in more than a few cases.

The discussion which follows is intended to emphasise that in a large variety of energy transfer-systems forces are involved. Some pupils may also see that movement is always involved at the same time.

▷ *Investigation 1.2* Devising a way to measure forces
Effects of a force:
1 changing the speed of an object

2 changing the direction of motion of an object (e.g. a string pulling a conker into a circle, rails holding a train on to a curve)

3 changing the shape of an object (e.g. bending a steel rule)

4 changing the size of an object (e.g. compressing the air in a bicycle pump)

5 overcoming another force (e.g. pushing a book along the bench against friction).

The most suitable effects for measurement are 3 and 4. Stretching a piece of rubber (e.g. a rubber band), and stretching or compressing a spiral spring are likely suggestions, although other possibilities exist. A rubber-based instrument has the advantage (from a teaching point of view) that the relation between force and extension is not a linear one: this means that calibration is certainly not a mere formality. Reference must be made to some sort of standard force (e.g. the pull of gravity on a certain spring by a specified amount). Attention must then be given to how a force of, say, twice the size is recognised, by combining two identical forces in a suitable way. Details of materials and construction are not given here because of the great diversity possible. Points to check include the extent of possible motion, stability in use, range of forces measured. Pupils keen on design may like to produce refined versions.

One suitable instrument has already been designed in *Patterns 1*, Section 1.

▷ *Investigation 1.3* Measuring forces

The time spent on this investigation will depend on how familiar pupils are with measuring forces and with the newton as a unit. Fairly large forces are involved so that they are of a magnitude which means something in terms of 'feel' to a pupil.

Part g

Weight on the Moon is about 1/6 of that on Earth. The significant forces for the 'personal weighing machine' are those applied at the two ends of the spring which is stretched. Because a lever system is used these (equal) forces are normally greater than the actual weight. Even with a simple spring balance, which is easier to understand, the forces measured are the equal forces applied to the ends of the spring, i.e. the force of the load on the spring (downwards) and the force of the support on the spring (upwards). This could be an extra problem for pupils to puzzle over.

Part j

The answer is expected to be the same as in part g.

Part k

Raising each end in turn and adding the results gives the weight of the table. This is frequently not obvious to pupils.

▷Part m

If the door behaves reliably, the expected result is: (force × distance from hinge) is constant ($F \times x = c$). Strictly it is the perpendicular distance from the hinge to the line of the force which should be measured, but most pupils will naturally pull in the most effective way, at right angles to the door. In this sort of example $F \times x$ is called the moment of the force. (Moment in the sense of importance, in this case with respect to turning the door.)

As an introduction to the next few investigations a discussion on what the meaning of the word 'machine' is can be useful. Many so-called machines (e.g. car, washing machine) have a non-mechanical energy transfer device operated by fuel, electricity etc. Omitting this aspect a machine can be said to be a mechanical device for applying a force more conveniently, or for transferring energy in a convenient way.

Investigation 1.4 The lever: a simple machine

Part b

Distance multipliers: fishing rod, long scissors (non-gravitational load).

An equal-arm lever is (in the simple sense intended) neither a force-multiplier nor a distance-multiplier.

Part c

(Force × distance) is the same for load and effort, quite closely (unless the pivot has a great deal of friction), i.e.

$$(F \times d) = c, \text{ or } (F_L \times d_L) = (F_E \times d_E)$$

▷Part d

The simplest way to consider the lever's weight is to think of it as an additional load, or an additional effort. It is assumed (without more than intuitive justification) that the weight can be considered to act at one point (the centre of gravity). If suffix zero refers to the lever,

$$(F_L \times d_L) + (F_0 \times d_0) = (F_E \times d_E)$$
$$\text{or} (F_L \times d_L) = (F_E \times d_E) + (F_0 \times d_0)$$

depending on the position of the pivot.

From the pupils' point of view this will probably seem a sensible suggestion, but certainly not so obvious that it does not need experimental checking. It is an interesting example of the interplay of theory and experiment that the pattern is 'simple' when once a certain viewpoint has been adopted, but would only be found by pure experiment (without any guiding theory) with extreme difficulty.

30

The discussion following can be used to bring out the significance of something $(F \times d)$ being the same at the 'input' and
'output' of the lever: it looks as if something is transferred, and as
if $(F \times d)$ indicates how much of this something is transferred.
Teachers not familiar with the suggestions in Nuffield Physics
Teachers' guide III, pages 24–27 (Note to teachers on 'work') are
recommended to read them: the same approach is followed in
Patterns and, in particular, work is treated as a measure of energy
transfer, *not* as a form of energy. The analogy of the cheque is a
good one (it shows how much money is transferred), and in fact
the analogy of money is an excellent one for energy in almost all
contexts, with the advantage that pupils know how the 'money-
transfer' system operates. (One might point out that energy is no
use as such, any more than a miser's hoard is. A tank of fuel oil is
useful only if burned, or spent. The analogy can be extended
much further.)

It should be noted that *Patterns* differs from Nuffield Physics
in that forms of energy are not emphasised. Instead of talking of a
transfer from 'chemical energy' to 'potential energy' it would be
more appropriate in *Patterns* to say that energy is transferred
from the chemicals which interact (one system) to the object which
is raised against gravity (another system). Similarly instead of a
transfer from 'kinetic energy' to 'heat' one would speak of the
energy of a moving object being distributed among the particles
of a system, although this anticipates some of the work of
Section 2.

Investigation 1.5 More machines
A distance-multiplier is in *Patterns 3*, Figure 1.7a; b and c are
force-multipliers and d is neither.

The machines suggested could be used in a circus arrangement.
For these machines it is approximately true that (force ×
distance) for the load is equal to (force × distance) for the effort.
Part e
This has strong links with ▷ Investigation 2.7 which extends the
work here to a more detailed examination of the body's muscular
system. The two investigations could be combined. A skeleton
may be useful, together with the topic book *Machines and engines*
which contains relevant illustrations.

Bones act as levers, invariably operating with a mechanical
disadvantage. They are therefore distance multipliers, and this is
true of the arm-biceps machine. Loads of 1, 2, 3, 4 and 5 kg
(10, 20, 30, 40, 50 N) can be placed in the hand of the model arm.
The force necessary to maintain the forearm in a horizontal
position for each of these loads can be measured on the force
meter (which is equivalent to the biceps). A graph can be plotted

to show force exerted by the 'biceps' against force exerted at the hand. By plotting the actual maximum force the biceps could apply (at the hands) on this graph the actual maximum force the biceps can exert can be found by extrapolation. An alternative approach would be to use $(F \times D) = (f \times d)$ for this system, remembering that the fulcrum is the elbow joint. (This will necessitate somewhat crude measurements of distances in the actual arm.)

The average biceps muscle has a mass of about 0.1 kg and weighs 1 N. The force it can exert is of the order of about 400 N. Thrust to weight ratio is thus about 400. In a jet engine it is about 4!

Part f

A single pulley changes the direction of an effort. Many muscle-bone systems change the direction of the effort, for example the thigh muscles straightening a bent leg. The tendons connecting the muscle to the bone of the lower leg enables this change of direction to occur. It is analogous to a single pulley system.

The pattern, work = force × distance, implies not only the numerical relation, but also joules = newtons × metres or 1 joule = 1 newton × 1 metre.

This is typical of all mathematical patterns involving measurable quantities, which all have a numerical value and a unit. It is important that the direction of the movement that matters is recognised as being in the direction of the force. Movement perpendicular to this 'does not count', and (in suitable examples) does not need a source of energy. For example sliding a mass on polystyrene beads requires very little energy compared to lifting it against its weight. This can later be extended to show that it is the component of the motion in the direction of the force which is significant (or equally the component of the force in the direction of motion). If the pupils have done a considerable amount of vector work in a mathematics course it is even possible to point out that work is the scalar product of force and distance. The Nuffield Physics reference (*Teachers' guide III*, pages 37–39, 'Getting tired when holding a load at rest') is useful background for teachers not familiar with these ideas.

Investigation 1.6 Work and its measurement

This investigation provides experience related to the work pattern discussed above. Depending on the pupils, it may be appropriate to extend or curtail this, or possibly to provide additional practice at using the pattern on simple problems. In all cases it is (force × distance) taking due account of direction which must be calculated.

Investigation 1.7 What is a person's work worth? As with all of the 'social studies' investigations, the examples chosen could quickly date. Teachers will no doubt substitute current newspaper extracts and photographs for those which are given in the *Pupils' manual*.

It should be noted that work against gravity plays a minor role here. This is deliberate, to counteract the common misunderstanding that work is always connected with weight, which should be recognised as only one type of force among many.

Investigation 1.8 Still more machines

Various machines are appropriate here, among them a car jack, a wheel-and-axle, an inclined plane (probably sliding version), worm gear or other low-ratio gear, bicycle. Each different load would be entered as a separate line in the table. The fact that the input work (i.e. energy transferred to the machine) is always more than the output work (i.e. energy transferred from the machine) should emerge easily, but it may be less obvious that this is associated with friction. If this idea does not come at once, it can be left until the next few investigations have been done.

The definition of efficiency given emphasises that it is a quantity (strictly a ratio) which depends on what is wanted. This is taken up in later sections, but a simple example would be a lever pivoted so that its centre of gravity must be raised: different values of efficiency are obtained if the energy transferred to the lever itself is included or is excluded from the numerator. Similar considerations apply to raising a pulley block.

The efficiency of machines appears, at this stage, to be 100 per cent (approximately at least) or less. It might be useful to construct an efficiency chart for different machines to emphasise that the efficiency is never much more than 100 per cent, certainly not more than can be attributed to experimental errors, whereas it can be much less than 100 per cent.

The obvious suggestion is that energy is lost. This may or may not be acceptable to pupils. Discussion can bring out the fact that, to determine whether energy was really lost, one would need to measure all the energy transfers, and see whether the total transferred from the machine equalled that transferred to it. This is not possible at this stage. It is taken up again in Section 2. Again the Nuffield Physics reference (*Teachers' guide III*, pages 28–33, 'Conservation of energy') is valuable, although the suggested sequence is different, and in *Patterns* the calorie is not used.

It is suggested that, in the absence of direct evidence, pupils should be encouraged to be sceptical at this stage about the conservation of energy. At best one half of the principle has been established, and that only in a restricted field: it seems that energy might be destroyed or 'lost', but it cannot, in these experiments, be created.

Investigation 1.9 Perpetual motion machines

Examples of (apparent) perpetual movement include the planets round the Sun and molecules in the air. Strictly speaking the Académie des Sciences was less scientific than the Patents Office: it is an interesting question, however, whether practical common sense is not a better guide than scientific scepticism in many areas! The interactions which prevent perpetual motion machines working are the 'dissipative' phenomena such as friction, electrical resistance, viscosity. The characteristic of all these is that energy is transferred to the particles of the system (shown by a rise of temperature) whatever the direction of motion, unlike (for example) a spring, where the energy transfer is reversible. It is too early for pupils to gain a full understanding of this, but they should recognise that reversing the motion makes no difference – the interaction still hinders the motion, and leads to a 'loss' of energy. Again, half the principle of conservation of energy is established.

Investigation 1.10 Friction

The association of temperature rise with friction is made explicit here, as is the fact that a large amount of work (in human terms) produces a rather slight rise in temperature: it is not a practical proposition to warm a room by clapping hands! It is doubtful whether any pupils in a particular class have ever succeeded in lighting a fire by 'rubbing two sticks together'!

▷ *Investigation 1.11* The efficiency of a machine

For most machines the efficiency is greater at greater loads. This can be explained because the energy 'loss' usually includes two parts, that due to friction, and that due to energy transfers which are, at least in principle, reversible (such as raising a pulley block). The latter remains constant, while the friction increases with load. Consequently the total energy 'loss' does not increase as rapidly as the load does, leading to the observed result.

Pupils are often surprised by this result. It has a very practical application, in that machines are most efficient when used near to their maximum capability.

Investigation 1.12 Other ways of transferring energy

Energy for the home enters electrically, as various fuels, and possibly by means of the water supply, although this is not often utilised. Similarly, energy is transferred around the country by the transport of fuels (in trucks, tankers or pipelines), or by electrical transmission. On a smaller scale hydraulic and pneumatic systems are also used. In some parts of the world, energy is transported by moving material at a height (typically water to hydro-electric power station). All except fuel transport can be considered in terms of a cycle of building blocks, which deliver energy to one system and pick it up from another (in some ways like a belt drive, stretched on one side, less so on the other). Fuels, on the other hand, are not normally reconstituted, so that they represent a one-way transfer and a permanent change of the building blocks. They also need an atmosphere: the energy is not in the petrol, but in (petrol + oxygen).

In garages compressed air drills are used because of the absence of sparking, in addition to the reasons mentioned in the *Pupils' manual*. Vehicles with an electric motor for each wheel have been built, giving independent drive: wheel slip on one wheel does not (significantly) reduce the force exerted by the other. Suspension problems are also easier because a flexible lead can be used to a motor moving with the wheel: no drive shaft is needed.

The extension of the word work to hydraulic, pneumatic and electrical machines is a natural one. The electrical case is dealt with in Section 3, but the relation between (force × distance) and flow under pressure can be illustrated simply as shown below.

Figure 1.1

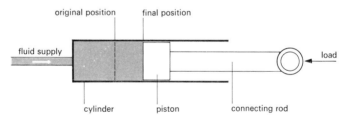

Suppose fluid (assumed incompressible) is supplied under pressure to an actuator (e.g. for a wing flap on an aircraft) which consists of a piston which can move in a close-fitting cylinder (see figure 1.1). The pressure of the fluid causes the piston to move, overcoming the load. Call the area of the cylinder A, the volume of fluid supplied V, its pressure p, the distance moved by the piston d, and the load F. It is clear that $V = A \times d$, and $F = p \times A$ (ignoring friction).

Then the work $= F \times d$

$$= (p \times A) \times \left(\frac{V}{A}\right)$$

$$= p \times V$$

35

Strictly the pressure p is the extra pressure in the fluid above that of the atmosphere. The result, obtained for a particular case, is quite general: $(p \times V)$ is what might be called 'fluid work', or 'pressure work', and is an equally good measure of energy transfer as $(F \times d)$.

Investigation 1.13   Transferring energy without transferring building blocks

The emphasis here is on showing energy transfer in a variety of ways in which building blocks are not transferred. In some cases building blocks are an essential part of the mechanism of transfer (e.g. sound, waves on liquids), but they do not 'carry' the energy along in the same way as does a flow of electrons or of water. Only brief demonstrations are intended because this is only an introductory investigation. It may be valuable to discuss possible ways of convincing a sceptic that energy is conveyed in each case. Other versions of the demonstrations would serve equally well.

Part c

i   To show waves on liquids, the transparent tank is ideal, but rather expensive. It also makes possible the demonstration of waves at an interface as well as a surface (see figure 1.2a). A small object in the interface shows almost circular motion in a vertical plane.

Figure 1.2a

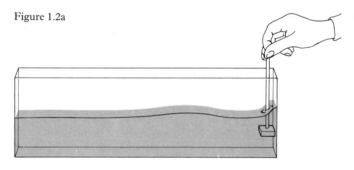

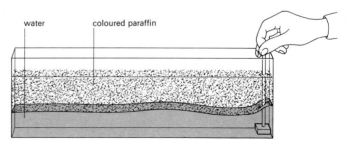

water   coloured paraffin

ii Waves on a string or rope are best shown with one of considerable mass per unit length, because the speed is less than with a lighter one. The fact that the tension also affects the speed will be obvious to pupils if they participate in the demonstration. Thick rubber tubing (possibly filled with sand) is also suitable for this demonstration. The floor may be found more convenient than a bench (see figure 1.2b).

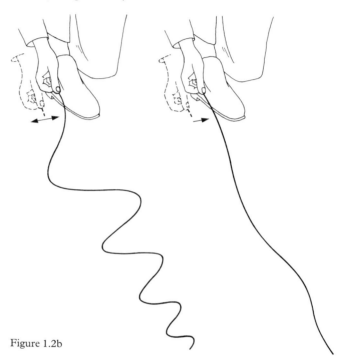

Figure 1.2b

iii A long slinky behaves in a similar way to a rope for transverse waves, but can also be caused to transmit a longitudinal wave. If the far end is firmly fixed and the bench or floor shiny, it is possible to see reflection of each type of wave at the fixed end. The speeds of longitudinal and transverse waves are not (in general) the same: this can be observed, with some difficulty, if a mixed pulse is started, i.e. a transverse and a longitudinal pulse with the same movement of the hand. See figure 1.2c on page 38.

iv Sound transfers energy, but this is not so easy to show, mainly because the amount of energy is small. The fact that some singers can shatter a wine glass is well known, but it hardly makes for a reliable demonstration! The possible damage caused by sonic booms could also be mentioned. Any actual demonstration will

37

Figure 1.2c

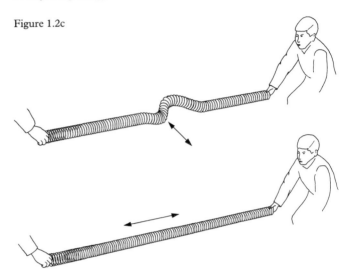

almost certainly have to rely on resonance to make the energy transfer noticeable. One possibility is to show that some of the (undamped) strings of a piano are set in vibration by a suitable sound, for example a loud note sung or played on another instrument.

v Light is an obvious example of the transfer of energy, which can occur through a vacuum, thus not depending on building blocks (apart from its production and detection). A Crooke's radiometer could be used to make the energy aspect clearer, but the explanation of how it works could not be given at this stage. Pupils may also suggest the similarity to infra-red ('heat') radiation and other forms, although these are not being emphasised here.

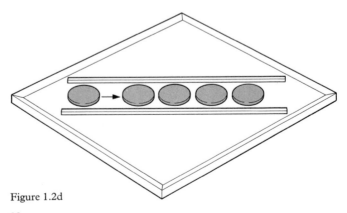

Figure 1.2d

vi Some teachers may like to show the way in which a line of ring magnets on a frictionless surface (air table or 'dry-ice pucks') can pass energy from one to the other, in effect producing a longitudinal wave (see figure 1.2d).

vii If plenty of dynamics trolleys are available it is possible to use these to construct spring-linked systems which will show longitudinal or transverse waves (see figure 1.2e).

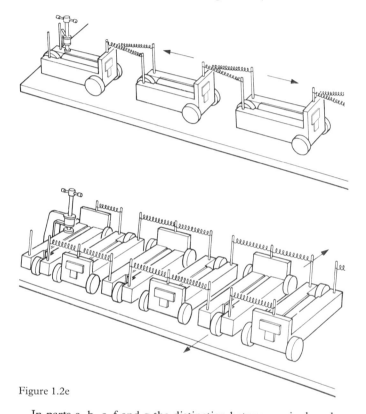

Figure 1.2e

In parts a, b, c, f and g the distinction between a single pulse and a continuous wave can be brought out. For parts d and e there is no clear evidence at this stage that the phenomena are similar to the waves in the other parts. The transfer of energy by sea waves and by earthquakes (see figure 1.16 in *Patterns 3*) do not involve the transfer of building blocks, and again it is not obvious that earthquakes are waves. A degree of scepticism could be encouraged.

Some form of 'wave machine' to simulate wave motion mechanically might also be shown at this point.

Investigation 1.14 Is there a pattern in the way ripples are reflected?
This is a relatively easy start to the search for common patterns in these new energy transfer mechanisms. The *Pupils' manual* is written on the assumption that the experiment will be done by pupils, but some teachers may prefer to make this and/or other ripple tank experiments demonstrations.
Part a
Pupils will need individual assistance if they have not used ripple tanks before. The Nuffield Physics *Guide to experiments III* gives additional details for those not familiar with the techniques. It is convenient to tell pupils the best volume of water for the model of tank used.
Part b
Circular patterns are an indication that the speed is the same in all directions (expected from symmetry anyway). Observant pupils may notice that the ripples are 'weaker' (i.e. of lesser amplitude) when they are of greater diameter. This can be linked to the greater length of circumference through which the energy flows.
Part c
The reflected pulse is also circular, with its centre behind the reflector. Two pulses started simultaneously and symmetrically on either side of the reflector seem to pass right through it, although each is reflected.
Part d
Straight pulses do not 'fade out' so much as circular ones. They also have a noticeable end effect.
Part e
This need not take long. No great precision is possible, and it should not be attempted. Various ways of stating the pattern are acceptable (e.g. the angle between the waves and the barrier is the same before and after reflection). It may be worth encouraging pupils to consider how the direction of energy flow is changed in reflection.
▷Part f
Extra for fast pupils. A focussing effect should be predicted, with the energy flow lines passing through a point about halfway between O and C. The experimental confirmation is quite dramatic.
▷Part g
The reverse of part f. A semicircular barrier will give a reflected wave which is straight in the middle, but curved at the sides, even with the best position for starting the pulse. A parabolic reflector gives a good straight pulse after reflection if the pulse is started at

the focus. Pupils could discover this by trial (although they could hardly know the name of the curve).

Part h

Important aspects of continuous waves arise here, and can arise directly from observation. It is advisable to let the pupils gain familiarity with the apparatus before making close observations.

The ripples show a constant spacing between crest and trough, i.e. a constant wavelength. (If very large amplitude ripples are used this may cease to be strictly true, since the speed depends on amplitude, if large, but this is not obvious to pupils.) It should be clear that the waves have the same frequency as the vibrator producing them.

The Earth goes round the Sun at a frequency 1.0 yr^{-1} and the tides occur at about 1.9 day^{-1} (i.e. twice every 24 hours 50 minutes). The mains frequency is 50 Hz in Britain and 60 Hz in North America. Radio station frequencies are given in *Radio Times*. (Medium and long wave stations are usually quoted in terms of wavelength.) The reflection pattern is the same here as before, and does not depend on frequency. Continuous waves represent a steady flow of energy.

Part i

The speed of the high frequency ripples is the same as that of others (approximately at least) but the shorter wavelength means that one wavelength is traversed in a shorter time, making it difficult for the eye to distinguish. The fact that a 'snap shot' taken by blinking gives a clearer impression shows that this is a time effect in the eye (or brain). Blinking at the same frequency as that of the ripples would give a sequence of identical images, so the waves would appear stationary.

Further explanation of the stroboscope, with demonstrations, will be needed beyond that which is given in *Patterns 3*. The propellor rotating at 8.0 Hz would appear stationary as it would at any integral multiple of 8.0 Hz.

The experimental side is not easy at first. However it does lead to separate measurements of wavelength (of the images on the paper) and frequency. Help from the teacher will be needed by many pupils in the calculation of the frequency, since this is not yet a thoroughly familiar concept.

Part j

The first part is in effect a simple problem using the pattern: distance = (speed × time). Combining this pattern with the definitions of frequency and wavelength leads to the pattern, $v = n\lambda$, which is derived without reference to the type of wave involved. The calculation of the speed of the image-waves on the paper is a straightforward application of the pattern; the water waves move more slowly (in proportion to the respective distances from the light source).

The speed is, within the limits of the experiment, independent of frequency. The inherent imprecision of the experiment may lead to spurious suggestions of variation, which can only be resolved by further data.

Additional problems using the mathematical pattern could be added at this point if this is thought desirable.

Investigation 1.15 How does the behaviour of ripples depend on depth of liquid? This experiment requires careful setting up. Those not familiar with it are advised to try it beforehand. For details see Nuffield Physics, Year III, experiment 4t.

Part a

The speed of the waves is less in shallow water, but the effect is noticeable only when the depth is so small that attenuation (i.e. fading out) begins to be significant. Levelling becomes very important in these circumstances. The observable difference (with or without stroboscopes) is a reduction of wavelength. Since the frequency is unchanged (there is clearly no change in the number of ripples passing any point in unit time), the speed change can be deduced using $v = n\lambda$. (This can be made quantitative if desired.)

Part b

The refraction of individual ripples can be considered as a consequence of (i) the speed change and (ii) maintaining continuity on the two sides of the interface.

This is a rather simplified view of refraction, but is adequate at this stage. It fits in with the analogy of marching soldiers (if that is used as a teaching point). Refraction of the path of the ripples is towards the normal when the ripples slow down.

Part c

Since there is no obvious 'memory' in a ripple, one would not expect the speed to depend on its past history. Therefore the prediction would be made that on passing back into deeper water the speed would revert to its original value, i.e. the waves would get faster, and the direction of travel be refracted away from the normal. This can be observed (with difficulty) using a triangular glass plate.

The film loops should be regarded as a less effective way of teaching this work, although more efficient in terms of convenience and time.

Investigation 1.16 Combining ripples

Part a

Ripples seem to pass through each other with no mutual effects (one is tempted to say 'without interfering with each other' but the expression would be misleading in this context!). The open-ended experimenting with two finger-dippers may lead more observant pupils to the surprising observation that the super-imposed circles can equally well be seen as 'bands' spreading out from the mid-point. This is clearly seen with the vibrating dippers when stroboscopes are used. A redistribution of the energy flow takes place, so that in certain directions it is zero.

Part b

This part forms the basis for a discussion to elucidate the concepts of displacement, superposition and interference (constructive and destructive), as applied to ripples. The concept of phase is a difficult one, and it is not suggested that any precise definition is attempted here; the phrases 'in phase' and 'out of phase' should be understood as descriptive terms. (If equal waves are in phase the displacements at similar points are exactly the same.)

Part c

The advantage of these physical models is that the concrete representation does not move.

Part d

The drawing exercise helps to reinforce what is happening with the ripples. The bold lines indicating the constructive inter-ference points spreading out are gentle curves, becoming effectively straight at a considerable distance from the sources. Destructive interference occurs between them: no energy flow occurs along intermediate lines.

Part e

The theoretical prediction is quite hard: reduction in the wave-length gives more constructive interference lines than before, so the spacing is also reduced. If the frequencies of the sources are different, interference patterns are formed which change con-tinually. The importance of the concept of coherence is that this is essential for steady interference effects.

▷Part f

Increasing the separation of the sources leads to closer spacing of the constructive interference bands, as can be predicted by drawing.

Part g

Diffraction is treated here simply as the spreading of waves from a straight line path when they meet a gap or obstacle. It is most noticeable when the obstacle or gap is comparable in size with the wavelength. (Details of diffraction patterns need not be con-sidered.) A narrow gap leads to diffraction rather evenly over a whole semicircle, but the amplitude is small because the energy transmitted through the gap is small.

▷Part h

The double gap produces an interference pattern identical with that from two coherent sources.

Investigation 1.17 Patterns of behaviour of sound

This is a series of demonstrations with class participation which shows a number of similarities between sound and ripples, and establishes sound as a wave phenomenon. Reflection can be demonstrated as shown in figure 1.3 (any hard surface will serve instead of a wall). The pattern of reflection is the same as with ripples (the tubes are necessary because of diffraction effects).

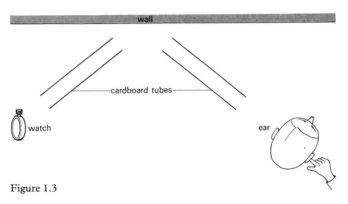

Figure 1.3

Both reflection and the speed of sound can be shown by using echoes, for example of hand claps, from a fairly distant wall. An elaboration of this, which enables the speed of sound to be found, uses a metronome, the interval between 'ticks' being adjusted until one coincides with the echo of the previous one. From the calibration (usually in minutes^{-1}) and the distance of the wall the speed of sound can be calculated.

Figure 1.4 shows one way to demonstrate the refraction of sound. The balloon full of carbon dioxide, which slows down the sound waves, acts as a converging lens, so that, if the distances are right, interposing the balloon makes the tick sound louder.

Figure 1.4

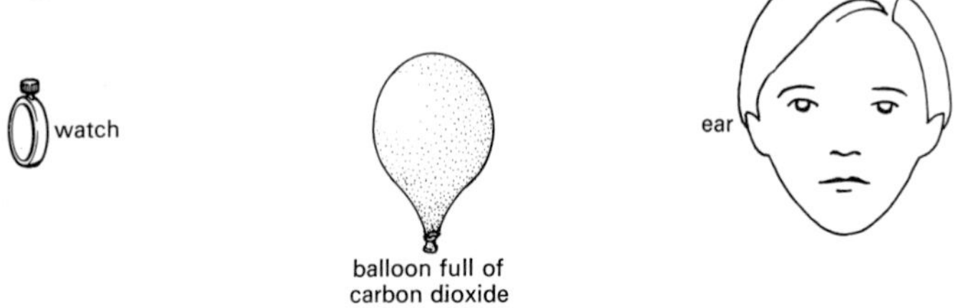

watch

ear

balloon full of carbon dioxide

44

Attempts to show the interference of sound waves are some-times not very convincing in the laboratory because of reflections from hard surfaces (walls, benches) and standing waves being set up. Consequently it is best done in the open, well away from buildings. There are several ways of showing the effect and it is probably worth doing more than one of these. The quickest is to attach the two loudspeakers (connected in parallel to the signal generator: see figure 1.5a) to a meter rule or lath (for example with stout elastic bands), and slowly rotate the rule around a vertical axis so that the speakers point towards different members of the class in turn. A frequency of about 2 000 Hz and a separation of about 0.5 m are suitable. The pupils hear the maxima and minima sweeping past them. (This works tolerably well in the laboratory, if outdoor work should prove impossible.) A second method is similar, except that pupils walk in turn in front of the stationary loudspeakers. Blocking one ear helps. The third method is to tell the pupils to 'find a loud place', and they then should line up on a series of lines as in figure 1.5b. In this situation reversing the connexions to one speaker reduces the loudness. Pupils hear a slight (50 per cent, 3 dB) reduction when it is dis-connected, and a considerable reduction (about 90 per cent, 10 dB) when it is reconnected.

In this destructive interference situation it is very effective to cover one loudspeaker with an absorbent cushion, which makes the sound perceived get louder. This is strange, even when expected! It is convincing evidence of the wave nature of sound.

Figure 1.5a

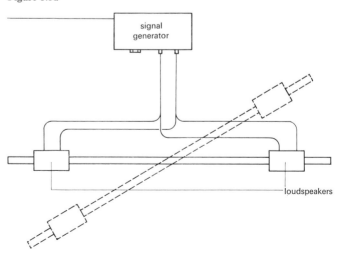

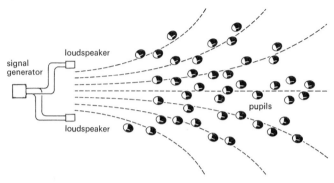

Figure 1.5b

Both the frequency and the separation can be varied, with results similar to those for ripples.

Diffraction of sound is so common that we take it for granted: one can hear the noise down the corridor through the open doorway. The fact that oscillating and vibrating objects emit sound enables frequency to be brought in naturally, and Savart's toothed wheels or the homemade equivalent show the relation between pitch and frequency. (Pitch is the term for what is perceived subjectively: how high or low a note is. An octave or a major fifth is an interval of pitch. Frequency is the objectively measured quantity. The fact that an interval of an octave corresponds to doubling the frequency is a matter of significance and of interest, not a self-evident tautology.)

It is not easy to show in any direct way that sound is a longitudinal wave. Probably the fact that a loudspeaker vibrates 'in and out', and the directions in which a tuning fork emits the loudest sound are the two best pieces of evidence.

Investigation 1.18 Noise
Part a
The distinction between sound and noise is a subjective (aesthetic?) one, not scientific. But scientific matters have a bearing on it, for example the level of sound power which is damaging.

Foulness (or Maplin Sands) is remote from centres of population: the numbers of people affected by low flying aircraft will be much smaller than at other sites: much of the flight path is over the sea. Other considerations are also relevant, such as distance from London and other destinations or starting points, links with other forms of transport, availability of airport workers, the likely advent of VTOL and STOL aircraft, and many others.

Part b

A tape should be prepared on which a sequence of five or six notes is recorded, all of the same frequency, but each louder by 6 dB than the previous one (i.e. at four times the intensity). This is easily achieved using a signal generator with voltmeter attached, as doubling the output voltage corresponds to quadrupling the power. Direct input to the tape recorder is best (possibly via an attenuator), rather than using a loudspeaker and microphone. The loudest note should just overload the recording. Fairly brief tones with even briefer pauses are best. It is convenient to record the sequence several times so that it can be repeated without rewinding.

The significant result is that quadrupling the sound power is perceived as a roughly fixed increase in loudness: pupils may well agree that the notes go up by equal steps of loudness, or at least nearly so. The relation between loudness and power is not one of proportionality: it is in fact logarithmic, as are several relations connected with perception. (If L represents loudness and I the intensity, then

$$L/dB = 10 \log_{10}(I/10^{-12}\,\mathrm{W\,m^{-2}}).$$

For two intensities such that $I_2 = 4I_1$, corresponding to loudnesses L_1 and L_2,

$$L_1/dB = 10 \log_{10}(I_1/10^{-12}\,\mathrm{W\,m^{-2}})$$
$$L_2/dB = 10 \log_{10}(I_2/10^{-12}\,\mathrm{W\,m^{-2}})$$
$$\therefore (L_2 - L_1)/dB = 10\{\log_{10}(I_2/10^{-12}\,\mathrm{W\,m^{-2}})$$
$$- \log_{10}(I_1/10^{-12}\,\mathrm{W\,m^{-2}})\}$$
$$= 10 \log_{10}(I_2/I_1)$$
$$= 10 \log_{10}4$$
$$\approx 10 \times 0.606$$
$$\approx 6$$

So, $L_2 - L_1 \approx 6$ dB.

This calculation is not intended for pupils.

It may be helpful for pupils to construct an additional column to the table showing the loudness in bels.

The distance of a sound need not be specified very exactly on account of the logarithmic nature of the scale. Doubling the distance might give a quarter of the intensity, but this means only 6 dB difference in loudness.

It is of interest to compare the intensity of a loud sound with other energy flows. For example an electric fire might easily radiate more than $1.0\,\mathrm{kW\,m^{-2}}$ through a surface 0.5 m from it.

This is 1 000 times greater than a painful sound.
▷ Part c
The sounds should be recorded from a calibrated signal generator, with a separate voltmeter to ensure equal power if one is not provided on the generator. Some planning is necessary to obtain a good sequence of sounds, covering most of the audible range. The following is a set of 9 frequencies at approximately equal pitch intervals (chosen not to be a simple musical interval): 190, 300, 470, 750, 1 200, 1 900, 3 000, 4 700, 7 500 Hz.

If these are recorded in a jumbled sequence, with each possibly identified by a code letter, pupils can compare the nuisance caused. A fairly prolonged sound is needed, with the briefest gap between (this is why recording is suggested: producing the sounds 'live' leads to an awkward gap, or a sliding note). It may be found that the loudspeaker in use has pronounced resonances. If so, frequencies near the resonant frequencies should be avoided. Similarly frequencies outside the limits of good quality reproduction of amplifier or, more probably, speaker, should not be used. Many people find the extremes of the range of frequencies cause more nuisance than the middle range, but this is not universal.

For the second experiment in this part recordings need to be made of sounds varying widely in loudness and in 'nuisance-value'. Those used in trial situations and found to be effective were as follows: wind whistling through trees, two year old child crying, underground train (recorded inside), mains (50 Hz) hum, spin drier, circular saw, clock ticking, conversation, traffic, running tap.

Each sound should last for about one minute in order that pupils can do a simple task as they listen. This will enable them to compare the degree of nuisance more effectively. Suitable tasks would be punctuating a piece of prose, straightforward sums or drawing a diagram of some apparatus.

This section of the tape should be played twice. The first time the maximum loudness should be assessed on the scale i to v, and the second time the nuisance should be assessed on the scale A to E (see *Pupils' manual*).

Good agreement is usually found in the assessment of loudness, but much less in the assessment of nuisance. Also certain sounds (e.g. child crying) are much more disturbing to most people than others (e.g. clock ticking) irrespective of loudness. This illustrates the subjective nature of nuisance as opposed to loudness.
Part d
The loudness reduction to increase the 'percentage acceptance' from 50 per cent to 80 per cent is from 81 dB to 75 dB, i.e. a 6 dB

reduction (approximately), corresponding to reducing the intensity to a quarter of its previous value. The graph refers to the noise from motor vehicles. To reduce the sound intensity to one quarter would be a formidable engineering undertaking, although probably not impossible. To reduce the loudness by a further 10 dB (to 1/40 of the original intensity) would be totally impracticable, although this would still not be acceptable to 5 per cent of the population.

Notes on the discussion questions

Warning noises need to attract attention (fire bell, baby's cry). There is evidence that people strongly dislike working in an environment so noisy that they cannot easily communicate with each other. Reducing the noise level so that they can speak to one another makes the situation much more tolerable.

▷ *Investigation 1.19* Musical instruments

Part a

Instruments can be classified in terms of range, type (brass/ woodwind/string/percussion), and in several other ways. Display of the wave forms on an oscilloscope shows distinct differences between different instruments, but little difference (other than frequency) between different notes from the same instrument. Considerable skill would be needed to identify an instrument from the trace. Most brass instruments played softly produce a good approximation to a simple sine curve, but if played loudly a more complex wave form results. Woodwind and stringed instruments usually have fairly complex wave forms (showing the presence of harmonics – see below). The position at which stringed instruments are bowed is chosen to create many harmonics, giving the note produced 'brilliance'.

Part b

Details of demonstrations of standing waves (also called stationary waves) are given in Nuffield Physics, Year V, experiments 94 to 98.

The resultant waves from the incident and reflected waves for times 0, 0.10, 0.20, 0.30, 0.40 s are shown below. Those for the

Figure 1.6

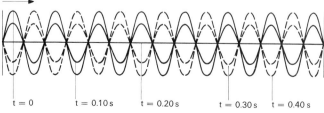

t = 0   t = 0.10 s   t = 0.20 s   t = 0.30 s   t = 0.40 s

subsequent instants coincide with those for 0.30, 0.20, 0.10, 0 s respectively. These are based on the reflected wave being equal in amplitude to the incident wave, a fair approximation in many cases.

The nodes are half a wavelength apart. Any two equal waves at the same frequency travelling in opposite directions would be expected to interfere so as to produce a standing wave pattern, in which the amplitude is zero (at all times) for certain points (nodes) and a maximum at intermediate points (antinodes).

Part c

The observation that $l = \frac{1}{2}\lambda$, i.e. $\lambda = 2l$, for the fundamental, and $\lambda = \frac{2l}{2}, \frac{2l}{3}, \frac{2l}{4}$ etc. for higher harmonics leads to the frequencies n, $2n$, $3n$, $4n$ etc. The sound energy derives from the kinetic energy of the string.

Figure 1.7

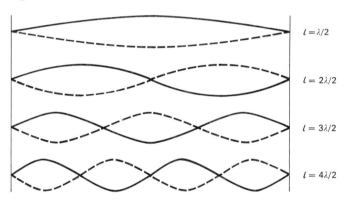

$l = \lambda/2$

$l = 2\lambda/2$

$l = 3\lambda/2$

$l = 4\lambda/2$

Part d

Similarly here (with a pipe closed at one end), the open end is an

Figure 1.8

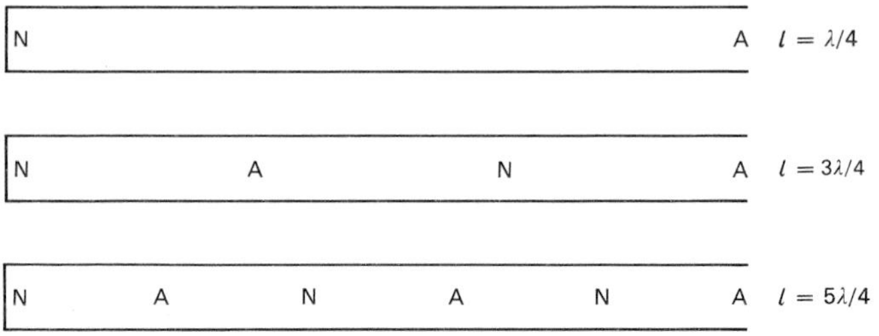

| N | | | | | A | $l = \lambda/4$ |

| N | A | | N | | A | $l = 3\lambda/4$ |

| N | A | N | A | N | A | $l = 5\lambda/4$ |

antinode for particle movement, whereas the closed end is a node. (It is necessary to mention particle movement because pressure has a node at the open end and an antinode at the closed end: it is as well not to introduce this complication to the pupils in the first instance.) This leads to the length being $\frac{1}{4}\lambda$ so that $\lambda = 4l$, for the fundamental, and $\lambda = \dfrac{4l}{3}, \dfrac{4l}{5}, \dfrac{4l}{7}$ etc. for higher harmonics (see diagrams). This gives frequencies n, $3n$, $5n$, $7n$ etc. Reed instruments have many harmonics, and in some cases a selection of those mentioned are prominent. This is because the vibrations of both the air column and the reed are important.

Part e

At a resonant frequency, the source of vibration causes another object (e.g. the table top or the air column) to vibrate at the same frequency, because this is near to its natural frequency. This leads to a more rapid dissipation of energy, i.e. a louder sound. Stringed instruments use resonance of both an air volume and one or more thin layers of wood to produce an even resonance over a wide range of frequencies.

The question of why a Stradivarius is so much to be preferred to a modern violin was the subject of a fascinating television programme in 1971. Two important features of the old violins from Cremona, Italy, emerged: a loud resonance and an even resonance over the whole range. Cheap violins tend to have little bass response, and excessive resonance above 3000 Hz. Violins by Stradivarius particularly were shown to have the attractive 'singing' tone, which is associated with the absence of excessive high frequencies. Orchestral soloists now frequently prefer instruments by Guarneri which have a louder response, but are not quite as mellow as a Stradivarius which is preferred for quartets and so on.

The even resonance is achieved by making the resonance of the body around the frequency of the G-string, and that of the air in it around that of the D-string. The age may well be important, but the varnish, contrary to rumour, does not seem to be a crucial factor. See also 'The physics of violins' by Carleen Maley Hutchins, Scientific American offprint no. 289 (November 1962).

The frequency meter shown in the photograph in the *Pupils' manual* is used by sliding the rod out of its holder until it can be observed to vibrate with maximum amplitude. The frequency can then be read off on the scale, previously calibrated from a vibrator of known frequency.

Resonance is the cause of considerable design problems in loudspeakers, because it is all too easy for one particular frequency (or rather a narrow range) to be reproduced much louder than others.

Vibration at particular vehicle speeds is another common example. If obtainable the film or film loop of the Tacoma Narrows bridge collapse is a dramatic illustration of the possible large effects of resonance.

There are two approaches to reducing the effects of resonance: preventing the transmission of frequencies which might produce it, and the introduction of damping to dissipate the energy and avoid large oscillations building up. The rubber suspension for a car engine probably does both, and 'sound absorbing' kits are sold in large numbers.

▷ *Investigation 1.20* Earthquakes and energy

Part a

Figure 1.30 in *Patterns 3* shows the narrow zones of major earthquakes. Here we have a hint of plate tectonics.

In the Peruvian earthquake, the epicentre was 80 km offshore. The shock waves' source (the focus) was at shallow depths (50 km, but up to 700 km at the deepest point). The measurements quoted in the investigation were difficult to make and so patterns are imprecise. This leads to difficulty in making predictions.

Part b

The fact that mechanical waves originate from some sort of vibration and convey energy without the transfer of building blocks suggest that earthquakes might be waves.

Liquids cannot sustain shear forces: attempting to deform a liquid in this way leads to flow. The 'sound' wave is the longitudinal one: it involves pressure changes. The transverse wave would not be expected in a liquid, because it would involve shear forces.

Three seismometers give full information about ground displacement because this is a vector quantity with three components.

Part c

To use speed differences to locate earthquake epicentres it is necessary to know (or assume) that the type of rock traversed by the wave is similar to that from which the calibration was made. This may well not be the case, although speeds in different types of rock are not greatly different. The shorter distances would be subject to less error on account of the Earth's curvature. Stations at greater distances would over-estimate the speed, if the surface distance was used for calculation.

These speeds are as shown (to calculate them it is necessary to know the time of occurrence of the earthquake: 0800 hours, with epicentre in Washington DC (USA)). The stations have been re-arranged in order of distance, and the surface distance used in calculation.

Seismograph Station	Distance from Washington/km	Speed of P-wave/km s^{-1}	Speed of S-wave/km s^{-1}
New York, USA	339	8.9	4.35
Chicago, USA	988	8.65	4.66
Houston, USA	2010	8.1	4.5
Mexico City, Mexico	3120	9.0	4.95
Los Angeles, USA	3810	9.5	5.2
San Francisco, USA	4040	9.6	5.33
Bogota, Colombia	4840	10.0	5.5
London, UK	6060	10.7	5.95
Stockholm, Sweden	6800	10.9	6.1
Moscow, USSR	8040	11.8	6.5
Buenos Aires, Argentina	8640	13.0	6.6
Cairo, Egypt	9590	12.7	6.1

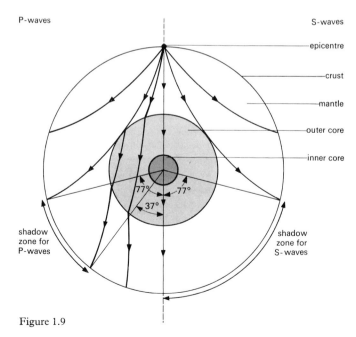

Figure 1.9

Part d

The non-arrival of S-waves is a clear indication that they are transverse and that there is probably liquid inside the Earth. The shorter time of arrival of P-waves than predicted from speeds derived from shorter distances shows that the speed is greater at certain depths than at the surface. The Earth is likely to show spherical symmetry (approximately) because of the very large gravitational forces: denser materials are expected nearer the centre. A model at this stage might be a central liquid core and a solid outer part, with little knowledge of dimensions of the core.

Speed changes lead to refraction. Figure 1.9 on page 53 shows how the refraction relates to the suggested structure: the curved paths are a consequence of the speed variation.

Part e

The interior of the Earth must be considerably denser than the surface rocks. The density of iron is about $7\,800\,\mathrm{kg\,m^{-3}}$, ignoring any increase due to compression.

Another relevant matter is the Earth's magnetic field, which may be caused by electric currents in the core, maintained by motion of the fluid (a self-acting dynamo). This would necessitate a core of conducting material. (An alternative cause of the Earth's magnetism could be currents outside the Earth, i.e. charged particles in motion.)

Both hypotheses about the Earth's interior may have some truth in them, or both may be incorrect.

Part f

The additional waves can be explained in terms of (partial) reflection at the interfaces.

Part g

A change in the stress imposed on part of the Earth's surface can lead to small movements. Liquid seems to lubricate the movement, or assist it in some way. This might be used to release the accumulated stress in small stages, relatively safely. It would be necessary to find ways of (i) producing small Earth movements (ii) ensuring they did not trigger off a major earthquake (iii) controlling the time and place of the movements so that the stress is progressively reduced.

▷ *Investigation 1.21* Moving objects

Part a

Pupils should have no difficulty in designing simple ball-reflection experiments. The pattern of reflection is 'angle of incidence equals angle of reflection' only for the (ideal) perfectly elastic case. Considerable deviations occur with certain types of ball, which are not very near to being perfectly elastic.

The discussion about particle-reflection must be hypothetical since no direct experiments are available. It will raise questions of interations (forces) between the particles, and whether collision could be elastic or not.

Part b

Increase of speed causes refraction towards the normal, in contrast to the behaviour of waves. Electrons are 'refracted' in a cathode ray tube, in a way broadly similar to the refraction of the ball bearing. Speeding an electron up, by means of the potential on an anode, causes refraction towards the normal (ignoring effects of the special shape of the anode). This is shown in several of the film strips available from Mullard's agents.

Part c

Diffraction and interference are hardly to be expected with ball bearings, and cannot be observed. This makes it all the more surprising that electrons can show both effects. At this stage it is unlikely that pupils will find this easy to believe. If a relevant film or a special electron diffraction tube is available either would provide evidence for this surprising fact.

▷ *Investigation 1.22* Does a centimetre-radiation transmitter produce waves?

This investigation gives an opportunity for pupils to devise experiments to find whether the radiation emitted has wave-properties. For this reason the term 'microwaves' is avoided. If the word appears on the apparatus it would be advisable to cover it with a label.

The key patterns will be those of diffraction and particularly interference. Reflection (from a metal surface) and refraction (e.g. through a hollow prism filled with paraffin (kerosene) and/or a wax lens) can also be demonstrated.

Many microwave transmitters produce a signal modulated at an audio frequency, so that the output from the detector can be amplified and used to operate a loudspeaker. The danger with this system is that pupils may think there is some connexion with sound, which is merely the means used to show the intensity of microwaves: the easier perception must be balanced against harder comprehension.

Diffraction is easily shown with a slit made by supporting two metal plates in a vertical plane. When the slit is smaller than about 100 mm, diffraction effects begin to be more noticeable. Interference can be demonstrated with a double slit made in a similar way. Varying the separation is a little more difficult to achieve, but two (or more) overlapping vertical metal strips make it possible. The effect is clearer if a diode probe is used rather than a horn detector.

The fact that interference can be observed may lead to the measurement of wavelength.

There are several ways pupils might suggest for measuring the wavelength: the simplest would be to see what size gap produces a diffraction pattern like a single slit. This does not work too well because the horn transmitter itself produces a diffraction pattern, but it can give an order of magnitude result. Much better in practice is a double slit experiment, which is straightforward, but involves the same calculation as with light, except that the approximations are more serious (see Nuffield Physics, Year V experiment 10.7b). The most effective method is probably to form standing waves by reflection (at normal incidence) from a plane aluminium sheet. Nodes and antinodes are easily found by means of the diode probe, and by measuring the distance for perhaps ten or twelve nodes a good estimate of wavelength is obtained. Near the reflector the nodes are of almost zero intensity, but further away they are not because the incident wave is of greater amplitude than the reflected one. The node-antinode distance of about 15 mm gives a wavelength close to 30 mm. If the speed is given as $3.0 \times 10^8 \, \text{m s}^{-1}$, the pattern $v = n\lambda$ can be used to determine the frequency, which is about 10^{10} Hz or 10^4 MHz. The idea that something could be vibrating or oscillating so rapidly may be quite amazing to pupils.

Investigation 1.23   Is light a wave?

Part a

A rapid, not very precise, experiment is best here. The degree of inventiveness required is slight. Faster pupils can move on to work investigating the curved mirrors. It should be clear that the result does not contribute directly to solving the major problem.

▷Part b

Using the reflection pattern, the positions of a point object and its image in a plane mirror can be proved, by geometrical means, to be symmetrical positions with respect to the mirror (regarded as a symmetry plane). Formal proof will be beyond many pupils at this stage, but it may be found that the emphasis on symmetry operations in many mathematics courses will mean that they have at least an intuitive understanding of the situation. Some mathematics courses regard it as almost axiomatic that reflection occurs according to the pattern 'angle of incidence equals angle of reflection' which can, of course, be known only by experiment and observation.

The idea of a virtual image, from which light only seems to come, is introduced here also.

Part c

Pupils should find without difficulty that light is refracted towards the normal on entering any liquid or solid from air, and vice versa. For parallel-sided blocks the final path is parallel to the original one.

If light were a wave it would be travelling more slowly in the other media than in air, but if it were a stream of particles it would be natural to think of it moving faster in the other media. The very great speed of light means that ingenious indirect means of measurement had to be devised. The results indicate, but hardly conclusively, that light may well be wave-like.

▷ Part d

The answer to the first problem may have already been found in part c. But putting the lamp in the water gives the possibility of total internal reflection, which is not predictable from the refraction pattern (although a few pupils may notice in part c that the angle of refraction is never greater than a certain value and wonder about the implications).

The simplest sort of explanation is: 'All the possible angles (of refraction) in air correspond to a limited range of angles (of incidence) in water. For angles in water greater than these, there is no matching angle in air, so the light stays in the water and is reflected.' This takes no account of the mechanism, but is probably satisfactory at this stage.

Part e

In the quotation from Newton he uses 'motion' to mean, in effect, waves.

Some pupils should be able to recognise that, if the wavelength is very small, diffraction effects would not be observed except on a similar scale.

The bending of light round finger and thumb suggest that possibly light has small-scale wave properties. The ball-bearing experiment is rather effective. If the source is symmetrically behind the ball as seen by the observer a tiny point of light can be perceived, apparently in the centre of the ball. This point moves as the observer moves slightly. Assuming (!) the light does not pass through the metal, it must be bent in some way round the edge. This is a diffraction effect, although conceivably an explanation might be considered in terms of refraction and/or reflection.

Part f

The term 'coherent' must be explained. Sources of light are coherent if frequency and phase are the same. It is hoped that pupils will be able to suggest, without prompting, that if light is a wave it must have a very short wavelength. They will probably need help in designing a Young's slits experiment, but may well offer many sensible suggestions. This discussion is at least as important as the experiment (see the reference). Doing the

57

experiment should convince them that light really must be a wave: the conclusion is inescapable. (But wait!) The question of the wavelength of light takes the Young's slits experiment as far as making actual measurements in order to obtain a rough estimate of the wavelength: it should be stressed that even a very approximate answer is very useful. For details see the reference.

Part g

Most pupils will probably give answer iv to the introductory question. This part stresses the importance of the unexpected, the new way of looking at a question. It may be of interest for pupils to learn something of Einstein's background and biographical details.

Notes on the questions

1 The object can break up into parts.
2 No. The energy may divide (as in partial reflection, or part passing through a gap, but not into 'many small parts'.
3 No, he explicitly denies this.
4 The generation and transformation of light, i.e. its interaction with building blocks.
5 A particle theory.
6 A 'packet' or 'unit' of wave energy.

▷ *Investigation 1.24* Perceiving light

Part a

Throughout this investigation structural and functional relationships should be emphasised. The iris controls the amount of light passing into the eye through the pupil. The control of pupil diameter is a reflex action stimulated by the amount of light impinging on the retina. The two eyes are 'linked' in the sense that light shone in one eye will also cause a reduction in the diameter of the pupil of the other.

At a certain point the black dot should disappear from view and then reappear. This is sometimes difficult to appreciate and this may be because (i) the movement of the eye is too rapid so that the dot disappears and reappears almost instantaneously (ii) the distance the book is held from the eye is usually wrong: experiment with different distances. The fact that the spot disappears at all is due to the fact that, at this moment, light from it impinges on the blind spot. This is the point the optic nerve leaves the eye. (See below.)

Part b

An alternative dissection of the eye to the one given can be found in Nuffield Secondary Science, Field of Study 3.41. The dissection of the eye should reveal the lens. In fresh eyes this is transparent but may have clouded when taken from eyes of animals which have been dead for some time. Depending on its freshness its texture may or may not be slightly flexible. (See ▷ Investigation 1.25.) The outer 'skin' of the eye (the sclerotic layer) is tough and attached to it are the small muscles which insert on the bone of the eye socket. These are the muscles which enable the eye to rotate in the socket. The sclerotic layer and the bony socket into which the eye fits are protective. The optic nerve should be seen emerging from the back of the eye.

The lens is attached around its circumference by the suspensory ligaments to the choroid layer (inner wall). It is positioned immediately behind the pupil. The retina is black. This contains light sensitive elements (the rods and cones) connecting with nerve cells which eventually come together to form the optic nerve. The point at which the optic nerve leaves the eye contains no rods and cones and hence is insensitive to light. The black colouration of the retina prevents light being reflected. The eye is filled with a watery jelly whose outwardly acting pressure helps maintain the shape of the eye. It also has some small refractive properties (see part c).

Part c

i With a single small pinhole the image is determined by the straight line paths of light (ignoring diffraction), and can easily be described in terms of mathematical similarity. A large hole gives a brighter image, but a blurred one. Many holes give many overlapping images.

ii With the lens, if the distances are appropriate, all the images can be made to coincide, giving a single, clear, bright image.

iii An image located by using a screen is still observable without the screen. Pupils often find it difficult to see images directly (i.e. without a screen) because they put their eye too close, and the image is formed nearer than the least distance of distinct vision.

iv All have a lens to refract the light, an illuminated object (the scene in the case of the camera), and a place to receive the image. The size relation between object and image is one of proportionality to distance from the lens (assumed simple and small). The image is inverted in every case.

v The parallel between eye and camera can be brought out here. Since the eye is filled with fluid, refraction is to be expected at the curved cornea as well as at each lens surface. The corneal refraction is in fact greater than that at the lens.

The retinal image in an eye can be predicted to be inverted. To test this cut a small square hole in the back of the eye. Cover this with a small piece of tracing or greaseproof paper (it will usually stick). Hold the eye to a window so that light enters the pupil, passes through the eye and falls on the paper. An image of the window should be seen which is inverted.

The work on images could be extended considerably, if desired.

▷ *Investigation 1.25* How does the eye focus on near and far objects? Moving the object nearer to the lens causes the image to become blurred, but moving the screen further away enables a sharp image to be located again. Some animals (such as fish) are able to move their lens backwards and forwards within the eye.

Human eyes, similar in structure and texture to that of a sheep, produce the effect of replacing the $+14\,D$ lens by the $+20\,D$ one by means of a change of shape of the lens. By examining the different shapes of the two glass lenses this possibility should occur to at least some pupils, especially if the lens tissue has been found to be slightly flexible.

They may, of course, already have read or been told how the human eye accommodates. It should be quite straightforward for the prediction to be made that a 'fatter' lens would be needed to

Figure 1.10 Accommodation in the mammalian eye. The ciliary muscles contract, the suspensory ligaments slacken and the lens is allowed to thicken

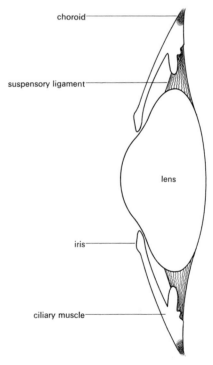

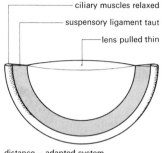

ciliary muscles relaxed

suspensory ligament taut

lens pulled thin

distance – adapted system

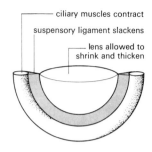

ciliary muscles contract

suspensory ligament slackens

lens allowed to shrink and thicken

near – adapted system

focus near objects. The pattern can be expressed as 'fatter lenses are more powerful', using the word power in its technically correct sense in optics. Accommodation in the mammalian eye is brought about as shown in figure 1.10.

The large-scale demonstration makes the point effectively (see the reference). It is assumed that the lens of the eye is, inside the eye, acting as a converging lens. This is equivalent to assuming it is made of an optically denser material (higher refractive index) than the fluid on either side of it, which is correct, but not obviously so.

▷ *Investigation 1.26*   Improving perception
Part a
The pattern developed in ▷ Investigation 1.25 should make easy the suggestion that two thin lenses close together will be more powerful than either separately. Equally pupils may suggest that slight distortion would lead to the two lenses forming a single 'fatter' lens.

Figure 1.11 shows the correction of the defects. The demonstration using fluorescein solution in a large flask is direct and rapid.

Figure 1.11

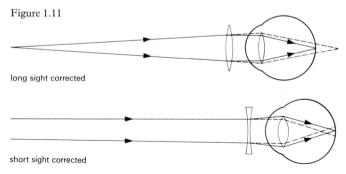

long sight corrected

short sight corrected

61

Part b

Human vision is limited in respect of range of frequencies, intensity, and discrimination between near objects. Humans can also only look in one direction at once, because of coordinated vision, in contrast to other organisms (e.g. horses, some birds, fish). Cats and owls can perceive lower intensities of light than people. Some organisms appear to respond to frequencies outside the 'visible' region.

Discrimination is improved by bringing the object nearer to the eye, leading to a larger retinal image, but this is limited by the inability of the eye to form a clear image of objects nearer than a certain distance. (This is usually quoted as about 250 mm, but for most pupils this will be a gross over estimate.)

A magnifying glass (simple converging lens) allows the object to be placed nearer to the eye, and thus to form a larger retinal image. The eye is, in effect, looking at a magnified, virtual image of the object.

The limit to optical microscopes is set by the wavelength of light: it is impossible to distinguish two objects separated by a distance less than this wavelength, whatever magnification is used, on account of the inherent diffraction effects. To do better a shorter wavelength would be needed. Ultra-violet microscopes have been designed, but the advantage is not very great in comparison to the complications. The beam of electrons in an electron microscope is refracted by magnetic lenses in much the same way as light is in an optical microscope. Whether there would be any limit to such microscopes on account of wave effects is not a question pupils could be expected to answer adequately at this stage. The 'particle' aspects of light have been referred to, but the wave aspects of particles are not dealt with in *Patterns*.

To 'see' atoms a wavelength of 10^{-10} m or less would be needed. In the electromagnetic spectrum this represents the X-ray region.

Extending the wavelength used to 'see' with, for example by infra-red photography, could also be discussed.

▷ *Investigation 1.27* Cameras and photography

The *Pupils' manual* describes one way of approaching very simple photography, starting from a cardboard box. The advantage of this is that it dispels the mystery attaching to photography, although quality is low, and the inconvenience considerable. It is as well for teachers to try this out for themselves first to get an idea of appropriate exposure and development times. There is ample opportunity for extending this work in a number of directions, and for forming links with other departments (see suggestions in the 'Sample scheme').

▷ *Investigation 1.28* Colour

Part a

The demonstrations are best if done on a large scale. This necessitates a small, bright source of light, such as the Nuffield Physics compact light source. In each case a converging lens is used (ideally an achromatic doublet) to form a real image of the source on a screen. Interposing the prism or grating then creates the spectrum, at the same distance (approximately) as the original image.

Without going into details it should be obvious to the pupils that in glass different colours travel at different speeds, whereas in air this does not occur (at least noticeably). Use of the wave pattern can then lead to the conclusions that light travels more slowly in glass than in air, and violet more slowly than red. In contrast, using the diffraction grating the red is deviated most, the violet least, corresponding to the greater wavelengths of red light.

Part b

It is relatively easy for pupils to discover:

red + green = yellow

green + blue = peacock blue

blue + red = magenta.

However, to obtain even a moderate approximation to white by mixing all three requires close control over the relative intensities. Consequently various answers may be obtained in a pupil experiment. It is a curious fact that while the ear can distinguish a mixture of frequencies from the (average) single frequency, the eye cannot do so.

Any two good 'primary' filters in combination should produce a good approximation to complete absorption of light of all colours. On the other hand combinations of two secondary filters will transmit the appropriate primary colour. In fact real filters have a smoothly increasing and decreasing curve of transmission against frequency, so the phenomena are more complex than this simple description implies.

Part c

Pigments are more complex than filters, because only rarely is any frequency completely absorbed. Consequently red paint, for example, reflects a fair proportion of the blue and green light falling on it, and does not appear black, as might be predicted, if viewed through blue or green filters. Mixing pigments usually gives darker colours, but not anything like black. The best known example of blue and yellow giving green indicates that both pigments reflect a good deal of green light.

Part d

'Optical whiteners' contain dyes which are fluorescent, absorbing ultraviolet radiation and emitting visible radiation. Such substances glow brightly under ultraviolet light, and in daylight look significantly 'whiter than white'. However, artificial light, particularly tungsten filament light, has little ultraviolet content, so the effect is much less.

Part e

This introduces the subjective aspects of colour as well as the subtleties of colour mixing and illustration.

Part f

Under normal conditions, it is the red mercury(II) iodide which is stable. (At higher temperatures, the yellow version is the most stable.) Yellow mercury(II) iodide can be prepared by the teacher (or technician) in advance by rubbing red mercury(II) iodide with a spatula over a large sheet of filter paper. The paper is warmed (coated surface uppermost) over a flame in a fume cupboard, moving the paper with gentle circular motion.

The mercury(II) and iodide ions are arranged differently in the two different forms. (The technical term is enantiotropy.) The application of pressure to the yellow iodide causes the particles to rearrange to the red form.

Sample questions

1 The sketch shows the biceps muscle and its attachments to the skeleton of the arm.

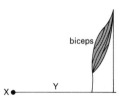

Select from the list below to complete the following statement. The biceps could support a load at Y which is . . .

A considerably more than X (correct)

B a little more than X

C the same as X

D less than X

2 A refrigerator normally is operated by gas or electricity. A housewife defrosts her refrigerator by switching it off and letting it

reach room temperature with the door open. She then switches it on, but forgets to close the door. Which of the following is correct?

A the refrigerator will cool down the kitchen because energy from the air molecules will continuously be absorbed by the cooler unit inside it

B the refrigerator will warm up the kitchen because there is a continuous input of energy from the supply (correct)

C the kitchen will neither cool down nor warm up because the energy given to the air by the radiator unit (at the back) is balanced by the energy absorbed by the cooler unit inside

D it is impossible to make any of the above statements with certainty on the information given

3 The diagram illustrates a possible design of machine, with a turbine and pump on the same shaft.

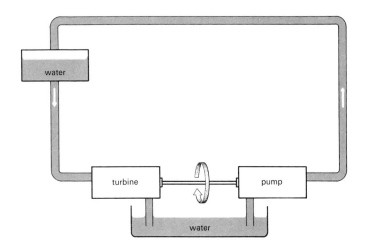

Which one of the statements about the machine is correct?

A this machine would continue to work because the turbine provides energy to drive the pump, which raises water (increasing its potential energy) which is used to drive the turbine

B the machine would continue to work because the water is continually supplying energy

C the machine would not continue to work because energy is being lost from it but not supplied to it (correct)

D the machine would not continue to work because the pump would have to rotate the opposite way to the turbine

4 Scales show a reading of 420 N when a boy stands on them. In order to balance on his toes, the boy's calf muscles must contract about 0.07 m. It is assumed the boy's weight acts along the

direction of the calf muscles. If his heels rise 0.14 m from the ground, the total force exerted by the muscles is

A 210 N
B 294 N
C 420 N
D 840 N (correct)

5 ′The diagram represents a toy car running on a smooth surface towards a rough surface, where friction between the wheels and the surface is considerably greater.

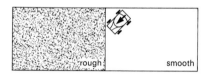

Assuming that friction at the axles is unimportant, which one of the following is correct?

A this is a useful model of particle refraction
B this is a useful model of wave refraction (correct)
C this is a useful model of both particle and wave refraction
D this could not be a model of either particle or wave refraction

6 Which one of the following diagrams could represent the paths of light entering a fish's eye?

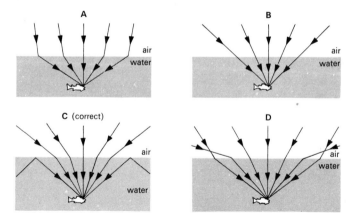

▷7 The pigments extracted from a plant had the following absorption spectrum:

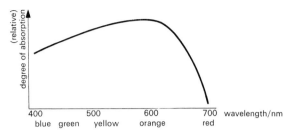

The colour of this plant is

A red (correct)
B yellow
C green
D blue

8 The table below compares certain aspects of some present form of transport. The information relates to the transportation of 640 people from, say, the suburbs of London to the suburbs of Birmingham and assumes no congestion and easy linking facilities between modes of transport. The cost includes maintenance of machinery and the transport system (e.g. roads and rail). Remember that electricity generating stations cause pollution even if the vehicles using electricity might not do so.

Method	Time by this method	Total transit time	Number of passengers per vehicle	Cost per head	Total degree of chemical pollution	Total noise pollution
diesel train	90 min	130 min	640	£3.00	moderate	moderate
electric car	180 min	180 min	4	£0.50	nil	low
electric train	90 min	130 min	640	£3.00	nil	low
petrol car	150 min	150 min	4	£0.70	moderate	moderate
bicycle	2 day	2 day	1	nil	nil	nil
jet plane (VTOL)	30 min	100 min	80	£6.00	moderate	moderate

If you were involved in planning transport for the future, which one of the methods indicated would you recommend? Give three reasons for your choice. State briefly why you would reject each of the other methods.

9 Light passes from a source S to a detector D in straight lines, being reflected at a mirror M.

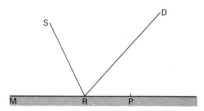

By measuring the actual path (SR + RD) and other paths such as (SP + PD), find out what is special about the original path followed (in accordance with the pattern of reflection of light).

10 Storms at sea (for example in the Atlantic) create waves by wind action, and these waves have a wide range of wavelengths. A few kilometres from the storm the waves of all wavelengths are mixed up, but at the coast, some hundreds of kilometres from the storm, the low-frequency waves always arrive first, and the higher-frequency waves later. Which one of the following is a possible explanation of these observations?

A the short wavelengths die out more easily

B the short wavelengths travel slightly slower than the longer wavelengths (correct)

C the long wavelengths die out more easily

D the long wavelengths travel slightly slower than the shorter wavelengths

11 Light going from air to two substances X and Y is refracted as shown.

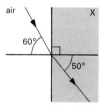
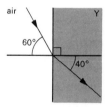

Which of the following diagrams best represents what would happen to light going from X to Y?

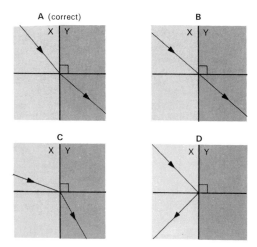

▷12 Which one of the following is the best explanation of the fact that some (electromagnetic) wavelengths starting from any point on the Earth's surface can reach any other point on the Earth's surface?

A the waves follow a curved path because of interference

B the waves are reflected back and forth between the Earth and a certain layer in the upper atmosphere (correct)

C the waves are electromagnetic waves with wavelengths much larger than the diameter of the Earth, so they travel all over the Earth's surface

D the waves are transverse waves, and oscillations occur only in the vertical direction, so they can curve round in a vertical direction

13 When a cotton thread is pulled and one end is vibrated up and down, standing waves are set up (see diagram).

Which one of the following is the best way of apparently stopping the motion?

A illuminate it strongly

B use a magnifying glass

C use a stroboscope (correct)

D use a camera

14 Which one of the following can be explained by the combined patterns of interference and diffraction?

   A certain stretches of the coastline are subject to erosion by sea waves

   B radio waves can reach the internal aerial of a transistor radio even when it is in a house

   C the sound outside a factory from a machine operating continuously seems much louder at some places than others when several windows are open (correct)

   D the fact that the light is on in a closed room can be detected from the crack of light under the door

15 When two substances being tested are placed in a flame, each makes it look the same colour (bright red) to the naked eye. Which conclusion is correct?

   A the substances are the same

   B the substances contain the same element

   C an instrument such as a prism or diffraction grating would be necessary to tell whether the substances are the same

   D an instrument such as a prism or diffracting grating would be necessary to tell whether the substances contained the same element (correct)

▷16 A professional photographer wishes to take a picture of a flower from a distance of 100 mm, but his camera will only focus down to 500 mm. He considers the following courses of action:

   i changing the lens on his camera

   ii adding a special extra lens to the camera

   Which of these could he use?

   A i only

   B ii only

   C i and ii (correct)

   D neither

▷17 An airline operator says that his new engines produce only half the sound intensity of the old ones, so the aircraft will make only half the noise nuisance they used to. Which one of the following comments is correct?

   A the statement is accurate but incomplete

   B the statement is inaccurate because the quality of the sound from the new engines will be different

   C the statement is inaccurate because the new engines will take longer to get the aircraft out of earshot

   D the statement is inaccurate because halving the sound intensity does not halve the loudness (correct)

18 A new type of wave with the following properties is discovered:

   i it conveys energy

   ii it travels through vacuum

iii it is transverse
iv it has a very short wavelength (about 10^{-15} m).
Which one of the following is correct?
A this could be an electromagnetic wave (correct)
B this could not be an electromagnetic wave because of ii
C this could not be an electromagnetic wave because of iii
D this could not be an electromagnetic wave because of iv

19 The diagram represents a grating with a spacing between equivalent points of 10 mm.

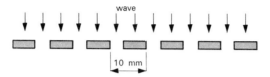

If a wave (for example a sound wave) of wavelength 100 mm fell on the grating, which one of the following would you expect to happen beyond the grating assuming the wave was not completely reflected?
A the wave would be diffracted considerably at the grating
B the wave would form an interference pattern
C the wave would continue unchanged, but might be reduced in intensity (correct)
D the wave would be refracted

20 The spectra of three elements and an unknown substance X are as shown:

From this information, which one of the following statements about X is correct?
A X contains L, M and N
B X contains L and M (correct)
C X contains L and N
D X contains M and N

▷21 Write an essay about the various types of any one optical instrument you know about, and the important features of the design of each type.

▷22 Devise an experiment to investigate the differing extent to which people are distracted by noise.

23 For which one of the following electromagnetic waves might ionic crystals act as a (three dimensional) diffraction grating?
   A gamma rays
   B X-rays (correct)
   C ultraviolet rays
   D infrared rays
   E microwaves

▷24 The table gives information about four systems of communication on the Earth's surface. Systems of communication should ideally be convenient and inexpensive to use and involve simple techniques. Unfortunately not all of these desirable factors can be achieved at the same time.

Communications system	Amount of information which can be handled	Cost	Relative use at present
wires (e.g. telephone)	low	low	high
radio waves	moderate	high	moderate
microwaves (e.g. Post Office link)	high	high	low
light (i.e. direct vision)	very high	zero	universal

Suggest explanations for the extent of present use of each of the systems given in the table.

25 Which one of the following is the clearest example of diffraction? Assume that reflection and refraction do not occur.
   A a stone is thrown into a pond and waves spread out in circles from the point where it enters the water
   B light from a very small source spreads out and passes through a hole in a card, giving rise to a sharp shadow
   C sound from a bell spreads out through a doorway so that a person who cannot see the bell can hear it (correct)
   D radio waves spread out from a transmitting aerial and some of the energy is received by a receiving aerial

▷26 Compression waves (P-waves) travel faster in rock than in water. An explosion in the sea at E (see diagram) gives rise to a pulse of P-waves travelling outwards in all drections. Which one of the diagram best represents the path of the waves *after* reaching X?

A (correct)

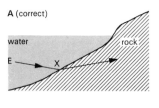

B

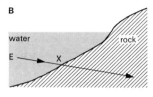

C

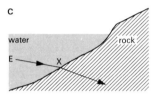

D

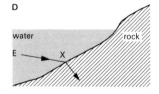

2 Energy and particle interactions

Introduction

Power is first introduced by experiments on pupils' own power, and this leads to consideration of the way man's use of power has grown (including social effects). The origin of most of this power is fuel which is burned in engines of various sorts. These show the patterns of increasing the temperature of the surroundings and of using oxygen and producing carbon dioxide and/or water. These patterns are found to be paralleled by the human body, the cells of which act as engines with food their fuel. The circulation of blood is treated as a fuel (energy) transport system.

Investigation of the particle interactions by which fuels and foods release energy leads to the concept of a chemical bond, and the need to be able to measure the energy released gives rise to a study of the patterns involved in temperature rise, and the kinetic picture of temperature.

Respiration is treated as a series of problems using the patterns already developed, and in turn leads to problems relating to the effects of increasing the power of the body, particularly on temperature and breathing. The work on breathing concludes with an investigation dealing with the health hazards of smoking.

The section ends with investigations relating energy needed for change of state to forces between particles.

Objectives

Skills

1 To recall and to understand the following concepts: system, energy transfer, energy spread, energy conservation, power, rate, fuel/food, bond, interaction, blood, artery, vein, capillary, mass, (specific) thermal capacity, (specific) latent heat, proportionality, combustion, respiration, organism, solid, liquid, gas, temperature, particle, engine.

2 To recall and understand the following patterns:

a Power is the rate of transferring energy, i.e. (energy transferred) ÷ (time taken) (2).

b Energy can be made available by burning fuel with oxygen, an interaction which usually produces carbon dioxide and water (combustion) (2).

74

c When fuels are burned some or all of the energy transferred raises the temperature of the surroundings and some may be transferred mechanically (measured as work) via engines (2).

d Blood circulates round the body in a system of arteries, veins and capillaries (2).

e Energy is required to break a chemical bond; energy is released when a chemical bond is formed (2).

f Rate of reaction depends on temperature and the presence of a catalyst (2).

g When a temperature rise of a system occurs, an energy transfer can always be identified which corresponds quantitatively to the rise in temperature. This can be explained in terms of temperature rise being associated with additional energy shared among the particles of the system (2).

h For most systems increase in temperature is proportional to energy transfer if no particle interactions or changes of state are involved. Hence (temperature rise) × (thermal capacity) can be a measure of energy transfer (2).

i The thermal capacity of a quantity of any substance is proportional to the mass but depends on the substance. (The thermal capacity of a unit mass of a substance is called its specific thermal capacity.) (2).

j Energy tends always to be transferred from objects at higher temperatures to objects at lower temperatures, thus distributing itself more evenly. (Energy is useful when unevenly distributed.) (2).

k Respiration is a characteristic of organisms (2).

l Energy is required to turn a solid into a liquid and a liquid into a gas at the same temperature. The amount of energy required is proportional to the mass and depends on the substance (2). (These patterns are linked with patterns in the *Teachers' handbook* as follows: a with 33; b with 22 and 48; c with 22, 36 and 37; d with 38; e with 21 and 22; f with 78; g with 19, 36 and 37; h and i with 35; j with 37; k with 22 and 23; l with 9, 19 and 20.)

3 To solve problems using the above patterns (4).

4 To understand that the growth of the use of engines (and the associated machines) has had highly beneficial effects on people's lives in developed countries, for example making possible labour-saving devices, rapid and easy transport, and new forms of building. It has also created considerable social problems such as unpleasant work and working conditions, large concentrations of population, and atmospheric pollution, which are only gradually being alleviated (6).

▷ 5 To be able to write an essay about the advantages and disadvantages of industrialisation (i.e. the use of engines and machines) including suggestions for overcoming or avoiding the disadvantages by the application of scientific principles (5).

6 To use reference books to compare the energy required to vaporise and to melt unit mass of various substances, and to compare the specific thermal capacity of various substances (3, 4).

7 To design and perform experiments to find out if respiration is a characteristic of all organisms (8).

▷8 To be accurate in reporting the experimental results of an investigation into anaerobic respiration of yeast (7).

9 To understand (i) that the body is a relatively inefficient 'machine' and (ii) to look for relationships between different physical activities and mechanical efficiency (6, 3).

10 To make an appraisal of data obtained in an investigation relating volume of air breathed to the amount of work done (3).

11 To design and perform experiments to measure the energy required to melt and to vaporise unit mass of different substances (8).

Attitudes

12 To cooperate in investigations of the power of pupils (9).

13 To cooperate in investigations into relationships, physical activity and the 'quantity' and 'quality' of air breathed in and out (9).

▷14 To be sceptical about increase of temperature being proportional to energy transferred (10).

▷15 To be concerned about the effects (including side-effects) of man's increasing use of fuels (11).

16 To be concerned about the effects of smoking on health (11).

▷17 To be sceptical about reaction rate increasing when the temperature increases (10).

Flow diagram

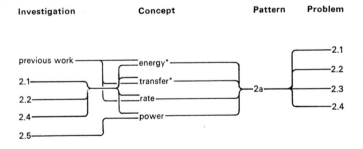

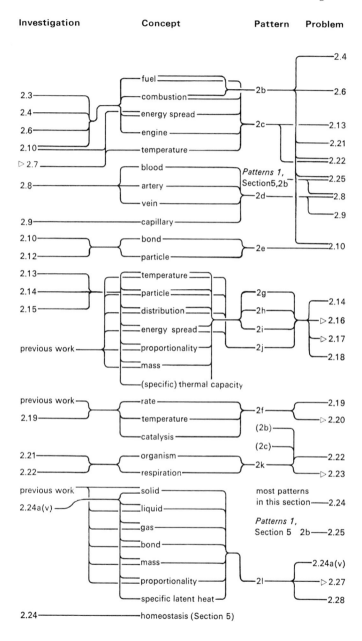

*The concepts of energy transfer and conservation, interaction and system are implicit throughout this section.

Sample scheme
Time allocation for this section: $6\frac{1}{2}$ weeks

	Description	Reference	Notes
R	*Biology of man*	NSS Theme 3	Relevant to much of this section
▶2.1	Pupil power	NSS Fields 3.11, 4.25; NP year IV expt. 112	
▶2.2	What is your maximum power?		Experiments and calculations
▶2.3	How much are you worth?		Calculation
▷T	Wallchart	Made by teacher	Comparison of power of man and animals
▶2.4	Increasing the available power		
▷R	*Energy, work and leisure*	Durnin, J. and Passmore, R., Heinemann, 1967	Draws on everyday experience
D	How the power used by man has grown		Links with history
2.5	The effects of greater power		Social implications
▷T	*The motor industry*	Jackdaw Publications no. 77, Cape	Survey of common experience and experiments/demonstrations
▶2.6	Engines and fuels		
B	*Machines and engines*	*Patterns* topic book	
▷2.7	The 'muscle–bone' machine	NSS Field 3.16	Examines the relationships between muscles (the 'engines') and bones (the 'machinery')

	Description	Reference	Notes
▶2.8	Transporting fuel in the body	NSS Field 3.14 *Patterns 1*, Section 6	
	Part a		Structure and function of villi
	Part b		Glucose in blood
	Part c		Pattern of blood-flow
	▷Part d		Structure and function of heart
▷T	*The heart in action*	Film loop, Macmillan	
▶2.9	How does blood get from arteries to veins?		Capillaries
▷T	*Capillary circulation of blood*	Film loop, NBP 45	
▷T	*Harvey and the circulation of blood*	Jackdaw Publications no. 56, Cape	
▶2.10	Some chemistry of a selection of fuels and foods		
▷2.11	The products of combustion		Some pollution problems
2.12	Fuels and food: an explanation		Energy transfer and particle interactions
▶2.13	How can we compare fuels?		Introduction to following experiments
▶2.14	How does energy transfer affect temperature?		Preliminary pattern finding experiments
D	Is the energy still there?		

	Description	Reference	Notes
2.15	What is the connection between work and temperature?		
▷R	*Count Rumford, physicist extraordinary*	Brown, S. C., Science Study Series no. 26, Heinemann	Also suitable for some pupils
D	Conservation of energy	NP *Teachers' guide IV* pp. 273–302	Includes survey of historical development of the idea
▷►2.16	Is water the best substance to put in a hot-water bottle?		Use of data book
▷►2.17	Using thermal capacity		Calculation and 'think' investigation
►2.18	Comparing fuels and food as energy sources	NB Year III 4.3, NC Section 23.1, NP Year IV expt 106c	Experiment and demonstration to answer original question, Investigation 2.13
►2.19	Temperature and the effect on particle interaction		
▷►2.20	Enzymes and particle interactions	*Patterns 1,* Section 6	
►2.21	Predicting the composition of expired air	NSS Field 3.12	
D	Combustion and respiration		
B	*Machines and engines*	*Patterns* topic book	Section on respiration
►2.22	Do all organisms respire?	NB Year III and *Teachers' guide III* Ch 1 and 3	
▷►2.23	Could an organism respire in an oxygen free environment?	NB Year III Ch 3	Anaerobic respiration

	Description	Reference	Notes
▶ 2.24	Explaining the effects of increasing 'pupil-power' output on body functions		A related series of discussion, demonstration and class experiment
	Part a The effects on body temperature		Includes latent heat
	Part b The effects on breathing	NSS Field 3.12	
	▷ Part c Why do we breathe more heavily during exercises?		Extension of part b to test prediction that more oxygen is being used
	▷ Part d		Efficiency of body
	▷ Part e		Efficiency in different activities
▶ 2.25	How does breathing take place?	NSS Field 3.12 NB *Text III* Ch 2, *Teachers' guide III*	
▷ T	Part a *Breathing* Part b *The cleaning mechanism of the lung* Models	Film loops, (a) Macmillan, (b) NSS Longman	To show breathing mechanisms
2.26	Smoking and health		
▷ R	Smoking and health now	Report of the Royal College of Physicians, Pitman Medical Publications, 1971	
▷ B	Pamphlet: The Dangers of Smoking	Central Council for Health Education	
▷ T	*Dying for a smoke*	Film, Central Film Library	Amusing cartoon film: the villain, Nick O'Teen is finally put to rout
▷ ▶ 2.27	The motorist's problem		'Think' problem

81

Description	Reference	Notes
▷▶2.28 Energy and change of state		Should include discussion on change of state, energy and particle interactions

Teaching progression

The first group of investigations, 2.1 to 2.4 are intended to develop objective 2a, use the pattern, and achieve objective 12. The most important contributory concept is that of rate, and the relation between power and energy is typical of several similar relations. It may be thought valuable to emphasise the graphical representation of this relation by sketching a linear graph of energy transfer against time, and showing that the power is represented by the slope (gradient) of this graph. This would enable links to be made with work in mathematics on rates and gradients, as well as with work on proportion and rates earlier and later in *Patterns*.

Figure 2.1a

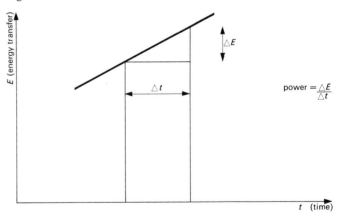

$$\text{power} = \frac{\triangle E}{\triangle t}$$

Investigations 2.3 and 2.4 also contribute to achieving objective 4, and lay a foundation for objectives 2b and ▷5. Some of the social implications of greater power are discussed in Investigation 2.5.

The introduction to objective 2b in Investigations 2.3 and 2.4 is taken further in 2.6, which also gives the first opportunity for consideration of the important pattern, objective 2c, which is related to the second law of thermodynamics.

Figure 2.1b

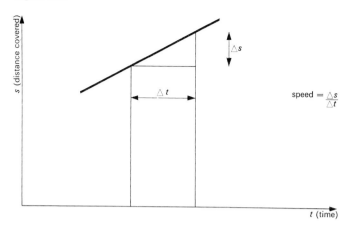

$$\text{speed} = \frac{\triangle s}{\triangle t}$$

▷ Investigation 2.7 considers the analogies between the muscular and skeletal systems of the human body, engines and machines. The topic book *Machines and engines* also considers this comparison.

Investigations 2.8 and 2.9 achieve objective 2d. Blood transports food from the gut to all parts of the body. The pattern of blood flow around the body is a circular one. In mammals there is, in fact, a twin circulation (Figure 2.2 on page 84) which keeps the lung circuit separate from the body circuit. This idea is best dealt with after Investigation 2.25 which considers the oxygenation of the blood in the lungs. The topic book *Machines and engines* contains some details. The twin circulation, achieved by the division of the heart into two 'sides', keeps oxygenated and deoxygenated blood from mixing. Although work on the heart is optional the topic book contains sufficient information to establish the functional significance of the heart's structure. The idea of a circular pattern of flow of blood round the body can easily be achieved without necessarily performing the investigation on the heart. In Investigation 2.8 all the evidence points to a circulation of blood from the heart to arteries, to veins and back to the heart. If this is so then there must be some link, which can be predicted, between the arteries and veins. Looking for this link (the capillaries) is the subject of Investigation 2.9.

Investigation 2.10 is a straightforward testing of the products of combustion (objective 2b). Energy is transferred in this process. Combustion of food in organisms is called respiration. A more detailed discussion of the similarities and differences between these two processes follows after Investigation 2.21.

Figure 2.2

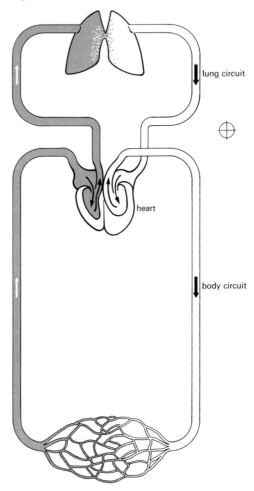

lung circuit

heart

body circuit

▷Objective 15 is achieved in ▷Investigation 2.11. Objective 2e is introduced in Investigation 2.12 where simple calculations are attempted using given data.

Since it is not possible to measure bond energies as such, these must be approached indirectly, by measuring the energy released in known reactions, and the way this can be done is treated in Investigations 2.13 to 2.18, achieving objectives 2g, 2h and 2i. It is important for pupils to realise that the energy associated with temperature rise is not transferred to the particles of the system individually, but to all the particles of the system collectively. This is why the word 'shared' is used in objective 2g. Individual particles will vary in speed and distance from other particles, so one could speak of the kinetic and potential energy of any particle changing, but the energy shared is unchanged. This work takes up the ideas about friction leading to temperature rise first developed in Section 1. Here the apparent loss of energy associated with friction can be identified with the rise of temperature. The important feature is not that one can think of this happening, but that when measurements are made, there is a quantitative correspondence between the temperature rise and the energy 'lost' (measured as work, or in some other suitable way).

The concept of thermal capacity (defined as the energy transfer per unit temperature rise) is used rather than others which could have been chosen (water equivalent, specific heat) because it fits the development more naturally. This leads on to the concept of specific thermal capacity (identical with what has commonly been called specific heat), but the names are deliberately introduced only after the phenomena have been investigated experimentally, towards the end of Investigation 2.15.

▷Investigation 2.16 contributes to achieving objective 6. Objective 2j is closely related to 2c, and is another pattern developing ideas close to the second law of thermodynamics. The pattern itself is rather obvious, but its practical applications are of great importance. Thermal conduction and convection are not considered in detail in *Patterns*, but pupils should be aware that substances differ greatly in their ability to conduct energy.

The fact that temperature rise of a system is not always proportional to the energy transferred to it is investigated later, but scepticism (objective ▷14) can be encouraged in this series of experiments, since they deal with a limited range of systems (or substances).

Objective 2f is achieved in Investigation 2.19 and ▷Investigation 2.20, although the catalyst part of the objective is optional in this particular section. The optional investigation is also used to achieve objective ▷17.

The concept of rate is again important here. Since the rate of any change is defined as (change occurring) ÷ (time taken) if the same change is always considered, as here, the rate is directly proportional to $1/t$, i.e. inversely proportional to t. So $1/t$ can be used as a measure of the rate of reaction. For many pupils this may be too mathematically sophisticated (see 'Teaching notes').

Investigation 2.21 uses pattern 2b. The transfer of energy from food in organisms is called respiration and results in, amongst other things, muscle contraction. Since foods have already been established as fuel and since these use oxygen and produce carbon dioxide when energy is transferred, it should be a relatively simple matter for pupils to predict that, in expired air, carbon dioxide will be present in a higher proportion and oxygen in a lower proportion than in inspired (atmospheric air). The ensuing discussion should clarify the distinction between combustion and respiration.

In respiration the energy is made available in controlled amounts in small enzyme catalysed stages. This is considered in more detail in the topic book *Machines and engines*. It is important to avoid the impression that there are little 'fires' in the body's cells. Respiration proceeds at relatively low temperatures

Figure 2.3a The combustion of sugar

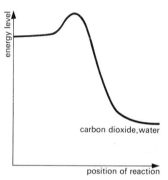

carbon dioxide, water

position of reaction

Figure 2.3b The respiration of sugar

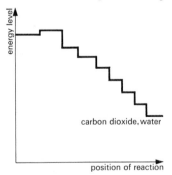

carbon dioxide, water

position of reaction

(governed by the optimum temperature for enzyme effectiveness, see ▷ Investigation 2.20). Combustion and respiration will be linked into the overall pattern of events known as the carbon cycle in *Patterns 4*, Section 11 'Stability' (see pattern 48 in the

Figure 2.4 When sugar is oxidised the available energy is transferred to adenosine triphosphate (ATP) and some will raise the temperature of the cells. But because the oxidation proceeds in a series of small steps this temperature rise is easily controlled and dissipated to the surroundings (see Investigation 2.24a). ATP acts as a sort of energy 'currency' making energy available for work such as contraction of muscle (see topic book *Machines and engines*) and chemical synthesis, e.g. the production of protein from amino-acids

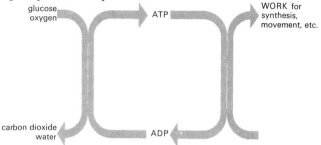

Teachers' handbook). When fuels are burned some of the energy is transferred to raise the temperature of the surroundings (pattern 2c). This is as true of respiration as of combustion. Thus there are two pieces of evidence which can be used to detect respiratory activity (temperature rise of surroundings and gaseous exchanges) and these are explored in Investigation 2.22 (objective 7). That respiration is a characteristic of organisms (objective 2k) emerges in this investigation. Sometimes however it is difficult to detect in green plants (see 'Teaching notes').

The logical prediction made in answer to ▷ Investigation 2.23 is: no, respiration cannot take place. However, the evidence gained suggests otherwise, since the temperature of the surroundings rises and carbon dioxide is released (see ▷ objective 8).

Much of the work in Investigation 2.24, part a, is based mainly on patterns 2b, c and d. ▷ Part a iii uses pattern 2f (in conjunction with ▷ Investigation 2.20); part a v introduces objective 2l, and achieves objective 11. Part b of Investigation 2.24 starts out by taking pattern 2b and asking pupils to suggest another pattern which would relate the amount of work done (as physical activity) with the amount of air breathed. Part b i gathers information and the resulting relationship appraised in terms of that predicted (objective 10). Part b ii and ▷ part d achieve objective 9i. ▷ Part e achieves ▷ objective 9ii. This is a particularly useful pattern-finding activity and interesting projects could result. ▷ Part c extends part b i by looking at changes in the 'quality' of air breathed during and after exercise.

The whole of Investigation 2.24 will contribute to the achievement of objective 13. The relative inefficiency of the body can be related to the resultant need for the body to dissipate energy to the surroundings.

Investigation 2.25 makes use of structure and function patterns. Surface area to volume relationships are also significant when considering gaseous exchange at the lung surface.

Objective 16 is achieved by Investigation 2.26.

Objective 2l is used in ▷ Investigation 2.27, which makes the quantitative relations more explicit by means of a structured example. Further (qualitative) aspects of the same pattern are developed in Investigation 2.28 which is a series of small problems, and also enables pattern 2l to be explained in terms of pattern 2e.

Teaching notes

Investigation 2.1 Pupil power

The sequence of parts is one in which the pattern (2a) is developed and then used, first numerically and then symbolically. In part f, strictly, the word 'average' should be included before 'power' and 'speed'. It would be important if a situation were considered which was not one of constant rate.

The 'units' pattern is watts = joules/seconds

or joules = watts × seconds

Notes on arm and cycle ergometers

If the handle is turned fairly quickly and steadily the forcemeter should only give a small reading.

The rope is in the grooved circumference of the wheel. If the wheel is not being turned or held by hand then the weight of the sandbags will extend the forcemeter fully.

When the handle is turned the rope 'slips' in the groove but the sliding friction between the rope and the wheel will almost be sufficient to support the sandbag(s). There will now almost certainly be only a small reading (F) on the forcemeter.

As always 'weight' means the force with which the object is pulled down by gravity.

Investigation 2.2 What is your maximum power?

The clear difficulty here, which pupils should see fairly easily, is that only by trial can it be decided whether an activity can be maintained for a long time. Precision is not important here: what is needed is a rough estimate, or even an order-of-magnitude answer.

Investigation 2.3 How much are you worth?

Suppose the maximum power is 50 W. Then the calculation is as follows i Energy transfer per day (6 hours) $= 50 \times 60 \times 60 \times 6\,\text{J}$

$$= 1\,080\,000\,\text{J}$$

$$= 1.08\,\text{MJ}$$

ii $3.6\,\text{MJ}$ costs $0.9\,\text{p}$

$\therefore\ 1.0\,\text{MJ}$ costs $0.9 \times \dfrac{1.0}{3.6}\text{p}$

$$= 0.25\,\text{p}$$

iii So a day's work is worth $0.25 \times \dfrac{1.08}{1.0}\text{p}$

$$= 0.27\,\text{p}$$

iv Assuming $6 \times 80\,\text{W}$ fluorescent tubes are used to illuminate the laboratory.

Total power $= 480\,\text{W}$

So the power of 10 pupils would be adequate to light the lamps, working near to their long-term maximum (assumed to be $50\,\text{W}$). Man-power is clearly tiny in comparison with what is used by people in Britain. Also the value of a man's time (about £5 per day for unskilled work) is several thousand times the value of the energy transfer he can achieve. These facts show some of the most important differences between developed and underdeveloped countries, the latter being largely dependent on human work (which is more readily available).

Investigation 2.4 Increasing the available power

The Archimedes screw is still used in some parts of the Middle East, powered by man-power, to raise water for irrigation. One important reason is ease of control, others are the expense of keeping animals or using engines (using fuel) compared with the cheapness and availability of people who have to be fed anyway!

The percentage of man-power may decrease to a very small value, but could hardly become zero.

The control of machines is considered in Section 5.

The origin of energy will be some sort of fuel: this name is in fact given to substances which provide useful energy by means of combustion. Most contain carbon and hydrogen. This will probably not be known to pupils until they have searched out the relevant information.

Investigation 2.6 Engines and fuels

The development of engines is a fascinating study in the history of technology, with a great bearing on the development of much that is now taken for granted. In 1698, Thomas Savery patented a steam engine for raising water and other purposes, although it has been suggested that Thomas Newcomen (1663–1729) had in fact invented his version before that. The first steam engine made by Newcomen for practical purposes was used at a coal mine near Dudley, Staffordshire in 1712, and was the earliest engine to use atmospheric pressure in the working stroke. An example of a Newcomen engine dating from 1725 is preserved at Dartmouth, his birthplace, and is open to the public.

Part a

A card folded and cut into a 'windmill' shape, and pivoted in a near horizontal plane above a flame is a very simple form of engine. Many others are possible.

Part b

Some technical studies departments have car engines either sectioned or in operating condition. Many books have illustrations of internal combustion, gas turbine and jet engines. The motorcycle's fins enable energy to be transferred more readily by conduction to the air. Without them the temperature of the cylinder block would become excessive. (A few motorcycles have water cooling systems.)

Part c

The body's engines are clearly the muscles, or more specifically the cells in them. The skeletal system is essential for the muscles to operate. (The same might be said of the circulatory system, but that is not the obvious answer here.)

▷ *Investigation 2.7* The muscle-bone machine

The reference given in the 'Sample scheme' contains all that is required and includes useful illustrations. The demonstration suggested is a dissection of the leg muscles of a chicken and this is described in detail in the reference.

Investigation 2.8 Transporting fuel in the body

Part a

This part is to elicit the suggestion that food, once absorbed by the villi (see *Patterns 1*, Section 6), passes into the blood with which the villi are well supplied. The microslides or photomicrograph transparency chosen to illustrate villi should have been prepared from a specimen in which the blood vessels have previously been injected to make them stand out clearly in the subsequent sections. Transparencies of photomicrographs are usually better for class teaching and are certainly more economical of time in a brief exercise of this sort. An illustration of an injected villus is shown in figure 2.5. Blood vessels stand out as dark lines.

Part b

This part of the investigation looks briefly at the structure of blood but is designed mainly to establish its function in transporting food from the gut to other parts of the body.

The photomicrograph of blood shows the biconcave red blood cells.

90

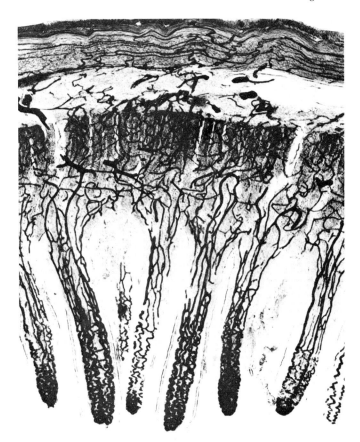

Figure 2.5

The function of these red cells is dealt with in Investigation 2.25. The red blood cells circulate round the body in the liquid plasma. Blood can usually be obtained from slaughterhouses or butchers but must be from a freshly slaughtered beast. To prevent clotting it must be citrated (5 g of sodium citrate per 100 cm³ blood). Hospital blood banks are sometimes an alternative source. Centrifuging will drive the red blood cells to the bottom of the tubes, leaving clear yellowish plasma at the top. Trials have shown that centrifuging sometimes fails to separate cells and plasma. If this happens (test before the lesson) it is best to try an alternative source of blood.

Once obtained the plasma can be tested for sugars. Clinitest tablets (a tablet form of Benedict's reagent) can be used as an alternative to Benedict's reagent. A tablet is dropped into 15 drops of the liquid under test. Even simpler is Clinistix, a cardboard strip which is dipped in the liquid, but it is specific for glucose. If any of these sugar tests have not been performed previously, control tests on a solution of known sugar, such as glucose, and on distilled water should be run. The opportunity to mention the other major functions of the blood could be taken: sealing off wounds by clotting and destroying invading micro-organisms for example. White cells may be visible in photomicrographs or prepared slides. The loop film *Phagocytosis* (NBP 20) illustrates clearly the action of white cells in engulfing bacteria.

Blood plasma contains a protein, fibrin, which precipitates in long threads on exposure to air. (There is no need to go into details.) These threads trap corpuscles and so form a clot. Fibrin can also be precipitated by stirring. Slaughterhouse blood will probably have been stirred, removing the fibrin. Blood from a butcher's shop may not have had the fibrin removed. A clean glass rod may gather fibrin threads if stirred in the blood.

Part c

This can be done at home or, if in school, the services of a male member of staff conscripted! It should not be performed on pupils. A tight tourniquet will not be necessary. The Jackdaw publication, *Harvey and the circulation of the blood*, provides a useful historical perspective. During the course of the experiment it will become clear that blood cannot ebb to and fro. Slight

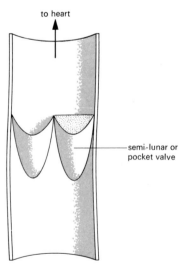

Figure 2.6 A vein cut open and laid flat to show the structure of a valve

bulges in the vessels indicate the position of the valves which prevent backflow. Pupils should be able to suggest their presence and 'design'.

The term vessel has been used in referring to Harvey's experiment. This is to avoid pre-empting the latter part of the investigation which asks some questions about arteries and veins. The heart pumps blood into the arteries which have thick, elastic walls to withstand the high pressures generated. Blood is helped on its return to the heart by normal muscular action squeezing on the thin-walled veins. Because of the valves blood can only travel towards the heart.

▷Part d

Slaughterhouses and butchers sometimes cut away the top part of the heart and thus vessels and auricles are damaged. Make a point of asking for a complete heart. This may entail getting a complete set of lights (lungs) as well but, if refrigerated, these can be used later in the section. The practical work and questions are designed to elicit the relationship of structure to function and pupils will appreciate that the heart is an incredible piece of 'engineering'. The film loop, *The heart in action* can be used as consolidation. Some teachers may wish to show this film loop even though the practical work is not attempted.

Investigation 2.9   How does blood get from arteries to veins?

Xenopus tadpoles and trout alevins can be anaesthetised in MS 222 Sandoz (see *Technicians' manual 3*). The pupils will easily see the capillaries containing blood corpuscles.

A number of other observations are worth making on the specimens if time allows:

i   the action of the heart

ii the flow of blood into and out of it

iii the jerky nature of the flow in the arteries and the smoother flow by the time blood reaches the veins.

By examining of the circulation in an amphibian or fish pupils should be beginning to appreciate that the circular pattern of blood flow in arteries, capillaries and veins is also a pattern applicable to other organisms.

Investigation 2.10   Some chemistry of a selection of fuels and foods

Part a

All of the substances burn in excess air to give carbon dioxide and water. This shows that both carbon and hydrogen are present in the original substances.

One suitable form of the experiment is shown in figure 2.7. It will be necessary to have a control experiment with the fuel (or food) absent.

Figure 2.7

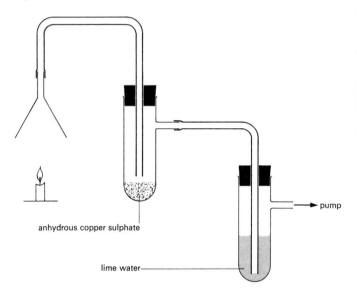

anhydrous copper sulphate

lime water

pump

Ways of burning the materials must be devised. The *Technicians' manual* gives suggestions.

The equation for the burning of paraffin is

$$C_{12}H_{24}(l) + 18\,O_2(g) \rightarrow 12CO_2(g) + 12H_2O(g)$$

and that for glucose is

$$6\,O_2(g) + C_6H_{12}O_6(s) \rightarrow 6\,CO_2(g) + 6\,H_2O(g)$$

▷Part b

Energy is released when sulphur burns in oxygen

$$S(s) + O_2(g) \rightarrow SO_2(g)$$

($S(s)$ represents one mole of atoms of solid sulphur; no assumptions are being made about molecular structure by writing S_8.) The residue (molten sulphur) and the product (sulphur dioxide) are both unpleasant and so sulphur could not be used as a fuel. (However, many tonnes of sulphur dioxide *are* released into the atmosphere, particularly from coal-fired power stations.) Ammonium dichromate(VI) reacts in a spectacular manner to produce chromium(III) oxide, which is used as a green pigment

$$(NH_4)_2Cr_2O_7(s) \rightarrow N_2(g) + 4\,H_2O(g) + Cr_2O_3(s)$$

Atmospheric oxygen is not required.

94

Investigation 2.12 Fuels and food: an explanation

It is important to emphasise in this investigation that all of the calculations are for 1 mole of molecules and not for individual molecules. The calculation for methane is summarised below.

Bond	Number	Energy per bond/kJ mol^{-1}	Total energy/kJ mol^{-1}
C—H	4	413	1 652
O—O	2	497	994

Total energy required for bond breaking $= 2\,646\,\text{kJ mol}^{-1}$. Energy released when bonds are formed:

Bond	Number	Energy per bond/kJ mol^{-1}	Total energy/kJ mol^{-1}
C—O	2	803	1 606
H—O	4	463	1 852

Total energy released when bonds are formed $= 3\,458\,\text{kJ mol}^{-1}$. Energy released when methane is burnt in air $= 3\,458 - 2\,646 = 812\,\text{kJ mol}^{-1}$.

A similar calculation can be done for ethane.

Investigation 2.13 How can we compare fuels?

The efficiency of any engine is rather low, and not necessarily always the same. Thus an engine is not suitable for measuring or comparing energies of combustion. Temperature rise will be the only effect of energy transfer whenever no work (including such non-mechanical forms as electrical work) takes place, and no conduction or other loss takes place. By ensuring that all the energy transferred in combustion is retained in a suitable system, and measuring its temperature rise, with no work involved, then a measure of the energy of combustion would be obtained. Efficient transfer of energy from the hot products of combustion to the measuring system, and adequate thermal insulation, would both be necessary.

Investigation 2.14 How does energy transfer affect temperature?

Parts a and b

Pupils will assume (correctly if the potential difference is constant) that the immersion heater transfers energy at a constant rate. Hence they will expect half the mass of liquid to take half as long to achieve the same temperature rise. They 'automatically' assume that, for a given temperature rise, energy is proportional to mass. This ignores the effect of the container, and any inequality in the power loss (e.g. because of incomplete immersion). The expanded polystyrene beaker has a tiny mass and is a good thermal insulator.

Part c

This should lead to the explicit pattern (for the same temperature rise):

energy $\propto$ mass

The number of particles is proportional to the mass, so the average extra energy per particle is the same for different masses of the same substance.

Part d

Differing results are obtained, most common liquids needing a much shorter time than water (and dilute solutions).

Part e

A good form of the experiment would be to observe the temperature at regular intervals and construct a temperature-versus-time graph. Pupils will probably expect a straight line, and may find a curve concave downwards. This is explained in terms of greater rate of loss of energy to the surroundings at higher temperatures. In any event this effect is small. There is not quite the strong, 'obvious' nature about the result here. It is easily conceivable that the relation may not be one of proportionality. Antifreeze (ethylene glycol) may well be found to give a different relation.

Part f

This involves using a block of aluminium, and perhaps other metals.

▷Part g

This is best attempted by mixing the material with a liquid, such as water or oil, whose characteristics (i.e. specific thermal capacity) are known. Nuffield Secondary Science gives details.

▷Part h

Some pupils may find the equation the simplest way to remember and use the pattern. Others may prefer a verbal form. These differences could be a reflection of mathematical ability, the type of mathematics taught, or differing cognitive styles. The equation is

$$t = k \times m \times T$$

where k is a constant depending upon the substance.

Investigation 2.15 What is the connection between work and temperature?

Part a

This approach to the relation between energy and temperature differs from the traditional one, and emphasises the importance of the historical slow development of the relevant ideas.

Part b

The answers to the questions on Rumford's paper are as follows:

i debatable

ii temperature

iii something which flows from a hot object to a cooler one

iv here it is apparently a fluid

v from small pieces of metal, from the air, from the water, from the iron bar, from the gun-metal neck

vi no fluid could be conceived of as inexhaustible.

Part c

Any of the conventional demonstrations will serve here. It is not of vital importance that high accuracy is achieved. It is important that electrical measurements are not used, since these are not considered until the following section. A joulemeter could possibly be used (as suggested in Nuffield Secondary Science) but the question of how it is calibrated could not be answered effectively. The Nuffield Secondary Science apparatus could be used if the mass of the block were known beforehand, and a value for the specific thermal capacity assumed.

Part d

Fairly consistent results should be obtained for the different substances.

Part e

$4\,200\,\mathrm{J\,°C^{-1}}$ is the thermal capacity of $1.00\,\mathrm{kg}$ of water

$\therefore\;1\,000\,\mathrm{J\,°C^{-1}}$ is the thermal capacity of $\dfrac{1.00\,\times\,1\,000}{4\,200}\,\mathrm{kg}$ of water, i.e. $0.24\,\mathrm{kg}$ of water.

Similarly $0.24\,\mathrm{kg}$ ($240\,\mathrm{cm^3}$) of any dilute aqueous solution would have thermal capacity approximately $1\,\mathrm{kJ\,°C^{-1}}$.

▷ *Investigation 2.16* Is water the best substance to put in a hot water bottle?
Water has the highest specific thermal capacity of any common substance, so will be the best of any (on a mass basis). Organisms will tend to change in temperature less rapidly than their surroundings (unless aquatic). Additional energy will not raise their temperature as rapidly as that of other substances.

▷ *Investigation 2.17* Using thermal capacities
For each mole of Y, $50\,\mathrm{kJ}$ is released. To raise the temperature,

$\frac{1}{2}$ mole of X needs $(40\,\times\,\frac{1}{2}\,\times\,300)\,\mathrm{J} = 6.0\,\mathrm{kJ}$

$\frac{1}{2}$ mole of W needs $(50\,\times\,\frac{1}{2}\,\times\,300)\,\mathrm{J} = 7.5\,\mathrm{kJ}$

Total needs for raising temperature $= 13.5\,\mathrm{kJ}$

So there is plenty available from the reaction: no extra energy input is needed. Energy is continually lost by conduction and radiation to the surroundings, and in the hot products as they are removed.

Investigation 2.18 Comparing fuels and food as energy sources

Notes on foods/fuels

Sugar

Fairly difficult to start, requiring oxygen; burns steadily until near end (with melting); oxygen needed to keep small quantity burning.

Albumen (powdered)

Oxygen necessary throughout; brilliant dazzling flame; difficult to keep alight.

Olive oil

Difficult to start; wick necessary (glass wool, asbestos wool, rocksil); burns very slowly without oxygen, leading to excessive losses.

Castor oil

Best avoided; requires wick and oxygen, and produces a lot of soot.

Lubricating oil

As castor oil but not quite so bad.

Meta fuel

Very convenient; burns quietly and slowly; very high energy output.

Methanol, Ethanol, Propanol, Butanol

Burn rapidly without wick or oxygen.

Paraffin

Should burn slowly with a wick.

In the simple form of the experiment only about one-half to two-thirds of the energy released goes in warming the water. This does not matter if the proportion is constant, which in practice means if the foods/fuels take similar times to burn. Thin spun aluminium containers are best, but baked beans cans would do. Squash bottle caps are suitable crucibles! A more sophisticated apparatus is described in Nuffield Biology *Pupils' text III* and *Teachers' guide III*, Chapter 4.

Complete combustion of 1 g of fat will ideally yield about 39 kJ, 1 g of dry protein will yield about 17 kJ, 1 g of carbohydrate will yield about 16 kJ. Oxygen will be necessary to complete a satisfactory 'burning'. 0.5 g of the foods will probably suffice. In the method described determinations will be rough but probably good enough to show that fats have twice as much energy available as proteins and carbohydrates.

Investigation 2.19 The effect of temperature on particle interaction

The graph shows that increasing the temperature causes the reaction to go more quickly. Everyday illustrations of this are cooking and refrigeration (the latter slowing down the reaction).

Discussion with pupils should lead to the idea that the energy needed for bond breaking is more readily available to interacting particles at higher temperatures, and the number of collisions per unit time is increased. (This is important because particles do need to touch in order for a chemical reaction to take place.)

▷ *Investigation 2.20* Enzymes and particle interactions

In this problem, the class discovers that there is an *optimum* temperature (approximately 40 °C) for the interaction starch → glucose.

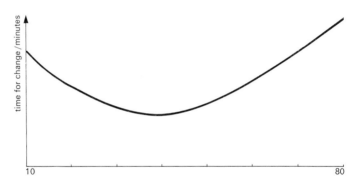

Figure 2.8   temperature/°C

The graph obtained is shown in figure 2.8.

The problem is two-fold:

a to decide (in class discussion) how to perform the experiment, including what apparatus to use and

b to explain the graph which is obtained.

a *Performing the experiment*

The previous investigation gives some hints for this. Important points are as follows.

i Equal volumes ($2 \, cm^3$ is suggested) of 1 per cent starch solution are put into graduated test tubes.

ii Test tubes are placed into water baths (thermometers required).

iii Equal volumes ($1 \, cm^3$ is suggested) of 10^{-2}–10^{-3} per cent amylase solution are added when the test tubes have reached the temperature of the water.

iv Every 5 minutes test for the presence of starch, using a glass rod and white tile. Starch is present if iodine/potassium iodide solution turns blue.

b *Explaining the graph*

The intention is that pupils should be sceptical about the pattern of particle interaction and temperature (see objective 2f). A steady increase was expected, whereas an optimum temperature of 40 °C was obtained. The explanation expected at this stage is that the enzyme catalyst is most active at 40 °C and this is reflected in the temperature-time graph. Denaturation of the enzyme begins to occur above 40 °C and at 70 °C most enzymes are completely denaturised.

This can be related in discussion to the fact that enzymes are usually found in living things and in mammals and birds the body temperature is between 37 °C and 40 °C.

Enzymes function by bringing molecules of reactants close together.

Investigation 2.21   Predicting the composition of expired air

Using the apparatus illustrated in the *Pupils' manual* the presence of carbon dioxide in expired air can easily be demonstrated. Sometimes bicarbonate indicator solution is preferred to lime water (and see also Investigation 2.22). Details of the indicator are given in Nuffield Biology *Pupils' text III* and *Teachers' guide III*, Chapter 1 and in the *Technicians' manual*. Its reaction to carbon dioxide should be demonstrated. Although it is assumed that colour changes in the indicator are due to carbon dioxide they are, of course, due to changes in pH.

A much more complete investigation can be performed which involves an analysis of inspired and expired air for oxygen and carbon dioxide content. This will allow any predictions concerning the oxygen content of expired air to be tested. It is suggested that this is demonstrated and the method used is that described in complete detail in Nuffield Secondary Science, *Theme 3*, Field of study 3.12 II. The method utilises large gas syringes rather than gas burettes (Nuffield Biology, year III) which are not recommended. It is important that pupils should read the section on respiration in the topic book *Machines and engines*.

Investigation 2.22   Do all organisms respire?

There are two pieces of evidence which indicate respiration:

a a temperature rise of the surroundings (energy transfer)

b gaseous exchange – utilisation of oxygen and liberation of carbon dioxide.

The apparatus suggested in the *Pupils' manual* should enable pupils to investigate a variety of organisms along these lines. It

100

Figure 2.9

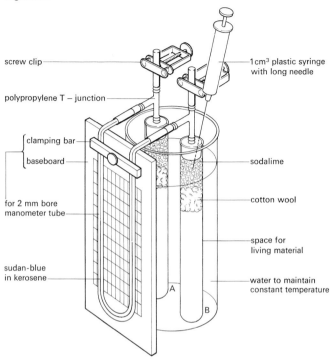

screw clip

1 cm³ plastic syringe with long needle

polypropylene T – junction

clamping bar

baseboard

sodalime

for 2 mm bore manometer tube

cotton wool

space for living material

sudan-blue in kerosene

water to maintain constant temperature

A

B

will be noted that bicarbonate indicator is suggested as an alternative to lime water. Be wary of droppings or excretion from organisms. Vacuum flasks can replace the insulated jars used in the differential air thermometer. Asking pupils how this works could provide a good problem! An alternative method using thermistors to detect temperature rise is described in the reference given in the sample scheme. Figure 2.9 illustrates a more complex respirometer for determining oxygen uptake quantitatively. This could be used as a demonstration apparatus. It has the advantage of overcoming temperature effects on respirometers (see below). Full experimental details are given in the reference quoted.

Apart from peas other germinating seeds can also be used, and pieces of apple, growing roots, potatoes, mushrooms, etc. can all be tried (although with varying degrees of success). Unfortunately, green plant material is different because photosynthesis may interfere, especially in the experiments on gaseous exchange. Since pupils are not yet familiar with this process, light cannot reasonably be excluded from the experiment. However, germinating seeds usually give adequate results and the use of these may be justified by suggesting that these are 'active' (and therefore more likely to use larger quantities of oxygen and produce more carbon dioxide) stages in the life of a plant. In comparison with animals, plants show remarkably little activity most of the time so it is not surprising to find that respiration is harder to detect. This could be predicted. With pieces of plant, such as apple, temperature rises or oxygen absorption may be due as much to respiring decomposers as the actual plant material and these are not dealt with until Section 4. Hence there are difficulties in this investigation with respect to plants but they are not insurmountable. Seeds should be germinated by soaking in water beforehand.

In designing experiments controls will be essential. The small respirometers suggested can act as very effective air thermometers and so attention must be paid to the surrounding temperature. Results should be obtained fairly quickly (minutes in some cases). Different groups of pupils should test different living materials.

▷ *Investigation 2.23* Could an organism respire in an oxygen free environment?

Apart from boiling, oxygen can also be removed from the glucose solution by bubbling nitrogen (from a cylinder) through the solution. Anaerobic respiration or fermentation involves particle interactions resulting in the formation of ethanol and this is the basis of the wine industry. The work may be extended for example by practical distillation of a yeast/glucose mixture which has been allowed to ferment. The fact that ethanol (which itself can be a fuel) is the end-product of anaerobic respiration testifies to the inefficiency of this process in utilising the energy in food.

To check that oxygen has been removed from the glucose solution a few drops of Janus green B can be added to a small portion. This blue dye turns salmon-pink when oxygen is in short supply. Contrast this reaction with glucose solution which has not had oxygen removed. The thermometer (which should be sensitive) and bicarbonate indicator should be carefully observed over the next 24–48 hours.

The glucose solution should be 5 per cent. Yeast should be prepared ready for adding beforehand. (See *Technicians' manual.*) About one part yeast suspension to nine parts glucose solution should be adequate.

Investigation 2.24 Explaining the effects of increasing pupil power output on body function

Part a The effects on body temperature

i Energy transfer in respiration can result in mechanical work and a temperature rise in the surroundings. Hence the body temperature should rise especially during hard physical activity. However the experiment to be performed in ii indicates that this is not quite true. Although the skin temperature may rise internal temperature remains steadier.

ii To record changes in temperature thermocouples connected to a spot galvanometer can be employed. The apparatus is illustrated in figure 2.10.

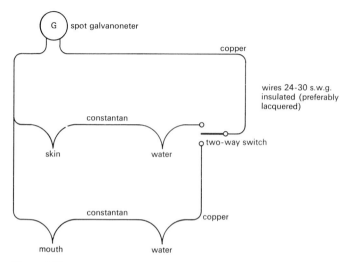

Figure 2.10

There is no need to calibrate the system (which is tedious) if we are only interested in relative temperature rises. Note the position of the spot for both skin (use plaster to tape a thermocouple on an arm) and mouth before and after exercise. Relative temperature rise after exercise will be indicated by the extent to which the spot moves. A volunteer should be chosen to perform the exercise which should be fairly heavy. It can be performed on the cycle ergometer.

It will be seen that the body (mouth) temperature remains relatively stable (although it may well rise somewhat) compared to the skin temperature. This can be explained as follows. During exercise we flush, indicating a larger rate of flow of blood in the capillaries near the skin surface. The amount of blood in these superficial capillaries can be controlled by the dilation and constriction of arteries supplying them. It is worth recalling the presence of muscle fibres in the walls of these vessels which enable them to do this. Blood in the skin capillaries has travelled (ultimately) from the active muscles. Hence energy transferred during respiration, some of which has caused the temperature of the muscle surroundings to rise, is quickly transported via the blood to the skin. Here it is dissipated, causing a temperature rise in the surrounding air.

Applying a tourniquet on an arm leads to a restriction of blood flow and the consequent fall in temperature of the skin is easily detected by a thermocouple. If this is demonstrated it should be done on the teacher, not a pupil.

During physical activity the heart rate and hence pulse rate rise to cope with the increased demands made to dissipate energy. It is also a consequence of the extra oxygen requirements and the need to remove carbon dioxide and other wastes. However the sample scheme has yet to establish the blood as the transporting medium for these materials (see Investigation 2.25). Tiredness is due to accumulation of wastes and especially of lactic acid (see the topic book *Machines and engines*).

iii If ▷ Investigation 2.20 was performed this question can be dealt with, otherwise it must be omitted. Advantages of a constant, high body temperature could be mentioned in terms of environmental independence.

iv This can be done for homework. It not only requires an account of the dissipation of energy to the surroundings but also its prevention. Hair, feathers and fat can be considered as insulators. The control of body temperature as a homeostatic mechanism is considered in Section 5.

v The effects of perspiration could be quickly and easily examined by placing a wet hand in the air stream from a fan explaining the results in kinetic terms.

One way of solving the practical problem is explained below. Pupils will need:

beaker, $100 \, \text{cm}^3$
thermometer, $-10\,^{\circ}\text{C}$ to $+110\,^{\circ}\text{C}$
Bunsen burner and hardboard mat
stop clock, or watch with seconds hand
graph paper

First, the energy supplied by the Bunsen flame per minute must be calculated. This can be done by placing a steady flame (about 5 cm high) below the beaker containing a known mass of water (about $50 \, \text{cm}^3$).

The thermometer is placed in the water and the temperature is recorded every quarter minute. A graph is plotted of temperature against time. The gradient of the best straight line gives the rate of temperature rise and hence the energy supplied per minute by the flame can be calculated, knowing the thermal capacity of (water + beaker). Without altering the flame, the water is allowed to boil for a known time (10 minutes is suitable). The

104

Bunsen burner is removed and the beaker and contents allowed to cool.

The beaker and water are weighed; the loss in mass of water is calculated. The amount of energy used in converting this mass of water into steam is calculated and, finally, the amount of energy required to change 1 mole of molecules of water (18 g) into steam can be obtained.

The energy is needed in order to change the close-packed, slow-moving water molecules into fast-moving, widely separated gas molecules. Energy is similarly required when water evaporates from the skin. (The energy required is not exactly the same: the lower the temperature of evaporation, or boiling, the greater the amount of energy required to change the liquid into a gas.)

Part b The effects on breathing

i The energy transferred can be measured as work. The energy conservation principle, dealt with in Section 1 and again earlier in this section, will mean that if the work is greater, more fuel (food) is necessary, more oxygen is used and more carbon dioxide produced. Hence there is an increase in the rate and depth of breathing. Therefore the simple pattern predictable is that the greater the work the greater the amount of air breathed. Choose a volunteer who is reasonably fit and willing.

The volume of air breathed over a three-minute period at rest should be measured. Full details for collecting and measuring volumes of air breathed using a breathing bag assembly can be found in Nuffield Secondary Science, *Theme 3*, Field of study 3.12. The measured amounts of energy (measured as work) should now be transferred on the cycle ergometer at some time in a three minute period. Arrange for the volunteers to be seated on the cycle ergometer and, at the beginning of the three minute period, to be breathing normally into the bag. At some time within the next minute the 500 J of energy should be transferred. The volunteer should then remain seated on the ergometer, breathing air into the bag, until the three minute period is completed. The need to collect air after the transfer has been completed should be obvious to pupils who will recognise that they pant after any exercise and this air should be considered. Whether this is explained in terms of an oxygen debt is left to individual discretion. During exercise, oxygen demands increase and wastes build up which must be removed afterwards. A sprinter will perhaps breathe only once or twice when he runs 100 m and does most of his breathing after the race, paying off the oxygen debt. Since there is a limit to the oxygen debt he cannot keep a sprint up for very long. Long distance runners keep their oxygen debt small and are able to balance it by careful pacing and controlled breathing.

Repeat the exercise on the same volunteer for different amounts of work. To achieve the larger quantities of work the volunteer's power must rise in order to complete the work and allow time for recovery during the three minute period.

If time allows, the exercises could be repeated with different volunteers. Plot the energy transferred (i.e. the amount of work) against extra volume of air breathed. The predicted pattern should emerge.

ii The efficiency of the volunteer in the cycle ergometer activity can be calculated using the information given in the *Pupils' manual* (Nuffield Secondary Science uses the phrase 'energy cost' to indicate the total energy transferred per unit time. Some useful data are given of the energy turnover in various activities.) The relationships between useful energy output (work) and the total energy transferred should illustrate clearly the necessity for dissipating energy to the surroundings after heavy physical activity if the body temperature is to remain more or less constant.

▷ Part c

This optional investigation tests the assumption, made in part b i, that more oxygen is used and more carbon dioxide is produced during heavy physical activity. The method is exactly the same as that used in Investigation 2.21 to analyse the oxygen and carbon dioxide content of inspired and expired air. To save time data for inspired air obtained from that investigation can be used again.

▷ Part d

This allows a more precise determination of efficiency to be made. Use data from the same volunteer as in part b i.

▷ Part e

The methods used for this investigation are the same as for part b i but different activities should be investigated. These could include arm ergometer, step-ups etc. Cycling is a fairly efficient activity. Different individuals will vary in efficiency in the same activity. The opportunities presented for pattern-searching are obvious. The effect of training on efficiency in performing certain activities would make an interesting project. The results of training are complex, including increased forces which muscles can apply; more effective application of these forces, more effective oxygen absorption in the lungs and transport by the blood system. There is opportunity for coopera- tion with the P.E. department.

Investigation 2.25 How does breathing take place?

It is essential that lungs be supplied with trachea and bronchii intact. (Sometimes they are sliced open.)

The investigation takes pupils through a series of steps:
Part a
Evidence to illustrate that air moves into the lungs, via the trachea. The lungs are spongy, a feature explained by the presence of many 'air spaces'.
Part b
For this part it will be useful to have available various models. A full discussion on the use of these models and of breathing can be found in the Nuffield Biology references given in the 'Sample scheme'. The apparatus shown in figure 2.11 can be used to illustrate the action of the diaphragm. This model has severe limitations. The rubber sheet is flat whereas the diaphragm is domed inwards even at forced inspiration. It is never domed outwards as the rubber sheet is when pulled. The rubber sheet

Figure 2.11

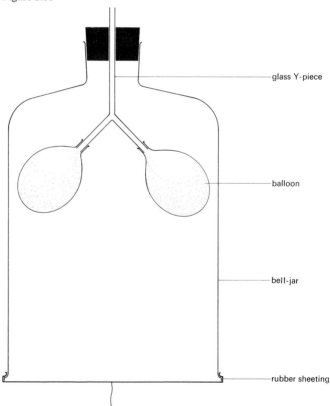

glass Y-piece

balloon

bell-jar

rubber sheeting

107

is stretched during the simulated respiration, whereas the diaphragm contracts.

The apparatus shown in figure 2.12 can be used to illustrate the action of the intercostal muscles located between the ribs.

Figure 2.12

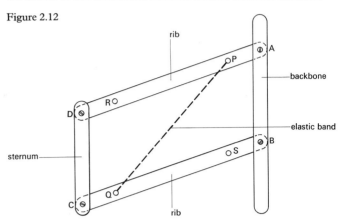

Figure 2.13 shows the appearance of the intercostal muscles.

Figure 2.13

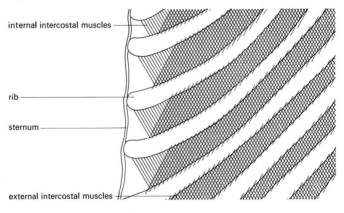

The direction PQ (figure 2.12) represents the external intercostals and RS the direction taken by the internal intercostals. It is normal to suggest that inspiration is due to the contraction of the external intercostal muscles and that the internal intercostals are expiratory. Electromicrographic recording techniques have shown electrical activity in the intercostal spaces during inspiration and this increases with inspiratory effort. However, in normal or slightly forced expiration there is no intercostal activity except in coughing. Cutting the nerves leading to the intercostals greatly reduces the rib movements. It is not possible to say if one or both sets of intercostal muscles are active in inspiration. There is some evidence to suggest that the internal intercostals may have some function in speech (during which air is forced past the vocal cords in the larynx).

The expansion of the thoracic (chest) cavity in which the lungs lie, either by lowering the diaphragm or raising the rib cage or both, reduces pressure on the lungs. Air thus moves into the lungs. Raising the diaphragm and lowering the rib cage forces air out of the lungs. The lungs also have a natural elasticity which helps push air out.

Figure 2.14 Simultaneous recordings of intra-oesophageal pressure and tidal air volume during the breathing cycle. To aid interpretation the pressure curve has been inverted

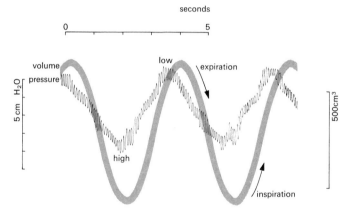

This explanation can be backed up with evidence shown in figure 2.14. The explanation is simplified to the extent that no mention of the pleural sacs has been made. The pleural sacs are often represented in diagrams (see for example that in *Patterns 3*) as a pair of airtight hollow cavities in which the lungs lie. In fact, the cavity of each sac is virtually eliminated, there being only a trace of lymph acting as a lubricant between the two layers. Pupils find this difficult to reconcile with the simplified explanation. We have to regard the pleural cavities as potential spaces. It also, incidentally, emphasises another limitation of the bell-jar-balloon model described above because the pleural cavity is much smaller than the model indicates. Changes of pressure inside the thorax can be measured by injecting a very small volume of air between the two pleural layers and connecting the hypodermic needle to a manometer. The record obtained is essentially the same as that shown in figure 2.14. Puncturing a pleural sac causes the lung to collapse.

Part c

The material presented here is designed to provide evidence for the exchange of oxygen and carbon dioxide between the lungs and the blood system, which is responsible for the transport of these gases to and from the rest of the body. Haemoglobin in the red blood cells is responsible for oxygen transport. In low oxygen concentrations as in the muscles oxyhaemoglobin readily dissociates into oxygen and haemoglobin.

▷ *Investigation 2.27* The motorist's problem

The answers are as follows:

i $3.0 \times 2\,250\,\text{kJ} = 6\,750\,\text{kJ}$

ii $6\,750 \times \dfrac{100}{80}\,\text{kJ} = 8\,440\,\text{kJ}$

iii $\dfrac{8\,440}{45\,000}\,\text{kg} = 0.183\,\text{kg}$

volume of this $= 0.183 \times 1.25\,\text{litres}$
$= 0.230\,\text{litres}$

iv $(0.230 \times 12)\,\text{km} = 2.8\,\text{km}$

v say 1 to 2 km

vi drive 2 km in the most likely direction!

Investigation 2.28 Energy and change of state

Part a

Loss of energy because of evaporation of water. The air temperature could be raised (expensive) or the humidity kept high (uncomfortable and inconvenient).

Part b

High humidity due to exhaled moisture. Energy released on turning to liquid water is transferred out through window. Air double glazing acts as insulator, so slower energy loss. Also cuts down sound transfer.

Part c

Energy absorbed from freezing compartment is used to vaporise liquid. At higher pressure this condenses, releasing energy to the surroundings. Net flow of energy is from surroundings into freezer, into working fluid, to condenser, to surroundings. Also energy is transferred electrically to motor, to pump, to fluid, also to condenser and to surroundings.

Part d

Ablative means literally carried away. Material should have high energy of vaporisation, should not melt, should conduct in layers but not through layers. Composite materials are used.

110

Part e

High energy to melt, poor conduction, excellent reflection.

Part f

Icebergs are large enough for the surface area to be so small in comparison with volume that transfer of energy melts only a small proportion per day. The size effect is similar to that with organisms.

Part g

Gas is too bulky. Energy is removed (by placing in contact with cold objects, e.g. pipes containing refrigerant) so as to condense gas to liquid. During a journey in an insulated tanker some energy reaches the liquid gas leading to 'boil-off'. Storage in refrigerated chambers also entails small energy transfer, and consequent evaporation. Energy must be supplied (e.g. from a river) to evaporate gas ready for use.

The topic book *Weather patterns* discusses examples of energy transfer and change of state on a very large scale but the book is best used in Section 4.

Sample questions

1 Study the following diagrams illustrating an investigation

That combustion and respiration have certain characteristics in common would be best shown by the experiments that contain

A i **C** i and iii

B i and ii **D** i and iv (correct)

2 A person runs a 1 500 m race. Which one of the following would most directly indicate that he is respiring more?

A his skin becomes 'flushed' with extra blood

B his heart beats faster

C his body temperature may rise a little (correct)

D he sweats more

3 The number of men per 100 000 people dying of lung cancer each year is as follows.

non-smokers	pipe smokers	cigarette smokers
10	39	135

Classify the statements below according to the following key:
a the statement is a reasonable interpretation of the data
b the statement is an unreasonable interpretation of the data
c the statement is data, not an interpretation of data.

i   Smoking causes lung cancer. (b)
ii More cigarette smokers die of lung cancer than pipe smokers. (c)
iii Smoking decreases the efficiency of the lungs. (b)
iv Whatever it is that causes lung cancer, it is more likely to cause it in the lungs of people who smoke. (a)
v   Pipe smoking does not cause lung cancer. (b)
4   The average rate of breathing for a man when in an awake, sitting position was 12 breaths per minute.

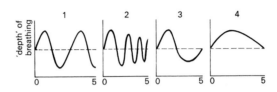

rate of breathing: time/s

What would be the order of the records which demonstrates sleep, running a 1 500 m race, reading?
A 3-1-4   C 3-4-1
B 4-2-3 (correct)   D 4-2-1

Read the following brief description of an iron lung and answer questions 5 and 6.

An iron lung consists of a cylinder in which the pressure alternates from higher than atmospheric pressure to lower than atmospheric pressure. A person who has had polio may be put in an iron lung, but their head must be outside the cylinder with an air-tight seal around the neck.

5 From the description above an iron lung must replace which one of the following in a human?
A lungs
B trachea
C diaphragm and intercostal muscles (correct)
D ribs

6 In an iron lung, such as described above, which one of the following would result in air passing into the lungs?
A the air-tight seal round the neck
B the elasticity of the lungs
C atmospheric pressure (correct)
D the patient's diaphragm and intercostal muscles

7 The gills of fish have the purpose of allowing exchange of carbon dioxide and oxygen with the surrounding water. Which of the following is the least important feature of gills with respect to this purpose?

A they have a large surface area

B the blood in the gill flows in the opposite direction to the water flowing past the gill

C they are connected to the back of the mouth behind the head region (correct)

D they have a skeletal framework to prevent them from sticking together

8 A person weighing 510 N climbs to the top of a hill 1 000 m higher than the point at which he started. To do this he uses up 200 g of food. If 1 g of food has an energy value of about 17 kJ what is his efficiency in climbing the hill?

A about 0.17 per cent

B about 1.3 per cent

C about 7 per cent

D about 15 per cent (correct)

9 Approximately £1 000 million is collected annually in tobacco taxes. The good that this does far outweighs any damage to individual health through smoking. Comment.

10 What is your power output in trying to push down the classroom wall? Explain the answer you give.

11 The pumping action of the heart follows an orderly sequence.

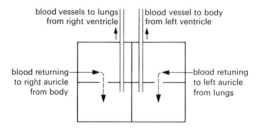

The contraction of the auricles is followed by contraction of the ventricles. There is then a brief period when all four heart chambers are relaxed. The graph represents a single cycle.

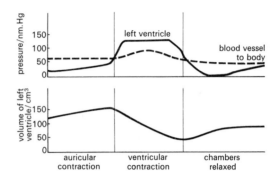

Which one of the following occurs during the contraction of the left ventricle?

A the left ventricle fills with blood

B the pressure in the vessel to the body remains constant

C the pressure in the left ventricle exceeds that in the vessel to the body (correct)

D the auricles empty

12 Water gas is manufactured by passing steam over red hot coke. The interaction can be summarised as

$$H_2O(g) + C(s) \rightarrow CO(g) + H_2(g) \qquad X$$
$$\text{(water gas)}$$

The water gas burns in oxygen, and the interactions are shown below:

$$CO(g) + \tfrac{1}{2}O_2(g) \rightarrow CO_2(g) \qquad\qquad Y$$
$$H_2(g) + \tfrac{1}{2}O_2(g) \rightarrow H_2O(g) \qquad\qquad Z$$

The transfer of energy to the chemicals in reaction X is $7.5\,kJ\,mole^{-1}$. The transfer of energy from the chemicals in reactions Y and Z are $16\,kJ\,mole^{-1}$ and $14\,kJ\,mole^{-1}$ respectively.

Which one of the following represents change in energy due to reactions X, Y and Z?

A $7.5\,kJ\,mole^{-1}$ **C** $22.5\,kJ\,mole^{-1}$ (correct)

B $9.5\,kJ\,mole^{-1}$ **D** $37.5\,kJ\,mole^{-1}$

13 The transfer of energy from the chemicals when the alcohols CH_3OH, C_2H_5OH and C_3H_7OH are burnt in oxygen are shown:

alcohol	$kJ\,mole^{-1}$
CH_3OH	42
C_2H_5OH	80
C_3H_7OH	115

Predict the approximate value of the energy transfer when the alcohol C_4H_9OH is burnt in oxygen.

14i What is the increase in energy (measured as work) when 2 kg of water is raised from the bottom to the top of a waterfall 42 m high? (Weight of 1 kg = 10 N.)

A 840 J (correct)

B 210 J

C 8.4 J

D 2.1 J

ii When 2 kg of water, specific thermal capacity = $4\,200\,J\,kg^{-1}\,K^{-1}$, falls from the top to the bottom of the waterfall its temperature rise (in K) will be

A 0.05

B 0.10 (correct)

C 0.20

D 0.40

▷15 On his honeymoon in Switzerland, J. P. Joule measured the temperature of water at the top and at the bottom of a waterfall, using a sensitive thermometer, and discovered the water was slightly warmer at the bottom. Which one of the following statements explains the observation?

A the air is colder, i.e. has less energy, at the top of a mountain than at the bottom

B the water loses potential energy and gains kinetic energy, which at the bottom is shared among the molecules of water (correct)

C the water is travelling faster at the bottom than at the top, i.e. it has more kinetic energy

D the water has more chemical potential energy at the top than at the bottom, and the chemical potential energy lost turns into kinetic energy

▷16 The temperature difference found by Joule was only small because

A a large amount of work only warms objects slightly (correct)

B the waterfall must have been a small one

C the water in Swiss rivers is very cold to start with

D he must have been careless making his observations (perhaps because he was on his honeymoon)

17 The four graphs show how reaction rate is affected by an increase in temperature for four different interactions.

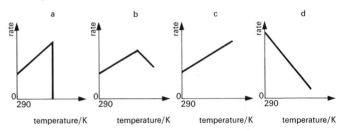

i In which case does the increase in temperature bring an increase in the rate of the reaction for the whole temperature range? (c)

ii In which case is there a best temperature for the interaction? (b)

iii In which case does the increase in temperature bring a decrease in the rate of the reaction for the whole temperature range? (d)

iv In which case does the interaction cease at a certain temperature? (a)

18 The table shows the energy required to change selected compounds from the liquid state into a gas at atmospheric pressure, and also the temperature at which this occurs.

Substance	Energy/kJ mol^{-1}	Boiling point/°C
carbon monoxide	6.03	−191.5
oxygen	6.82	−183.1
methane	8.20	−161.5
hydrogen sulphide	18.7	−61.8
ammonia	23.4	−33.4
sulphur dioxide	24.9	−10.0
tetrachloromethane	29.4	61.2
benzene	31.0	80.1
ethanol	38.6	78.5
water	41.1	100.0

Which of the following statements is best supported by the data?

A the higher the boiling point the more energy is needed to change one mole of a compound from liquid to gas (correct)

B the lower the boiling point, the more energy is needed to change one mole of a compound from liquid to gas

C compounds which are liquids at room temperature require less energy than other compounds to change from liquid to a gas

D there is no recognisable pattern

19 Increase in temperature can increase the rate of a reaction. To which one of the following could the pattern not be applied?
  A cooking potatoes
  B keeping milk in a refrigerator
  C burning coal on a fire
  D storing sugar (correct)

20 In an experiment different masses of four liquids were separately warmed by means of an electric immersion heater. The relevant data are given below:

Substance	Mass/kg	Specific thermal capacity/J kg^{-1} $^{\circ}$C^{-1}	Temperature rise/$^{\circ}$C
paraffin	0.70	2 400	9.0
olive oil	0.80	2 000	12.0
water	1.00	4 200	4.0
ethanol	0.60	2 600	10.0

Which one of the four liquids absorbed the greatest amount of energy?
  A paraffin
  B olive oil (correct)
  C water
  D ethanol

3 Energy and electricity

Introduction

Several different aspects of the relationship between energy and electricity are considered.

Quantitative work on current and charge leads into quantitative electrolysis. The mole of electrons is introduced and ionic formulae are used for the first time.

The concept of potential difference is developed (as the energy conveyed by unit charge). Electrical work and power are then discussed. A simple electrochemical series leads into applications which are disadvantageous (corrosion) and applications which are advantageous (cells).

Investigation of a variety of electrical components leads to the concept of resistance and to the power dissipated in a resistor.

The section closes with a discussion of electricity in the home.

Objectives

Skills

1 To recall and to understand the following concepts: current, time, rate, charge, conduction, electron, element, ion, atom, electron, mole, activity, (energy), (transfer), potential difference, resistance, power, proportionality, classification (1).

2 To recall and to understand the following patterns.

a Currents at a junction in an electric circuit behave additively, showing that the charge entering the junction is equal to the charge leaving it (2).

b Electric current (I) is the rate of flow of charge (Q) so that

$$Q = I \times t$$

where t represents time (2).

c The amount of a substance evolved, deposited or dissolved at an electrode during electrolysis is proportional to the charge which passes (2).

d Like charges repel, unlike charges attract.

e The mole is the amount of substance of a system which contains as many elementary entities as there are carbon atoms in exactly 0.012 kg of carbon-12 (2).

118

f   Elements require to gain or to lose simple multiples of one mole of electrons to deposit or to dissolve one mole of element (2).

g   Potential difference (V) is equivalent to energy (E) per unit charge (Q), so that (charge × potential difference) can be a measure of energy transfer. The relation between these quantities is

$$E = Q \times V \quad \text{or} \quad V = \frac{E}{Q} \text{ (2).}$$

▷h   For a transformer the voltage ratio is equal to the turns ratio:

$$\frac{V_1}{V_2} = \frac{n_1}{n_2} \text{ (2).}$$

i   An electrolytic cell is a source of (almost) constant potential difference, which depends on the two elements used for electrodes and on the nature (and concentration) of the electrolyte (2).

j   The elements can be placed in a series for which the potential differences are additive (electrochemical series), i.e. the energy per electron is additive (2).

k   The electrochemical series is an activity series. Activity can be explained in terms of the energy required for electron transfer (2).

l   Different types of conductor show different relations between the potential difference (V) across them and the current (I) through them. The fraction (V/I) is known as resistance (R), i.e.

$$\frac{V}{I} = R \quad \text{or} \quad V = IR.$$

For simple conductors at constant temperature R is constant (2).

m   Patterns b and g can be combined with the pattern defining power (P) to give

$$P = I^2 R = \frac{V^2}{R} \text{ (2).}$$

n   Because building blocks are diverse (either in structure or properties) a hierarchy of sets and subsets can be constructed based on the degrees of similarity and difference. This is the process of classification (which includes the periodic classification of the elements) (2).

(These patterns are linked with the patterns in the *Teachers' handbook* as follows: a with 39; b with 39; c with 8, 13 and 72; d with 72; e with 12; f with 13; g with 40 and 36; h with 70; i with 11 and 25; j with 25; k with 25 and 31; l with 41; m with 40 and 37; n with 17.)

3   To use quantitative data from experiments to derive the pattern

that (energy transfer per unit charge) is proportional to the number of cells (or to potential difference of a supply) (3).

4 To use the patterns above to solve problems (4a).
5 To understand something of the domestic and industrial importance of electrical means of transferring energy (6).
6 To understand that a cathode ray oscilloscope acts as a voltmeter of very rapid response, and by giving a visual display can be used to measure potential difference, time, and any quantity which can be represented by a potential difference (6).
7 To be aware of the importance, and in simple cases the action, of safety devices in electrical installations, without being afraid of electrical appliances (6).
8 To be accurate in reporting the results of experiments on the resistance of electrical components (7).

Attitudes

▷9 To be concerned about the problem of corrosion (11).
10 To be concerned about the correct use of electrical appliances in the home and at work (11).
▷11 To be willing to work as a group on a project on corrosion (9).

Flow diagram

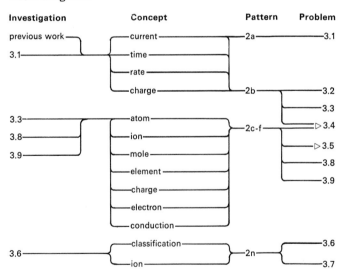

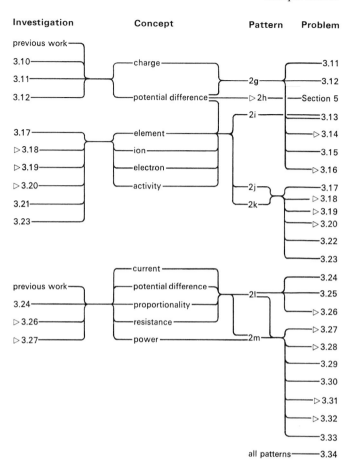

Sample scheme

Time allocation for this section: 4 weeks

Description	Reference	Notes
D Nature of electric current		
▶3.1 Current and charge		
▶3.2 Using the pattern of current and charge		

	Description	Reference	Notes
▶ 3.3	Relationship between quantities of charge and substance		
▷ ▶ 3.4	Is the pattern true for gases?		Experiment to be devised for homework, practical problem
▷ ▶ 3.5	What happens when two solutions are used?		Practical problem
▶ 3.6	Ions and the periodic table		Discussion and 'think' investigation for revision purposes
▶ 3.7	A pattern modified		Discussion problem
R	*Atoms into ions*	NC background book	
▷ T	*Electrolysis of lead bromide*	NC film loop	For revision
D	The mole of electrons		Revision of the mole as 'amount of substance'
▶ 3.8	Using the mole of electrons		
▶ 3.9	Formulae of ionic compounds		'Theoretical' problems and discussion
3.10	Current and energy	NP Year IV, expt 120	Demonstration
D	What affects the amount of energy?		An important question
▶ 3.11	Cells and energy		A crucial experiment for the concept of potential difference
▶ 3.12	How does the energy transferred depend on the current?		Prediction and experiment

122

	Description	Reference	Notes
▶3.13	Voltmeters	NP Year III, expts 91, 92b; NP Year IV, expts 125, 126, 128, 129	Includes oscilloscopes
▶3.14	Electrical work		Design of experiment and deduction
▶3.15	Electrical power		Develops patterns $E = ItV$ and $P = IV$
▷▶3.16	Alternating voltages	NSS Theme 4, Section 4.34; NP Year III, expts 89b, c, 90c	
▶3.17	Varying the electrodes in an electrolytic cell		Results should be exchanged
▷3.18	Varying the solution in an electrolytic cell		If time permits, NC Stage II, expt 16.5b could also be performed
▷▶3.19	Displacement reactions		
▷▶3.20	Uses of dry cells		Discussion investigation
▷B	*Michael Faraday*	NC background book	
▷B	*Faraday and electricity*	Jackdaw Publications, Cape	
R	*Corrosion*	NC background book	
3.21	Corrosion	Johnstone, A. H. and Morrison, T. I., *Chemistry takes shape*, Book 3, Heinemann, 1966	Reference gives further experiments suitable for science clubs
▷R	Corrosion and protection; protecting metals	NSS Theme 7, Sections 7.24, 25	

	Description	Reference	Notes
▶3.22	Problem searching		Optional project (e.g. for science club)
▷B	*Corrosion*	NC background book	
▷T	*Electrochemical shaping*	Project Technology Brief no 14	
▶3.23	Reversing the process	NC Stage II, expt 23.5	Demonstration investigation simple fuel cell
▶3.24	How does current depend on potential difference?		Wide variety, could be a circus of experiments
D	Electrical resistance		'Think' problem
▶3.25	Using the concept of resistance	NP Year IV, expts 139, 141, 142, 151	
▷▶3.26	Resistance of a lamp	NP Year IV, expt 140	Prediction which fails, design of experiment
▷▶3.27	Power and resistance		Deduction
▷▶3.28	Does a cell really produce a constant potential difference?		Introduce internal resistance
▶3.29	Electricity in the home		Mixture of thought, discussion and finding out
T	*Facts about flexibles*	Wallchart from Electrical Association for Women, 25 Foubert's Place, London W1	
▶3.30	Electrical power and safety		'Think' investigation

Description	Reference	Notes
▷T *Electric sense* ▷T *Home electric sense* ▷T *Electric entertainment*	Booklets from the Electricity Council, Trafalgar Buildings, 1 Charing Cross, London SW1A 2DS	
▷ ►3.31 Combinations of resistance		Deduction and experiment
▷ ►3.32 Photoelectric cells		Paper and pencil problem; design of experiment
►3.33 Rectifiers	NP Year IV, expt 129d; NSS Theme 4, Section 4.26	Experiment or demonstration
▷T Semiconductor diodes	Project Technology Brief no 25	Investigational project
▷3.34 Electricity and everyday life	'Baffled' Punch, July 10, 1968	Largely discussion
B *Electrification of* *British Rail*	*Patterns* topic book	Useful background reading

Early warning

See 'Teaching notes', Section 5, Investigation 5.12.

Teaching progression

The first two investigations and the associated discussion relate to objectives 2a and 2b, i.e. to the quantitative aspects of regarding an electric current as a flow of something identified as charge. At this stage there is nothing beyond speculation to indicate whether the charge occurs in pieces or not, still less to show the involvement of electrons. Additional simple quantitative problems can be added if desired. Pattern 2b is also used in Investigations 3.3 and ▷3.4. Periodic classification is again met (objective 2n) in Investigations 3.6 and 3.7. The quantitative work on electrolysis is used to develop ideas about the formulae of ionic compounds.

The first introduction to potential difference comes in Investigation 3.10. This is an important demonstration in that it shows conclusively that the 'obvious' idea (that the energy is dependent on the current) is not the whole truth.

A strong pattern-finding element is present in Investigation 3.11 (objective 3). The expected pattern is objective 2g in disguised form (the energy per unit charge available from a battery is directly proportional to the number of cells on series, i.e. $E/Q \propto n$).

The fact that the obvious answer is not always correct emerges from Investigation 3.12. How does the energy transferred depend on the current? The problem can be solved correctly only by clear thinking and quantitative patterns: a qualitative approach does not resolve the question. The concept of potential difference is central here.

A further help in understanding this subtle idea is for pupils to appreciate how, in practice, it can be measured, and this is done in Investigation 3.13, which also achieves part of objective 6. At this stage the actual name 'potential difference' is introduced, and the normal form of the relation between V, E and Q derived (objective 2g). This is deliberately left until after the experiences on which the concept and pattern are based.

This pattern is used (with earlier patterns) in Investigation 3.16, which could be extended if necessary with additional quantitative problems.

The fact that quantitative patterns can be combined to lead to more complex patterns is exemplified in Investigation 3.15. This very important technique is one of the major strengths of physical science, and explains much of the importance of mathematics in science. (The pupils are, in effect, working out the implications of simple, well-established, mathematical models.) ▷ Investigation 3.16 extends the achievement of objective 6, and can also lead to objective ▷ 2h. There is scope for considerable additional work for some pupils here, only hinted at in the Pupils' manual (see 'Teaching notes').

In Investigations 3.17–23 the previously developed quantitative work in electrolysis is extended to electrolytic cells and corrosion. Attitude objectives 9 and ▷ 11 are achieved here.

A possible modification of the sample scheme would be to deal with Investigations 3.24 to 3.28 immediately after 3.15.

Instead of presenting pupils with an experiment to establish Ohm's law (with consequent doubts about its validity in view of the way voltmeters are calibrated), the intention in Investigation 3.24 is to investigate a number of electrical components, only some of which will show a relation of proportionality between potential difference and current, achieving objectives 2l and 8, and leading directly to the concept of resistance. This is also the

126

opportunity for further work on mathematical models: it should become obvious that these are not perfect descriptions of what happens, but work very well within certain limits. Subsequent problems up to ▷Investigation 3.28 provide the opportunity to take this part of the work further, for more able pupils, developing objective 2m as another example of combining mathematical patterns.

Objectives 7 and 10 are linked to Investigations 3.29 and 3.30 which also use several of the patterns developed earlier. A nice balance has to be achieved here between over-familiarity and fear, and different children react differently. The intention is that the work should help to produce a realisation that electrical devices are potentially dangerous, but that adequate safety devices and arrangements exist to reduce danger to negligible proportions if they are used. Non-scientific questions are also introduced here in the discussion on design.

Additional optional problems are available as ▷Investigations 3.31 and 3.32.

The important idea of using a rectifier to obtain d.c. from a.c. arises in Investigation 3.33, which also brings together a number of the concepts of this section. The final humorous extract (Investigation 3.34) has a serious purpose, and the questions in the *Pupils' manual* have been designed to bring out the relations between the patterns of this section and the (sometimes subtle) misconceptions put forward in the article.

Teaching notes

Investigation 3.1 Current and charge
Pupils learn the language of electric currents, as they learn any new language, by picking it up as the natural way to speak. This investigation and the associated discussion inspect this language

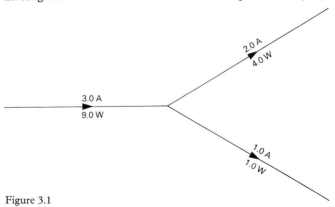

Figure 3.1

more closely. The fact that an ammeter (of any description) gives the same reading at any point in a simple circuit (without branches) is important, but the fact that it is possible to calibrate meters so that at a junction the readings 'add up' is of even greater significance. (Kirchhoff's first law: the algebraic sum of the currents at a junction is zero.) This has nothing to do with linearity of scale, or type of meter. There are measurable quantities which do not add up in this way (for example the power transfer in a standard piece of wire).

The power transferred in a $1.0\,\Omega$ resistor is indicated as well as the current (assuming that $1.0\,\Omega$ is a negligible resistance compared to the rest of the circuit).

The evidence for pupils that electric current is a flow of charge is the result of electrolysis (which needs a certain amount of interpretation) and the 'transfer of charge' experiment using a suspended conducting sphere (see *Patterns 2*). The water circuit board (Nuffield Physics Year II, Experiment 19) without pressure gauge can be introduced here. If the flow indicator is also omitted there is no evidence of a current of water, which is similar to the position when a wire is connected to a battery. Indirect means have to be introduced to show it. Pupils are invited to 'invent' the equation $Q = It$ (or $I = Q/t$). This involves familiarity with the idea of rate which some pupils find much easier than others. Analogies (water flow in a river, traffic flow on a road) help some, and introducing the units help others.

Investigation 3.2 Using the pattern of current and charge
The answers to the simple problems using the mathematical model are

Part a
$Q = (0.15 \times 15 \times 60)\,\text{C} = 135\,\text{C}$
Part b
$Q_1 = (43 \times 60 \times 60)\,\text{C} \approx 155\,\text{kC}$
$Q_2 = (57 \times 60 \times 60)\,\text{C} \approx 205\,\text{kC}$
$t_1 = Q_1/I \approx (155 \times 10^3/5)\,\text{s} = 31\,000\,\text{s} \approx 520\,\text{min}$
$t_2 = Q_2/I \approx (205 \times 10^3/5)\,\text{s} = 41\,000\,\text{s} \approx 680\,\text{min}$
Part c
$t_1 = Q_1/I \approx (155 \times 10^3/22)\,\text{s} \approx 7\,000\,\text{s} \approx 117\,\text{min}$
$t_2 = Q_2/I \approx (205 \times 10^3/22)\,\text{s} \approx 9\,300\,\text{s} = 155\,\text{min}$

A useful discussion might be based on the assumptions (e.g. constant current output, capacity of battery independent of charge rate, accuracy of labelling) leading to some appreciation of the strength and limitations of any mathematical model.

Investigation 3.3 Relationship between quantities of charge and substance
For each of the five currents, the loss in mass of the anode $(+)$ is

equal to the gain in mass of the cathode ($-$). At the anode, the following takes place:

$$Cu(s) \rightarrow Cu^{2+}(aq) + 2e^-.$$

(Energy is needed to form the copper ion from copper, although much more energy is released when the ion dissolves in water.) The reverse occurs at the cathode after the $Cu^{2+}(aq)$ ion has migrated from the anode to the cathode (see *Patterns 1*). The loss (or gain) in mass is directly proportional to the total charge which has passed. This experiment shows that for a fixed time, loss (or gain) in mass is proportional to the electric current. A further investigation is necessary in which the time is varied for a fixed current to show the whole pattern. Alternatively, both time and current can be varied in the same experiment, to show that $m \propto I \times t$.

▷ *Investigation 3.4* Is the pattern true for gases?

A simple gas voltameter should be substituted for the copper voltameter of the previous investigation. It will be found necessary to use a higher potential difference across the voltameter in this case.

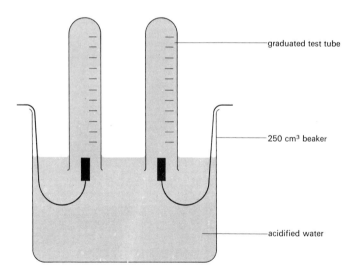

Figure 3.2

(Pupils should devise the experiment for themselves.) The pattern should also be true when gases are evolved, although errors may arise due to the initial dissolving of gas in water.

▷ *Investigation 3.5* What happens when two solutions are used?

The pattern still holds true: the same charge passes through both

129

cells. This is not necessarily true when the cells are in parallel. There is no reason to doubt the pattern, but it cannot be related to the observations without further measurements.

Investigation 3.6 Ions and the periodic table

The first part of the investigation is revision. Metals are in category A; ionic giant structures (electrolytes) are in category B; molecules and atomic giant structures are in category C. On the basis of the work done in *Patterns 1*, water is best classified as B.

Previous work has shown that the classification is not perfect. Elements to the left of the periodic classification (metals and hydrogen) usually form cations (i.e. they are positively charged) and elements to the right of the periodic table form anions (i.e. they are negatively charged). All elements can form ions, but those in the centre of the periodic table do not usually do so. The structures for each of the compounds are shown below.

Formula	Structure (room temperature)
$AlCl_3$	ionic, giant
CaF_2	ionic, giant
CCl_4	molecule
LiBr	ionic, giant
$MgBr_2$	ionic, giant
PCl_3	molecule
KI	ionic, giant
SiO_2	atomic, giant
NaCl	ionic, giant
$NaNO_3$	ionic, giant
SO_2	molecule
N_2O_4	molecule

Investigation 3.7 A pattern modified

Hydrogen usually forms the cation, H^+. However, in sodium hydride it forms the anion, H^-. (The formula for sodium hydride is Na^+H^-.) *Patterns 1* discussed this for carbon C^{4+} and C^{4-}.

Discussion: the mole of electrons

At this stage there should be time for revising the meaning of the term mole. The formal definition (this should not be remembered) is that the mole is the amount of substance of a system which contains as many elementary entities as there are carbon atoms in 0.012 kg of carbon-12. Mole refers to 'amount of substance' and here it is specifically 'amount of electrons'. If we have 23 g of sodium, the amount of sodium present is 1 mole, i.e. there are

130

6×10^{23} atoms of sodium. Similarly, 1 mole of electrons is 6×10^{23} electrons, and if we assume that one electron carries one negative charge, 1 mole of electrons carries a charge of 96 500 coulombs (i.e. 1 faraday). The model of the ion up to this point gives no indication of how much negative charge is removed from or added to the atom, although *Patterns 1* has shown that there can be different quantities of negative electricity (i.e. the same atom can form different ions).

Investigation 3.8 Using the mole of electrons

The completed table (apart from the last set of results) is shown below.

Electrodes	Electrolyte	Element discharged at cathode	(Relative) atomic mass of element discharged	Mass of element discharged/g	Amount of atoms discharged/mole	Current/A	Time/s	Amount of electrons discharged/mole	Ratio of B/A
				A				*B*	*C*
Graphite	Acidified water	Hydrogen	1	0.1	0.1	0.2	48 300	0.1	1
Graphite	Molten sodium chloride	Sodium	23	4.6	0.2	4.0	4 830	0.2	1
Silver	Aqueous silver nitrate solution	Silver	108	21.6	0.2	0.2	96 500	0.2	1
Gold	Aqueous gold chloride solution	Gold	197	39.4	0.2	0.2	96 500	0.2	1
Graphite	Aqueous zinc sulphate solution	Zinc	65	6.5	0.1	0.4	48 300	0.2	2
Aluminium	Molten aluminium oxide	Aluminium	27	2.7	0.1	6.0	4 830	0.3	3
Copper	Aqueous copper sulphate solution	Copper	64						2

The numbers in column C represent the charge on the ion. These numbers can vary for different elements (i.e. atoms can form more than one ion, e.g. Cu^+ and Cu^{2+}) but the ratio B/A will always be a whole number. Assuming that 1 mole of all stuffs contain the same number of particles, we now have the model:

$$X \longrightarrow X^+ + 1 \text{ electron}$$
(Neutral   (Ion)
atom)
$$X \longrightarrow X^{2+} + 2 \text{ electrons}$$

and so on.

The reverse (atom → anion) should also be discussed.

Investigation 3.9   Formulae of ionic compounds

This is the first time that the formulae of ionic compounds have been met. (The topic book *Chemical formulae and equations* did not mention ionic compounds.) Until now, formulae have been shorthand summaries of 'quantities of stuff'. For example, Cu has represented one mole of copper. We now move from the 'factual summaries' to the 'shorthand speculations' (i.e. ionic formulae).

The formulae are: $(Mg^{2+}O^{2-})$, (K^+I^-), $(Mg^{2+}2Br^-)$, $(Ca^{2+}2Cl^-)$, $(Sn^{4+}4Cl^-)$, $(2Al^{3+}3O^{2-})$, $Cu^{2+}O^{2-}$, Li^+F^-. It should be pointed out that these formulae are clumsy and for most purposes we shall be concerned either with the 'shorthand summary of quantities of stuff' (e.g. MgO, KI, $MgBr_2$, $CaCl_2$, etc.) or with quantities of ions (e.g. Mg^{2+}, Ca^{2+}, H^+, O^{2-} etc.).

Elements in group 1 of the abbreviated periodic table (Li, Na, K and Rb) usually form ions with a single positive charge. Those in group 2 form ions with a double positive charge; those in group 3 with a triple positive charge.

Elements in group 7 (F, Cl, Br and I) usually form ions with a single negative charge; ions in group 6 usually form ions with a double negative charge.

Copper(II) oxide is an ionic giant structure consisting of Cu^{2+} and O^{2-} ions. Copper(I) oxide consists of Cu^+ and O^{2-} ions. Whenever useful, the formulae of ionic compounds are written to indicate the size of the charge on the cation.

Investigation 3.10   Current and energy

This demonstration is very important to the development of this section, since it is the occasion for introducing, in an explicit way, the idea of potential difference.

The point may be emphasised by asking for predictions about first the current and then the power transferred (dissipated) when two lamps are connected in series. Most pupils, particularly if the discussion is theoretical, will predict equal current and equal power. Showing the different lamps may cause doubts, which can be resolved in the case of the current. Switching on the two lamps leaves no doubt that the power is quite different.

Details may be found in the reference. The two lamps should be rated as nearly as possible, the same in terms of current. Each will then give its normal brightness, since the potential difference across the low voltage lamp is very small in comparison with that across the mains lamp.

Because mains voltage is used with a low voltage lamp, this experiment must be done as a demonstration to avoid possible accidents.

Investigation 3.11 Cells and energy

This investigation should not be rushed. The preceding discussion should make it clear that the question being asked is 'What is the other factor (apart from current) which affects the amount of energy transferred electrically?'

Different pupils operate the immersion heaters from different numbers of cells, and measure the temperature rise produced in a known mass of water or paraffin in a certain time while also noting the current. Voltages from 14 V down to 6 V are suitable: below this the power is probably too small for reasonable results. Car batteries are a very convenient power supply. To obtain 14 V, two can be used in series. Temperature rises of 10–30 °C are suitable.

Knowing the specific thermal capacity of the liquid (and ignoring the very light container) the energy E supplied is calculated. The charge which flows is also calculated (using $Q = It$) and the ratio E/Q found. Before the experiment starts, it may be worth stressing the significance of this fraction, namely that it is the energy per unit charge left in the container. Different pupils with similar power supplies should find the same value for E/Q, but different power supplies lead to a different value for E/Q. So the value of E/Q indicates something about the supply.

If 2-V cells are used, E/Q is twice the number of cells. In any case E/Q is proportional to the number of cells, i.e. the energy transferred when unit charge flows through the immersion heater is proportional to the number of cells driving the current.

The scope of the experiment can easily be extended by using radio resistors (e.g. 1 W) instead of commercial immersion heaters. If paraffin is used, no insulation problems should arise. It is found that the effect does not depend on the resistor used, but only on the supply. A 'bright' class could be 'thrown in at the deep end' by starting with a variety of resistors, an average class might use their own choice of I and t (and hence Q) with standard heaters, and a weak class might need to arrange that everyone had the same Q, by adjusting the time for different groups. The calculation is simplest for 240 g of water (thermal capacity 1 000 J K^{-1}). At this stage the pupils should realise that the energy available per unit charge is a characteristic of the number of cells.

Variables which might be thought to affect the pattern are the substance, the temperature range used, the type of cell, the resistance of the immersion heater. Only the type of cell makes any difference to the energy transferred per unit charge. (This

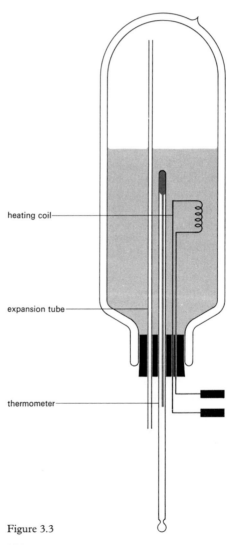

heating coil

expansion tube

thermometer

Figure 3.3

ignores internal resistance of the cells, which will not be significant if well below that of the immersion heater: see ▷ Investigation 3.28. Lead accumulators and NiFe cells are satisfactory, but some forms of mains operated power supplies may not be.)

A superior form of apparatus can be constructed from a vacuum flask (cheap domestic variety). Figure 3.3 is self explanatory. A suitable heater for 12 V can be formed from 660 mm of 26 s.w.g. constantan (Eureka, Contra).

Investigation 3.12 How does the energy depend on the current?

This problem is quite hard. Pupils may well predict that 'half the current means half the energy'. When they try it, they find the energy is near a quarter of its previous value. But consideration of how the previous pattern applies should lead to deeper understanding. In the first case half the energy of each coulomb is left in the heater and the other half in the rheostat. But in addition, the current is halved, so the power is only one quarter. Using the second circuit, all the energy transferred goes into the water (the ammeter and battery having negligible power dissipation).

Investigation 3.13 Voltmeters

Part a

Here the instrument used is found to (i) count cells and (ii) measure E/Q, these being equivalent statements. (A voltage range of a multimeter can be used instead of a voltmeter if this will not be confusing to pupils.)

By using the instruments also in a variety of circuits pupils should be able to gain confidence in the use of the term 'energy transferred per unit charge' or 'voltage' (which if strictly deplorable is hallowed by usage!) It should also become obvious that voltage has 'two ends' since the voltmeter probes have to be connected across part of a circuit. The additive nature of voltage should become clear, and this can be linked in discussion with energy conservation. If the energy available when unit charge flows between A and C were greater than the sum of the energies available when unit charge flows between A and B and between B and C, energy would be provided for nothing. One would just need to arrange a current to flow:

$A \rightarrow B \rightarrow C \rightarrow A.$

Figure 3.4

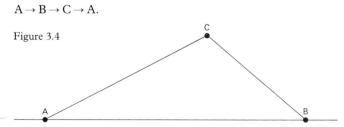

The energy obtained in the last step would more than compensate for that needed for the first two, contrary to experience. Resistors of resistance less than about $20\,\Omega$ are best avoided in circuits using dry cells, on account of excessive current drain.

Part b

An ideal voltmeter would not disturb the original situation when connected, i.e. it would draw no current. To measure the current, an ammeter (milli- or micro-) in series with the voltmeter is an obvious suggestion, which if desired, can lead on to the fact that a voltmeter is in fact a milli- or micro-ammeter with a high series resistor.

Part c

The oscilloscope is a measuring instrument of very wide application. If pupils recognise that it is, in effect, a voltmeter of very rapid response, it need not be a mystery to them. It is a distinct advantage to pupils to be able to handle an oscilloscope (simple version) for themselves: a demonstration is very much a second best here. Advantages over a moving coil voltmeter include rapid response and low current drain.

Part d

This part gives the opportunity to stop using the clumsy phrases 'energy per unit charge', 'energy available per coulomb', 'the value of E/Q' and 'number of cells used', which have been retained until now to stress the point that they are all equivalent but inconvenient. Clearly a special term is needed, and it is introduced and used here, with its defining equation $V = E/Q$.

This arises because a cell which provides $2.0\,\mathrm{J\,C^{-1}}$ gives a reading of $2.0\,\mathrm{V}$, i.e. the constant of proportionality is unity. This is treated experimentally here, but is of course the consequence of the definition of the volt.

The comparison of:

energy = charge × potential difference
energy = force × distance (position difference)
energy = thermal capacity × temperature difference
and
energy = pressure × volume difference

is useful both as an aid to memory, and also in understanding better the nature of energy transfers.

Throughout this investigation it is likely that a good deal of discussion and direct teaching will be needed. The concept of potential difference is one which has always presented problems, some of which may be traced to an attempt to present the idea in terms of logical definitions from the start, before pupils are old enough to accept this approach. Here the intention is that the experimental investigation should come first, so that the definition and pattern come as a convenient codification of experience. It may be that some pupils will need considerably more direct experience than is presented in the *Patterns 3*, and both qualitative and quantitative investigations and problems could be added as necessary. The central theme throughout is the association of potential difference with energy transfer. This is then refined to give energy transfer per unit charge.

▷ *Investigation 3.14* Electrical work.

Many additional problems on this pattern (2g) are available in physics text books and question books.

Part a

Energy transferred to the motor electrically would be measured by ammeter, clock and voltmeter (or using a supply of known constant voltage); energy transferred from motor to load by (force × distance).

Part b

The graph of efficiency against load must have a maximum at some value of the load, since efficiency is zero in both cases (i) and (ii).

Part c

Assuming a battery of constant potential difference (and no internal resistance),

energy dissipated $= (2.5 \times 0.15 \times 15 \times 60)\,\text{J} = 337.5\,\text{J}$.

This originates from the chemicals in the battery, is transferred chemically, electrically, and by radiation (mainly) finishing up distributed to the surroundings which become very slightly warmer. The assumption that each stage is 100 per cent efficient is poor, since energy is likely to be transferred to raise the temperature of the battery, and the connecting wires.

Part d

$Q_1 \approx 155\,\text{kC}$

$\therefore E_1 \approx 155 \times 12\,\text{kJ} = 1\,860\,\text{kJ} = 1.86\,\text{MJ}$

$Q_2 \approx 205\,\text{kC}$

$\therefore E_2 \approx 205 \times 6\,\text{kJ} = 1\,230\,\text{kJ} = 1.23\,\text{MJ}$

Part e

$V = E/Q = (600/25)\,\text{V} = 24\,\text{V}$.

Investigation 3.15 Electrical power

Charge is difficult to measure directly, so the derived pattern is often more useful.

Part a

$Q = It$

$\therefore E = QV$

$\quad = ItV$

$P = E/t$

$\therefore P = ItV/t = IV$

Part b
$P = (0.25 \times 240)\,\text{W} = 60\,\text{W}$
Part c
$V = P/I = (1\,500/6.0)\,\text{V} = 250\,\text{V}$
Part d
$I = P/V = (2\,000/12)\,\text{A} \approx 167\,\text{A}$
Part e
$I = P/V = (1\,200/120)\,\text{A} = 10\,\text{A}$
Part f
$I = 2\,880$ moles of electrons per hour
$\approx (2\,880 \times 10^5/3\,600)\,\text{A} = 8 \times 10^4\,\text{A}$
$P = IV = (8 \times 10^4 \times 0.2)\,\text{W} = 160\,\text{kW}$

Part g
Many situations could be considered appropriate fields for devising problems including domestic and automobile lighting, heating and motor circuits, cells, and applications of electrolysis.

▷ *Investigation 3.16* Alternating voltages
The argument for including a.c. in a course which will be the last formal science for many pupils is its ubiquity in everyday life.
Part a
Power supplies of various types, and transformers without calibration can be used. Attention should be given to safety considerations in respect of high voltages (greater than 50 V). Frequency and voltage can easily be measured.

The accepted meaning of '6 V a.c.' is that alternating voltage which will transfer the same power as 6 V d.c. when applied to a given resistor. Since power is proportional to the square of potential difference (at constant resistance), the 6 V is in fact the root mean square value (r.m.s. value) of the alternating voltage. In symbols the reasoning is as follows.

Suppose v and p represent the instantaneous values of potential difference and power, both of which vary with time, and R the resistance involved. Let V and P be the equivalent values of potential difference and power for d.c. (i.e. both steady value).
Then $p = v^2/R$ and $P = V^2/R$
If mean values are indicated by a bar,
$\bar{p} = P$ (definition)
But $\bar{p} = \overline{v^2}/R$
$\therefore\ V^2/R = \overline{v^2}/R$
$\therefore\ \ V^2 = \overline{v^2}$ (the mean square value)
$\therefore\ \ \ V = \sqrt{\overline{v^2}}$ (the root mean square value)
In the case of sinusoidal voltages, it can be shown that the r.m.s. value is $(1/\sqrt{2})$ times the peak value, i.e. about 0.7 times the peak value, or 0.35 times the peak-to-peak value.

Figure 3.5

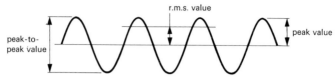

While this explanation is not appropriate for any pupils except the very brightest, they need some explanation of the observed fact that '6 V a.c.' gives a peak-to-peak value of about 17 V. For most the answer that this particular alternating voltage is found to give the same power transfer in a given resistor as 6 V d.c. is probably appropriate.

The average value of the voltage is clearly zero, so this could not be the significance of the term.

Part b

If one of the various types of demountable transformer is available, it could be demonstrated here.

In the pupils' own experiment it should be reasonably easy to find the relation:

$$\frac{V_1}{V_2} = \frac{n_1}{n_2}.$$

If they do not see how to make sense of the results it is worth suggesting that they keep the primary voltage and turns fixed for a start.

Part c

The obvious suggestion is to measure current and potential difference on input and output sides. However, a good transformer can easily have an efficiency of 90 per cent. Given the relative inaccuracy of the usual sort of meters available, it is not impossible that an apparent efficiency of over 100 per cent might be obtained. Better (more precise) meters would obviate this difficulty.

Part d

$$I_2 V_2 = I_1 V_1$$

$$\therefore \frac{I_2}{I_1} = \frac{V_1}{V_2} = \frac{n_1}{n_2}.$$

So a coil of few turns carries a larger current and needs to be of thicker wire, and conversely.

Investigation 3.17 Varying the electrodes in an electrolytic cell

Pupils should obtain the following order: magnesium, aluminium, zinc, iron, nickel, tin, lead, copper.

Different members of the class should obtain the same order, but the values of the voltages will probably differ. This is because no two cells are identical (e.g. the electrodes are of different areas, they are not equal distances apart, they will be immersed to different depths in the potassium nitrate solution. All these affect the 'lost volts', i.e. the potential difference used in driving current through the cell itself.)

A 'standard' cell could be constructed which removes some of the variables.

A detailed explanation is not appropriate at this stage. However, a discussion of 'possibilities' could take place. For example, in the case of iron and magnesium, at the magnesium electrode the following might be possible:

$$Mg(s) \rightarrow Mg^{2+}(aq) + 2e^-$$
$$2H^+(aq) + 2e^- \rightarrow H_2(g)$$
$$4OH^-(aq) \rightarrow 2H_2O(aq) + O_2(g) + 4e^-$$
$$K^+(aq) + e^- \rightarrow K(s)$$
$$NO_3^-(aq) \rightarrow NO_3^-.$$

Similar reactions could take place at the iron electrode. Observation of the electrodes and knowledge of the direction of the electric current should lead to an early elimination of some of the possibilities.

▷ *Investigation 3.19* Displacement reactions

The pattern obtained is summarised below:

magnesium
zinc
iron
nickel
lead
copper
silver.

Each metal can displace the metals below it from a solution of one of its compounds.

The list should be compared with that obtained in Investigation 3.17.

In the case of zinc and copper sulphate, the following take place:

$$Zn(s) \rightarrow Zn^{2+}(aq) + 2e^-$$
$$Cu^{2+}(aq) + 2e^- \rightarrow Cu(s).$$

The net effect is that zinc displaces copper from solution.

Similar pairs of reactions can be written for the other displacements. (The formation of cation from the metal is called oxidation; the formation of metal from the cation is called reduction.)

If time permits, pupils could make a 'Christmas tree' by suspending a piece of copper foil (cut to the shape of a Christmas tree) in a solution of silver nitrate.

▷ *Investigation 3.20* Uses of dry cells

The electrodes in a dry cell are the rod of graphite (the anode) and the zinc case (the cathode). The electrolyte is a paste of ammonium chloride. The black powder is manganese dioxide which prevents a sudden reduction in the flow of electric current.

In the lead accumulator, the cathode is lead and the anode is lead dioxide coated on lead.

Alkaline cells (Nife cells) use potassium hydroxide as the electrolyte. Nickel hydroxide is the anode and the cathodes are either iron or cadmium.

Investigation 3.21 Corrosion

Part a Class experiment

The most rusting occurs with copper and iron. Iron has changed to Fe^{2+}:

$$Fe(s) \rightarrow (rust) Fe^{2+}(aq) + 2e^-.$$

The least rusting occurs with magnesium and iron. A red colour shows the presence of alkali, i.e. $OH^-(aq)$ ions. This part of the experiment (and also the iron-zinc part) illustrate the way of preventing rusting which is called cathodic protection. Figure 3.16 in *Patterns 3* illustrates a commercial application of the principle.

Part b A demonstration experiment

It is suggested that the pairs of metals (iron-magnesium, iron-zinc, iron-tin and iron-copper) should be connected via a centre-zero ammeter (0.05 A) and placed in the indicator solution. The deflection in the ammeter will show that corrosion is electrical (and the direction of flow of electrons can be deduced from the ammeter deflection).

A further, more 'sophisticated' experiment is illustrated in *Patterns 3*.

Investigation 3.23 Reversing the process

Part a

In recharging a cell the energy needed to make the chemical reaction take place in the reverse direction is supplied electrically. This may be relatively ineffective because of secondary reactions which occur after the main (discharge) reaction, or because conditions are not favourable for the reverse reaction to occur.

Part b

With the cell connected to the bulb, at first nothing happens. This is predictable, in that the two lead plates are identical, i.e. the electrical circuit is symmetrical. It is important, however, for pupils to be sure that the energy transfer depends on initial charging. When the cell is charged from the supply, the positive electrode can be observed to acquire a brown deposit (lead(IV) oxide) showing that different interactions occur at the two electrodes. On discharging this deposit decreases. The bulb lights for a much shorter time than the cell was charged for, indicating low efficiency. The efficiency increases with repeated charging.

Part c

The lead-acid cell is convenient for many purposes because, in contrast to most other cells, its voltage varies very little with its state of charge. It is also the only common cell with a low enough internal resistance to enable it to supply the very high current needed to start a car.

Part d

This design owes much to that used in the Australian Science Education Project.

Investigation 3.24 How does current depend on potential difference?

Part a

In this investigation the relation between potential difference and current for wires (nichrome, eureka, perhaps iron), radio resistors, semiconductor diodes, Zener diodes, metal rectifiers, capacitors (current zero for any potential difference), thermistors, motors, electrolytes (acidified water, copper(II) sulphate solution) and neon lamp (demonstration only) should be discovered. Low voltages are used throughout, except for the neon lamp and pupils can select suitable meters for the very different currents involved. Multimeters could well be used. In some cases different meters or ranges are needed for forward and reverse directions. Any variable, low-voltage supply will serve, but if dry batteries are used currents should be arranged to be fairly low to avoid excessive battery drain. The work can well be arranged as a circus, and results can then be pooled.

Part b

The graphs reveal that certain components (wires, radio resistors, copper(II) sulphate solution) behave in a very simple manner, with current proportional to potential difference. It is useful to have some radio resistors of a power rating less than that actually dissipated at the higher voltages used. With these the breakdown of the proportionality is observed as the temperature rises. It is well worth the expense of letting pupils burn out these resistors, and letting them realise that the process of overheating can be irreversible. The same can be done with cheap semiconductor diodes, which, like various other components, can be bought in considerable numbers from the specialist suppliers at minimal cost (see the advertisements in *Practical Electronics* etc.).

Sketch graphs are probably appropriate, since it is the general shape rather than great precision which is important. If V/I is larger for A than for B, then it needs a larger potential difference to drive a certain current through A than B, i.e. A has a greater resistance. This leads to the defining equation for resistance,

$R = V/I$

Part c

For each component (i) is a simple description of the characteristic, whereas (ii) is in effect a description of the way the slope of the curve varies (in fact how the reciprocal of the gradient depends on V). Figure 3.6 shows examples. In figure 3.6a the resistance steadily decreases as potential difference increases (e.g. some semiconductor diodes in the 'forward' direction). In figure 3.6b the resistance is constant at relatively low potential

Figure 3.6

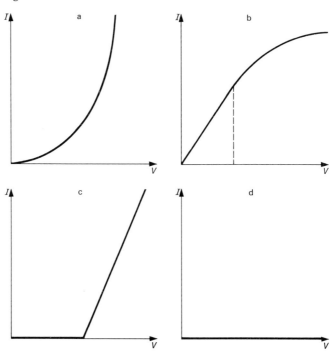

differences, but increases progressively beyond a certain value (e.g. a metal wire or radio-type resistor whose temperature rises significantly at voltages higher than this value). In figure 3.6c the resistance is very high below a certain potential difference, and above this gets progressively less (e.g. a voltameter containing dilute sulphuric acid with inert electrodes). And in figure 3.6d the resistance is always effectively infinite (e.g. a capacitor).

In the previous paragraph the answers correspond to the simple definition of resistance. However, in many applications it is the 'slope resistance'

$$R = \frac{\Delta V}{\Delta I}$$

which is significant, and this is clearly the case in figure 3.6c, where the slope resistance is constant above the critical potential difference. This suggests two different phenomena: a certain potential difference being necessary to effect electrolysis, and the resistance effect depending only on the extra potential difference above this value.

Part d

Most cheap multimeters are useful only for relatively high-resistance components. The reversed, non-linear scale arises because the instrument is a current meter with a resistance scale added. In the simplest forms, the circuit is as shown in figure 3.7, the rheostat providing the zero adjustment. Faster pupils could work out the requirements for a particular meter in more detail.

Figure 3.7

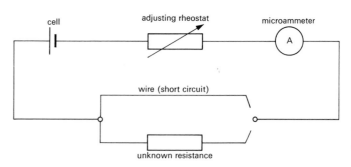

Investigation 3.25 Using the concept of resistance

Part a

If two cells (4.0 V) are used, a series resistor to drop 1.5 V is needed. At a current of 0.5 A, this corresponds to 3.0 Ω. Lamp

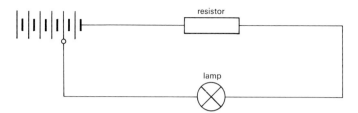

Figure 3.8

resistance is 5.0 Ω. Product of total resistance (8.0 Ω) and current gives battery voltage.

Part b

Assuming zero internal resistance of battery, in each case the maximum current through the 8 Ω resistor is $\frac{9}{8}$ A. The minimum in the case of figure 3.21a (*Patterns 3*) is $\frac{9}{20}$ A, but in figure 3.21b it is zero. The potential divider enables the load current to be reduced to zero at the expense of always having extra ('useless') current through the divider itself. A series resistor would be satisfactory for stage lighting, because no light is emitted from tungsten lamps below a moderate current. The volume control on amplifiers is commonly a potential divider (potentiometer) because a control over a wide range is required. In both cases resistors which are non-linear are frequently used, i.e. the increase of resistance caused by a certain adjustment of position depends on the starting position.

Calculating the currents in the other instances is relatively straightforward in figure 3.21a but more complex in figure 3.21b. The results are (in ampères):

	$\frac{1}{3}$	$\frac{1}{2}$	$\frac{2}{3}$
a	$\frac{9}{12}$	$\frac{9}{14}$	$\frac{9}{16}$
b	$\frac{9}{16}$	$\frac{9}{22}$	$\frac{9}{32}$

A much smaller resistance potential divider would draw a large current, but the potential drop along its length would be relatively unaffected by the presence of the contact for the 8 Ω load, i.e. a fairly linear response would result. If a much greater resistance were used, the control would approximate to that of a series resistor, because the current through the lower part of the

145

potential divider would be small in comparison with that through the $8\,\Omega$ load.

Part c

$$I = 2\,880 \text{ moles of electrons per hour}$$
$$= (2\,880 \times 10^5 / 3\,600)\,\text{A}$$
$$= 8 \times 10^4\,\text{A}$$
$$V = 0.2\,\text{V}$$
$$\therefore \quad R = (0.2/8 \times 10^4)\,\Omega$$
$$= 2.5\,\mu\Omega$$

Part d

$$V = IR$$
$$V_{\text{full}} = (2.0 \times 10^{-3} \times 2\,000)\,\text{V}$$
$$= 4.0\,\text{V}$$
$$V_{\frac{1}{2}} = 2.0\,\text{V}$$

Part e

$$I_s = V/R_a$$
$$= (12/0.05)\,\text{A}$$
$$= 240\,\text{A}$$
$$R_s + R_a = V/I$$
$$= (12/24)\,\Omega$$
$$= 0.5\,\Omega$$
$$\therefore \quad R_s = 0.45\,\Omega$$

Part f

$$I_1 = P/V$$
$$\therefore \quad I_1 = (3\,000/240)\,\text{A}$$
$$= 12.5\,\text{A}$$

$$R = V/I \qquad \text{or} \quad R = V^2/P$$
$$\therefore \quad R_1 = (240/12.5)\,\Omega \qquad \therefore \quad R_1 = (240^2/3\,000)\,\Omega$$
$$= 19.2\,\Omega \qquad\qquad = 19.2\,\Omega$$
$$I_2 = (2\,400/240)\,\text{A}$$
$$= 10.0\,\text{A}$$
$$\therefore \quad R_2 = (240/10.0)\,\Omega \qquad \text{or} \quad R_2 = (240^2/2\,400)\,\Omega$$
$$= 24.0\,\Omega \qquad\qquad = 24.0\,\Omega$$

i.e. a 20 per cent reduction in power results from a 25 per cent increase in resistance.

▷ *Investigation 3.26* Resistance of a lamp
The dry cell and milliammeter and voltmeter give a value of resistance an order of magnitude lower than that calculated from the rating of the lamp. The difference is accounted for by the increase of resistance of metals (including tungsten) with temperature: the temperature of the filament under normal operating conditions is between $2\,500\,\text{K}$ and $3\,000\,\text{K}$.

▷ *Investigation 3.27* Power and resistance.
This problem is largely concerned with selecting the appropriate

mathematical pattern from a small set. This is an important skill on a larger scale in science, and this problem is merely a simple indication of how to select, by identifying the appropriate variables.

i $R = V^2/P = (250^2/2\,000)\,\Omega = 31.25\,\Omega$

ii $P = I^2R = (2^2 \times 6)\,W = 24\,W$

iii $P = V^2/R = (12^2/0.1)\,W = 1.44\text{kW}$

The spanner could melt or fuse to the terminals. The energy dissipated could lead to a fire.

iv Formerly vehicles were mainly arranged with the positive terminal of the battery connected to the bodywork. Frequently now it is the negative terminal.

▷ *Investigation 3.28* Does a cell really produce a constant potential difference?

As each bulb is screwed in, those already alight become a little dimmer, i.e. the potential difference available from the battery must decrease as the current drawn increases. If (as assumed) the energy available per coulomb from the chemical interaction is constant, then some energy must be 'lost'. The only places energy can be 'lost' are the wires and the cell itself, and in either case a temperature rise would be expected. If thick connecting wire of negligible resistance is used, the effect still occurs. This leads to the idea of internal resistance, which is important not only with batteries but also with other power supplies.

Investigation 3.29 Electricity in the home

Part a

Windmills are commonly used to drive generators in many remote situations, watermills less commonly. Alternatively fuel could be burned to drive some form of engine.

Wind and water power are unlikely to be sufficient for keeping a building warm, and if fuel is to be burned it is clearly better to use this directly rather than distribute the energy through complex electrical devices.

Part b

All 'workers' are found to 'warm', but in general 'warmers' do not 'work'.

The refrigerator is in effect a heat engine (using the term in the thermodynamicists' way). In the compressor type, mechanical work is involved, but energy is also abstracted from the interior, so that the surroundings are warmed to some extent (until a steady state is established when leakage of energy into the interior balances that abstracted).

The 'warmers' normally have higher power ratings than the 'workers', the only common exception being incandescent lights (regarded as 'warmers'). Lighting generally does not readily fit into this classification.

The fact that high power is associated with low resistance becomes more realistic when actual domestic apparatus is involved.

It is easy to speak as though energy is often used to raise temperature. This is a temporary phenomenon, and the energy at once begins to spread to the surroundings. The final result of the expensive energy we bring into our houses is to warm up the atmosphere!

Investigation 3.30 Electrical power and safety

Part a

A single-pole switch other than in the live conductor would switch off the apparatus concerned, but leave part of the circuit live.

Part b

A ring main saves cable, and has an additional safety factor in that each socket can receive current by two routes. The earth wire, if correctly connected, makes it impossible for the body of any equipment to become live, because this would cause a fuse to blow. Apparatus without an earth wire needs to be double-insulated, with no conductors in any way accessible.

Every pupil should be able to wire a 13-A plug correctly: this is the commonest sort of electrical activity most pupils will have after leaving school. The wallchart from the Electrical Association for Women is useful for this purpose, and convenient cards are issued by the Home Office and Electricity Boards illustrating the correct connections.

Part c

Connections between one's body and earth are normally very high resistance paths, on account of the materials of which clothes and shoes are made. Actual body resistance is mainly skin resistance. When the skin is wet the resistance can be several orders of magnitude lower than when it is dry.

The 'galvanic skin response' (GSR) is well known in psychological literature in rather broader contexts than lie-detection. It is quite possible for pupils to design an effective system. Attention needs to be given to sensitivity of the meter, good contact with two skin areas (e.g. palm and back of the hand), and wide variation in normal skin resistance between individuals.

Part d

The completed table of current and power is as follows. The current is implicated as the lethal factor, but the situation is in fact quite complicated, and people with weak hearts are more susceptible than others.

Source of current	Potential difference/V	Current μA	Power
dry cell	1.5	1.5	2.25 μW
car battery	12	12	144 μW
mains*	240	240	57.6 mW
h.t. supply*	200	200	40 mW
e.h.t. supply	5 000	50 max	0.25 W
Van der Graaff	60 000	20 max	1.2 W

*Can give lethal shocks

Treatment for apparent death from electrocution is designed to restart breathing and heart beat, and mouth-to-mouth resuscitation would be the usual approach for a non-professional helper. It is of course assumed that the sufferer is first removed from the source of current or the current is switched off. It is worth informing pupils that wool, silk and most synthetics are quite good electrical insulators, but cotton is less good.

▷ *Investigation 3.31*   Combinations of resistance

Here the particular case is dealt with first, and this forms an example to follow for the general (symbolic) case.

Part a

$$V_5 = (2.0 \times 5)\,V = 10.0\,V$$
$$V_7 = (2.0 \times 7)\,V = 14.0\,V$$
$$\therefore \quad V_T = (10.0 + 14.0)\,V = 24.0\,V$$
$$\therefore \quad R_T = (24.0/2.0)\,\Omega = 12.0\,\Omega$$
$$V_1 = I \times R_1$$
$$V_2 = I \times R_2$$
$$\therefore \quad V_T = IR_1 + IR_2 = I(R_1 + R_2)$$
$$\therefore \quad R_T = V_T/I$$
$$R_T = R_1 + R_2$$

Part b

$$I_4 = (12/4)\,A = 3.0\,A$$
$$I_2 = (12/2)\,A = 6.0\,A$$
$$\therefore \quad I_T = (3.0 + 6.0)\,A = 9.0\,A$$
$$\therefore \quad R_T = V/I_T = (12/9.0)\,\Omega = 1.33\,\Omega$$
$$I_2 = V/R_1$$
$$I_2 = V/R_2$$
$$\therefore \quad I = I_1 + I_2 = V/R_1 + V/R_2$$
$$\text{But} \quad I = V/R$$
$$\therefore \quad \frac{V}{R} = \frac{V}{R_1} + \frac{V}{R_2}$$
$$\therefore \quad \frac{1}{R} = \frac{1}{R_1} + \frac{1}{R_2}$$

Part c

A piece of wire can be considered as a set of separate pieces connected in series. Hence the resistance would be expected to be proportional to length. It can also be considered as a set of pieces connected in parallel: doubling the area would be equivalent to two pieces in parallel, i.e. half the resistance. This suggests that resistance is inversely proportional to area. The argument can clearly be made more precise than the above.

The experimental aspects of all three parts are best done with low currents and high resistances. If mathematical computation is a problem, values should be chosen in advance to minimise difficulty. If pupils are mathematically competent, a free selection of (e.g. radio-type) resistors could be given.

▷ *Investigation 3.32* Photoelectric cells

Energy from the sun or other light source is reflected from the source viewed, radiated into the cell, and transferred electrically to the meter. In automatic cameras this is sufficient to control the adjustment mechanism and/or safety device.

The graph has a logarithmic scale on both axes. Increasing illumination by a factor of ten causes the resistance to decrease by a factor of ten: the product of illumination and resistance is constant within the limits indicated. It is perhaps more significant to state the above in the form 'conductance is directly proportional to illumination' which gives a clue to possible mechanisms.

Project work using either type of photoelectric cell is a fruitful field. The components are obtainable readily and fairly cheaply, and simple circuits can give good results.

Investigation 3.33 Rectifiers

Part a

The expected results are as shown in figure 3.9a and b. If the second trace is inverted, the connections to the oscilloscope should be reversed, or the diode reversed.

Figure 3.9

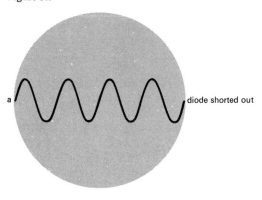

a diode shorted out

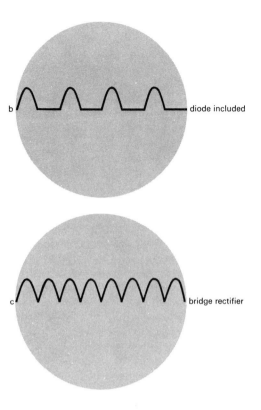

b — diode included

c — bridge rectifier

▷ Part b

The result is shown in figure 3.9c.

▷ Part c

Important uses of rectifiers include: in the power supplies of amplifiers etc. used on the a.c. mains; in vehicles fitted with alternators; and in electric locomotives, which use d.c. motors for reasons connected with control. In all cases they are now much smaller and more efficient than a few years ago.

To produce a.c. from d.c. is more difficult: a d.c. motor driving an a.c. generator is an effective method, but clumsy compared with a semiconductor rectifier.

Part d

A suitable circuit is on page 152, figure 3.10. Assuming the output is 16 V d.c., 12 V will be used in overcoming the battery e.m.f. (assumed constant) and 4 V in the resistor. Hence a 2 Ω resistor is suitable. The calculation is appropriate only at the peak value of the rectified p.d. The peak value of 240 V(r.m.s.) a.c. is

151

Figure 3.10

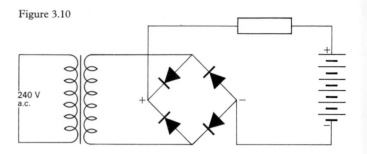

about $(240 \times 1.4)\,V = 336\,V$, so the turns ratio of the transformer would be $336:16 = 21:1$.

Investigation 3.34 Electricity and everyday life

Notes on the questions

a Not manufactured: driven perhaps?
b Yes, more or less! Charges separated in clouds lead to sudden discharges within clouds, between clouds or to earth.
c Return pathway (c.f. body of a car).
d Energy difference (to neutral or earth).
e Deep philosophical question! Negative could mean merely the absence of positive: but how could one tell?
f Batteries store energy.
g Electrons have charge: whether charge can exist attached to anything less massive, or smaller, is an interesting question.
h Air insulation.
i See the 'small ads' in the newspapers.
j To fuse!
k There used to be electrical engineers and electronics engineers. The distinction is now blurred, and even heavy electrical engineering involves techniques in the electronic field.

Sample questions

1 Someone who has studied no science says to you, 'I know that energy can be conveyed by a flow of water, or of air, or of electricity: what I can't understand is why electricity needs two wires, while water or air needs only one pipe'. Write several sentences explaining for him the similarities and differences between water, air and electricity in conveying energy.
2 The table below shows the power available from an electric motor at various speeds. Draw a graph to show how the power depends on the speed. From your graph find
a the maximum power developed by the motor and
b the speed at which this occurs.

Speed/rev. s^{-1}	Power/W
0	0
5	205
10	360
15	465
20	520
25	525
30	480
35	385
40	240
45	45

3 Which one of the following statements about an electric current is not always correct?

A it causes temperature rise in a conductor
B it consists of a flow of charge
C it affects a compass needle
D it creates a force (correct)

4 Which one of the following has the same number of particles as 1 mole of electrons?

A 3 moles of Al^{3+}
B 2 moles of SO_4^{2-}
C 1 mole of Cu (correct)
D 0.5 mole of Ca

5 1 mole of electrons is needed to neutralise unit positive charge on 1 mole of cation. A mole of aluminium ions is represented by Al^{3+}. The atomic mass of aluminium is 27. How many moles of electrons are required to deposit 54 g of aluminium during electrolysis?

A $\frac{2}{3}$ C 3
B 2   D 6 (correct)

6 1 mole of one of the chlorides of vanadium is represented as VCl_3. The compound dissolves in water to produce vanadium and chloride (Cl^-) ions. How many moles of electrons are lost by one mole of vanadium atoms in forming the vanadium ions?

A 1   C 3 (correct)
B 2   D 4

7 The strontium ion carries two positive charges. The nitrate ion carries one negative charge, NO_3^-. Which one of the following is the most correct shorthand way of writing 1 mole of strontium nitrate?

A $SrNO_3$ C $Sr_3(NO_3)_2$
B Sr_2NO_3 D $Sr(NO_3)_2$ (correct)

8 Write an essay describing what your day would be like without the use of electricity.

9 Which of the following use the principle of electromagnetic induction?

a electric motor   YES/NO (correct)
b dynamo   (correct) YES/NO
c generator   (correct) YES/NO
d moving coil meter   YES/NO (correct) used for damping
e immersion heater   YES/NO (correct)
f transformer   (correct) YES/NO
g semiconductor diode   YES/NO (correct)

10 What is the best explanation for the fact that if a permanent-

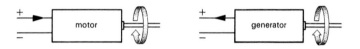

magnet motor is used as a generator, turning in the same direction, the direction of the current is reversed (see diagrams above)?

A the battery would have to be reversed to make it work like this

B the magnets would have to be reversed to make it work like this

C both battery and magnets would have to be reversed to make it work like this

D if the current went in the same direction the machine could drive itself (correct)

11 The relationship between charge and current is similar to the relationship between one of the following pairs. Which?

A width of river *and* rate of flow of water

B number of vehicles *and* rate of traffic flow (correct)

C temperature *and* energy flow in conduction

D air pressure *and* wind

12 What is the meaning of potential difference?

A the voltage available per unit charge (per coulomb)

B the product of charge (in coulombs) and energy (in joules)

C the charge (coulombs) required to transfer unit quantity of energy (one joule)

D the energy (in joules) transformed electrically per unit charge (per coulomb) (correct)

13 In purifying metals by electrolysis an impure block of metal is made the anode, and the pure metal is deposited on the cathode. What factors will the mass of metal purified depend upon?

A current and potential difference
B potential difference and resistance
C potential difference and time
D current and time (correct)

14 An element had the following properties:
  i it did not conduct electricity;
  ii the oxide of the element was not ionic;
  iii it reacted with hydrogen;
  iv it reacted with sodium to give an ionic giant structure.
Where in the periodic table is the element most likely to be found?
A right (correct)
B left
C centre top
D centre bottom

The following information about the charge required to produce a mole of a substance during electrolysis refers to questions 15, 16 and 17.

Substance produced	$g\,mol^{-1}$	$C\,g^{-1}$	$C\,mol^{-1}$
H_2	2.015	95 700	193 $\times 10^3$
O_2	32.00	12 070	386 $\times 10^3$
Mg	24.32	7 940	193 $\times 10^3$
Ag	107.9	894.5	96.5 $\times 10^3$

15 What is the common factor in the data for the number of coulombs required per mole of substance produced?
A 96.5 $\times 10^3$ (correct)
B 193 $\times 10^3$
C 2
D 1
E no common factor

16 How many electrons are transferred to produce one molecule of oxygen?
A 1
B 2 (correct)
C 3
D 4
E some other number

17 What is the approximate charge in coulombs represented by a single electron?
A 1.6 $\times 10^{-19}$ C (correct)
B 6 $\times 10^{23}$ C   **D** 1 C
C 96.5 $\times 10^3$ C   **E** 1.6 $\times 10^{26}$ C

155

18 An electrochemical cell in which hydrogen gas is produced is connected in series with a second cell in which silver is dissolved, as the same quantity of charge is transferred through both cells. For each gramme of silver dissolved, how many grammes of hydrogen are liberated?

A 0.01 g (correct)
B 1 g
C 2.0 g
D 0.1 g
E 108 g

(The last four questions are reproduced by permission of C.B.A., Chemical Systems, published by McGraw-Hill.)

19 If you were plating silver dishes, how many moles of electrons would be required to plate 2 g of silver? (Silver ions carry a single positive charge. Relative atomic mass of silver = 108.)

A 108
B 54
C $\frac{1}{54}$ (correct)
D $\frac{1}{108}$

20 Iron railings are often embedded in lead as the drawing shows.

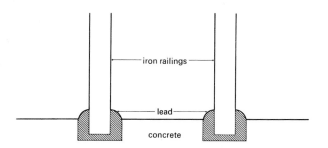

Where would you expect most corrosion to occur?

A corrosion would not take place
B on the surface of the lead
C at the base of the iron railing (correct)
D at the top of the iron railing

21 The aluminium ion carries three positive charges: the sulphate ion carries two negative charges. Which is the correct formula for aluminium sulphate?

A $(Al)_2SO_4$
B $Al_2(SO_4)_3$ (correct)
C $Al_3(SO_4)_2$
D $Al(SO_4)_2$

22 A manufacturer produces a new electrical component. Which of
    the following is he *not* likely to include in information about it he
    circulates to customers?
    A maximum power
    B resistance
    C maximum operating temperature
    D maximum size of connecting leads (correct)

23 Which of the following could *not* be measured with an oscillo-
    scope alone?
    A potential difference
    B time
    C power (correct)
    D current

4 Sources of energy

Introduction

This section deals mainly with food and fossil fuels as the immediate sources of energy available to man. Because of the demands made on these fuels there is considerable concern about their supplies and much scientific and technological effort is directed both to the search for non-fuel sources of energy (nuclear sources are not dealt with in this section), such as the direct utilisation of solar energy, and to improving food production.

The ultimate source of energy for fossil fuels and food (and also for many of the non-fuel energy sources) can be traced back to the Sun whose energy is transferred (radiated) to the Earth by waves (radiation). The essential link is the transfer of solar energy by green plants to form food in the process of photosynthesis. The transfer of energy through food webs in a community is also investigated.

Food, however, is much more than a mere energy source for organisms. It is a source of building blocks for growth and other materials essential for the maintenance of health. This section therefore also deals with the need for a balanced diet in order that food can fulfil its triple function.

Objectives

Skills

1 To recall and understand the following concepts: food (fuel), (balanced) diet, health, growth, food chain/web, producer, consumer, predator, decomposer, photosynthesis, system, energy transfer, wave (1).
2 To recall and understand the following patterns.
a A balanced diet is essential for health, to provide adequate building blocks for growth, and to supply sufficient energy (2).
b A model of a food chain can be expressed as
producer (plant) → consumer (herbivore) → predator (carnivore) along which energy and building blocks are transferred (2).
c A model of a food web can be expressed as follows (2).

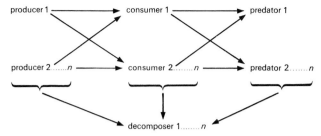

d Photosynthesis is a characteristic of organisms possessing chlorophyll, i.e. producers (2).

e The major part of the energy used on Earth is transferred from the Sun by waves (i.e. solar energy/radiation) (2).

(The above patterns are linked to patterns in the *Teachers' Handbook* as follows:

2a to 26; 2b to 27; 2c to 28; 2d to 22 and 24; 2e to 31.)

3 To solve problems using the above patterns and those from other sections (4).

▷4 To research a project on fuel or food and to present the results in a clear and interesting manner (5).

5 To understand the significance of science in relation to diet and health, both personally and for the community, and in relation to increasing food production (6).

6 To design and perform experiments to solve problems using the patterns mentioned above (8).

▷7 To understand the limitations of science in relation to decisions concerning aid and economic development (4, 6).

▷8 To observe accurately and report observations concerning red-brown leaves and their ability to photosynthesise (7).

Attitudes

9 To be concerned about the conservation of fuel resources in the light of increasing demand and limited world resources (11).

10 To be concerned about the increasing demand for food, and for the undernourished majority of an expanding world population (11).

Flow diagram

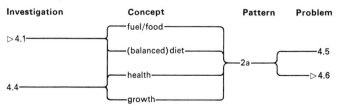

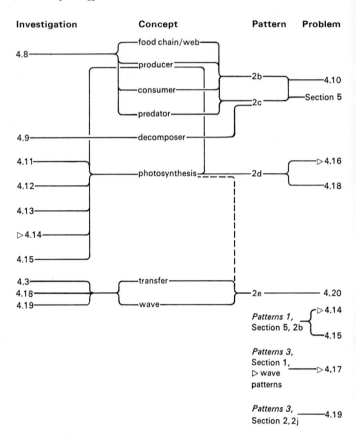

The concept of system is also useful throughout this section.

Sample scheme

Time allocation for this section: 3 weeks.

Description	Reference	Notes
▷4.1 Fuels and food		Project work: see 'Teaching notes' for sources of materials; food only as an energy source

	Description	Reference	Notes
B	The search for oil	*Patterns* topic book *Science and decision making*	
4.2	The conservation of fuels		
4.3	Non-fuel energy sources		e.g. tidal action, windmills
4.4	Food is more than a fuel		Balanced diet
▶4.5	Are you eating a balanced diet?		
▷R	*Biology by inquiry* Book 2	Clarke, R. A., *et al.*, Heinemann, 1970	Experiments on element content of food
▷T	*Nothing to eat but food*	Film, Unilever	Balanced diets: 18 minutes
▷T	*Vitamins*	Chart, Crookes Laboratories Limited	Rather detailed
▷▶4.6	Feeding the world		
▷T	*Food or famine*	Film, Petroleum Film Bureau	45 minutes
▷4.7	Deciding priorities for aid		Oxfam game
R	*The development puzzle*	Nance Lui Fyson (Ed), VCOAD 1972	Source book of materials for teaching about the rich-poor world divide
4.8	Energy transfer in a community		Food chains/webs

161

	Description	Reference	Notes
4.9	What happens to organisms which die?		Energy transfer by decomposers
▷T	Film loop: *The decay of leaves*	BBC publications	
4.10	Making use of food web patterns		
4.11	How do plants get their food?	*Patterns: Teachers' guide 1*, Section 8	Building block and energy requirements
4.12	Plants and the source of carbon	NB *Teachers' guide III* and *Text III* Ch 7 and 8	
T	*Carbon dioxide exchange in* Chlorella *using* $^{14}CO_2$	Film loop, NBP-9	
4.13	Testing a hypothesis		Photosynthesis
▷ ►4.14	Structure and function of leaves		
►4.15	What is the significance of chlorophyll?		
▷ ►4.16	Can plants with red-brown leaves photosynthesise?		
▷ ►4.17	Why are green leaves green?		
►4.18	Fossil fuels		Photosynthesis and the origin of fossil fuels

	Description	Reference	Notes
▶4.19	Other energy sources		Enlarges on Investigation 4.3
▶4.20	Why is it hot in the tropics?		
▷T	*Wind power plants*	Project Technology Brief no. 22	Constructional project
▷T	*Solar furnace*	Project Technology Brief no. 23	Constructional project
▷B	*Weather patterns*	*Patterns* topic book	Energy and weather

Teaching progression

▷Investigation 4.1 is a 'project' leading to the achievement of ▷objective 4. It also introduces some common sources of energy at present most utilised by man. Food is also included as an energy source. Ideally, different groups should attempt each of the four suggestions. If this investigation is omitted a brief preliminary discussion may be necessary to survey the variety of fuels and to prepare for the next investigation. The discussion could be based on the photographs in the *Pupils' manual* and on 'The search for oil' to be found in *Science and decision making*.

Objective 9 is achieved by Investigation 4.2 and to some extent by Investigation 4.3. Both of these investigations are intended to provide the basis for a discussion which need not be protracted. Investigation 4.3 also prepares the way for establishing objective 2e and, in addition, looks at energy originating from the interior of the Earth (hot springs, volcanoes, etc.). Nuclear fuels are not specifically brought to the attention of pupils but nuclear power is briefly mentioned in the extract included in Investigation 4.2 and the topic may arise in discussion. Whilst such an energy source cannot be ignored in the present context, detailed explanations must come later.

There have been instances in previous work in the sample scheme when food has been mentioned as the source of the building blocks necessary for growth. Of the three major groups of food, proteins are important as a source of building blocks (such as nitrogen atoms) essential for growth (and repair) of tissues. Carbohydrates and fats are important as energy sources,

163

the latter providing an important energy 'store' in the body (see Section 5, Investigation 5.1). Hence it is important that the diet should contain adequate supplies of these three groups of food. Investigation 4.4 opens with a practical examination of a variety of everyday foods, for carbohydrate, protein and fat (see also *Patterns 1*, Section 6). Pupils may be familiar with the basic tests and could already have tested a variety of materials from organisms (i.e. food, in this context) for protein (see *Patterns 1*, Section 7) Hence the tests suggested can be abbreviated as desired. The remainder of Investigation 4.4 consists of data and information leading to achievement of objective 2a. The Gowland–Hopkins experiment can be explained by hypothesising the necessity of some other factors in the diet to maintain adequate growth and health.

It is now known that these factors are vitamins. Other classic stories can be recounted (Captain Cook, vitamin C, and how the British sailor became known as a 'limey'). The illustrations of deficiency diseases, e.g. rickets, due to lack of vitamin D, and of 'Derbyshire neck', due to lack of the element iodine, illustrate the importance of food for the proper maintenance of health. These examples can be supplemented as desired. The question concerning plants is to help pupils recall an earlier pattern: that plants obtain some of the elements they require as ions from the environment (*Patterns 1*, Section 8). This can be contrasted with animals. This idea is picked up again both in Investigation 4.10b and in the introduction to Investigation 4.11.

Investigation 4.5 is a series of problems based on objective 2a. The final question in Investigation 4.5 is designed to help pupils appreciate that the molecules such as amino-acids must be rebuilt into proteins before being used in the growth of new tissues.

▷Investigation 4.6 also contains problem elements, but its main purpose is achievement of objective 10 and objective 5. The latter objective is also achieved by much other material in the section (it is one of the central objectives running throughout), but at this point the illustrations in *Patterns 3* and a selection of appropriate material from the sources mentioned in the 'Teaching notes' can be used. This work should not be allowed to drag on too long. ▷Investigation 4.7 achieves ▷objective 7 and will also contribute to others.

Energy transfer in a community is considered in Investigation 4.8. Studying a number of pathways of food transfer leads to an appreciation of the general pattern to which they all conform (objective 2b). Previous work can be drawn upon (*Patterns 2*, Section 9) and past and present observations of the mini-ponds utilised. The work is extended to objective 2c, which is then completed by a consideration of decomposers in Investigation 4.9. Here the temperature rise inside the unsterilised vacuum flask can be ascribed to micro-organisms utilising the grass clippings as food for their own respiratory and growth purposes. A proportion of the energy transferred is released to raise the temperature of the system. To test this hypothesis the bacteria (and probably moulds) can be cultured. It may be clear from smells (of, for example, ammonia) and putrefaction that a decomposing process is proceeding. The fact that decomposers release small-molecule building blocks, such as ammonia, as the waste products of their metabolism (in much the same way as man produces wastes such as urea), will be referred to later as this is a most important link in the pattern of events mentioned below.

Throughout the work on food chains and webs it should be borne in mind that building blocks as well as energy are transferred. In *Patterns 4*, Section 11 'Stability' the way in which energy and building block transfer through a food web fits into the overall pattern of events in an ecosystem will be considered (see figure 4.1).

A further dimension to the pesticide danger is examined in Investigation 4.10. Because some pesticides are persistent, they tend to be passed along food chains and accumulate in the bodies of the organisms involved. Since there is a cumulative effect, they tend to concentrate in the carnivores at the 'end' of the chain. This is clearly shown by the data supplied. The explanation cannot be based simply on a qualitative appreciation of food chains since there is a quantitative aspect which is not dealt with until Section 5. Bright pupils should appreciate this difficulty. The second part of Investigation 4.10 is more straightforward and should present no difficulties. Here the food chain pattern is obviously important and so is that concerning the uptake of elements (supplied in the fertilizer) from the environment by plants for growth. (See *Patterns 1*, Section 8.) Investigation 4.10 also helps achieve objective 5.

The next series of investigations (4.11 to 4.19) is concerned with photosynthesis (objective 2d). A study of food webs makes it clear that animals can obtain energy and building blocks for growth from other organisms. However all food chains begin with plants, the 'producers'. How then do plants obtain their energy and building blocks? The second part of this question is investigated by considering the widespread occurrence of carbon in living tissue and van Helmont's classic experiment – from which he drew the wrong conclusion (Investigation 4.11). If van Helmont's conclusion is acceptable (that the willow tree increased its mass solely by uptake of water from the soil) and if the original mass of the shoot was 5 lb (2.3 kg) then after 5 years' growth the tree would have an abnormally high water content.

Actual values for the water content of trees vary from 5 per cent for the wood to 80 per cent for the leaves. Allowing for this in the original shoot the final water content of the tree after 5 years would be in the region of 98.5 per cent! The discrepancy in the mass of soil at the beginning and end of the experiment could be due to experimental error, some soil loss and, perhaps, some uptake of building blocks. The latter can be deduced from the pattern that elements essential for growth are obtained from the environment other than the atmosphere (see *Patterns 1*, Section 8). By reminding pupils of another simple pattern: that there are large amounts of carbon in plant tissues it seems reasonable that atmospheric carbon dioxide is the only possible source of these carbon atoms. Investigation 4.12 and the film loop tests this idea and establishes that carbon dioxide is taken up by plants and used to manufacture carbohydrate.

Having established that foods such as carbohydrates can be manufactured from simple building blocks, such as carbon

Figure 4.1
General pattern of energy and building block transfer in a community. (A different way of regarding the same system is illustrated in figure 5.3.) The return of many building blocks to the environment via the decomposers (e.g. the nitrogen cycle) and the cyclic flow of oxygen have not yet been fully established. This is done in *Patterns 4*, Section 11 'Stability'

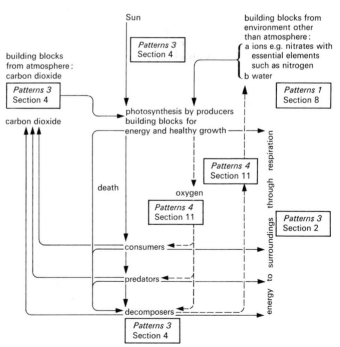

dioxide and water, attention is now turned to the source of energy for this process. Data presented suggests light (i.e. energy transferred from the Sun) is implicated. This is probably the obvious suggestion and Investigation 4.13 tests the hypothesis. The concept of photosynthesis can be introduced at this point. The interaction is: $CO_2 + H_2O \rightarrow (CH_2O)_n$. Although it looks as if oxygen should be released as the result of this interaction, there is no evidence yet. This is a prediction which will be followed up in *Patterns 4*, Section 11 (Stability).

If a variety of different plants are used this will contribute to the validity of the pattern concerning photosynthesis developed below. The question at the end of Investigation 4.13 is intended to assist the achievement of objective 2e. The pattern of events so far established is illustrated in figure 4.1.

▷ Investigation 4.14 relates the structure of leaves to their photosynthetic function and chlorophyll is drawn to the particular attention of pupils. The pattern of distribution of chlorophyll (chloroplasts are more concentrated in the upper cell layers of a leaf where more light will impinge on a leaf surface) is significant in terms of its importance in photosynthesis. Even if ▷ Investigation 4.14 is not performed this particular pattern should be discussed in relation to Investigation 4.15 which is designed to implicate chlorophyll in the photosynthetic process. This investigation helps achieve objective 6 and completes achievement of objective 2d.

In ▷ Investigation 4.16 the logical prediction is that photosynthesis will not presumably be able to occur. (It is essential to use young leaves in which a green tinge cannot be detected.) In the process of testing, however, the red pigment is readily extracted by ethanol and at this stage the chlorophyll may be detectable. Pupils should then go on to find starch. Hence there is no exception to the pattern. These apparently unexpected results will contribute to the achievement of ▷ objective 8. If, in the extraction process, chlorophyll is not noticed the results, which will show starch, will be even more puzzling. A simple chromatographic separation of leaf pigments obtained from an extract of the leaves in question may show the presence of chlorophyll, which is masked by the other pigments.

▷ Investigation 4.17 ties photosynthesis to visible light waves (wavelengths 350–450 nm and 650–700 nm are those approximately absorbed by chlorophyll). Illustrations (figures 4.34, 4.37 and 4.38) contribute to objective 5 achievement. The spectral curves shown are for warm white, ultraviolet and Gro-lux fluorescent tubes respectively. The suitability of the last for photosynthesis should be recognised.

With Investigation 4.18 the section covers full circle. A fossil fuel, such as coal, is seen to be derived from plant material. Hence the energy associated with such fuels has its origins in photosynthesis and, ultimately, the Sun (objective 2e). The origin of coal etc. as the forests of the Carboniferous era can be discussed.

Investigation 4.19 will also contribute to objective 2e.

Investigation 4.20 is primarily intended as an introduction to the topic book *Weather patterns*.

Teaching notes

▷ *Investigation 4.1* Fuels and food

There is a danger that pupils will produce long screeds of copied information.

The sources of material must be supplied, and it should be emphasised that pupils are expected to extract the relevant information. The results could be presented preferably in the form of a display to which all of the group should contribute. This will encourage diagrammatic presentation, and will enable other groups to benefit from what has been discovered. Additionally, each group could nominate a representative to talk for a few minutes about the findings. The project suggestions include some experiments which may require close supervision. Sources of materials for the projects are listed below.

Projects 1–3. Coal, Oil, Gas

The National Coal Board, Public Relations Officer, Hobart House, Grosvenor Place, London SW1

Institute of Petroleum Information Service, 61 New Cavendish St., London W1M 8AR

Shell International Petroleum Ltd, Shell Centre, London SE1

British Petroleum Co. Ltd, Britannic House, London EC2

The Gas Council, 4–5 Grosvenor Place, London SW1

West Midland Gas Board, Wharf Lane, Solihull, Warwickshire

Central Electricity Generating Board, Sudbury House, 15 Newgate St., London EC1

United Kingdom Atomic Energy Authority, 11 Charles II St., London SW1

Project 4 Food

a A table showing the energy value of foods is given on page 170. Since the values are given per 100 g a conversion into more realistic terms will be necessary; e.g. 1 level teaspoonful of sugar $= x$ g; 100 cm^2 of bread, 0.5 cm thick $= y$ g; and so on. This is not easy but determinations can be kept from year to year, gradually building up tables with realistic equivalents.

b Food firms produce free pamphlets on preservation. For example:
Batchelors Food Ltd, Wadsley Bridge, Sheffield 6
Smedleys, Whyteleaf, Surrey
Birdseye Foods Ltd, Station Av., Walton-on-Thames, Surrey
Food preservation, Unilever education booklet, Revised Ordinary
Series 3. Unilever Education Section, Blackfriars House,
London EC4

c National Milk Publicity Council, 5 John Princes St., London W1
Cadbury Bros Ltd (Schools Dept), Bournville, Birmingham.
(*Milk,* Project Notes 2)
White Fish Authority, 10 Young St., Edinburgh EH2 4JQ
Information Officer, Herring Industry Board, 1 Glenfinlas St.,
Edinburgh EH3 6AH
Fruit and Vegetables: National Federation of Fruit and Potato
Trades Ltd, Russell Chambers, Covent Garden, London
WC2

d Central Council for Health Education, Tavistock House North,
Tavistock Square, London WC1. (Food hygiene)

e Wheat
The Flour Advisory Bureau, 21 Arlingston St., London SW1.
(*The why and where of wheat*)
Allinsons Ltd, 210 Cambridge Heath Rd, London E2
McDougalls Cookery Service, McDougalls Mills, London E14
Kelloggs Ltd, Advertising Dept, Stretford, Manchester. (*Grains
are great foods*)

In general the above materials are free but small charges may
be made in some instances especially to cover postage. Most
firms do not appreciate large numbers of children writing for
materials. It is suggested that teachers write on their behalf
before the project begins so that material is available.

The following experiments can be used for practical work on
coal and oil.

Project 1 Coal

Pupils could distil coal using the apparatus on page 170. The
burning of coal gas can be shown to form carbon dioxide and
water. The alkaline water shows the presence of ammonia. Coal
tar is a viscous liquid containing a complex mixture of carbon
compounds. Some yellow/white sulphur might be detected in the
tar test-tube. Coke is left in the heated test-tube. The experiment
indicates the presence of carbon, hydrogen, nitrogen and sulphur
in coal.

Sources of energy

Figure 4.2 Apparatus for the distillation of coal.

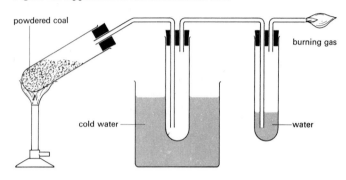

Project 2   Oil

If oil was not distilled in *Patterns 1,* then the experiment could be done here.

The following tables can be used in connection with ▷ Investigation 4.1 and Investigation 4.5.

Table 1

The energy value and protein, fat and carbohydrate content of food

Food	g per 100 g Protein	Fat	Carbo-hydrate	kilo-calories per 100 g	kilo-Joules per 100 g
Cereals					
Kellogs All-Bran	13	5	58	310	1 302
Biscuits, cream crackers	9	33	58	560	2 352
Biscuits, digestive	10	21	66	480	2 016
Biscuits, sweet mixed	6	27	67	560	2 352
Bread, brown	9	2	50	240	1 008
Bread, white (large loaves)	8	1	53	240	1 008
Kellogs Cornflakes	7	1	88	370	1 554
Oatmeal porridge	1	1	8	45	189
Puffed Wheat	14	2	75	360	1 512
Rice Krispies	6	1	85	350	1 470
Shredded Wheat	10	3	79	360	1 512
Weetabix	11	2	77	350	1 470
Milk products and eggs					
Butter	Tr	85	Tr	790	3 318
Cheese, Cheddar	25	35	Tr	430	1 806
Cheese, Cheshire	26	31	Tr	390	1 638
Cheese, Danish Blue	23	29	Tr	370	1 554
Cheese, processed	23	30	Tr	370	1 554
Cheese, Stilton	26	40	Tr	480	2 016
Cream, double	2	48	2	460	1 932

Food	g per 100 g Protein	Fat	Carbo- hydrate	kilo- calories per 100 g	kilo- Joules per 100 g
Cream, single	2	21	3	220	924
Milk, fresh, whole	3	4	5	66	277
Eggs, fresh, whole	12	12	Tr	160	672
Eggs, fried	14	20	Tr	240	1 008
Eggs, poached	12	12	Tr	160	672
Fats					
Margarine	Tr	85	Tr	800	3 360
Meat					
Bacon, fried, streaky	24	46	Tr	530	2 226
Beef, corned	22	15	Tr	230	966
Beef, roast, topside, lean only	27	15	Tr	250	1 050
Chicken, roast	30	7	Tr	190	798
Ham, boiled, lean only	23	13	Tr	220	924
Liver, fried, calf	29	15	2	260	1 092
Luncheon meat, canned	11	29	5	340	1 428
Meat paste	20	13	4	229	924
Mutton chop, grilled, lean and fat (weighed with bone)	15	34	Tr	380	1 596
Mutton, roast, leg	25	20	Tr	290	1 218
Pork, roast, leg	25	23	Tr	320	1 344
Pork, grilled, chop, lean and fat (weighed with bone)	15	42	Tr	450	1 890
Sausage, fried, pork	12	25	13	330	1 386
Fish					
Cod, fried	21	5	3	140	588
Fish paste	15	10	7	170	714
Haddock, steamed, smoked	22	1	Tr	100	420
Kippers, baked (weighed with bones and skin)	13	6	Tr	110	462
Haddock, fried, fresh	20	8	4	180	756
Sardines, canned	20	23	Tr	290	1 218
Fruit					
Apples, English eating (weighed with skin and core)	Tr	Tr	10	36	151
Bananas (weighed with skin)	1	Tr	11	45	189
Blackberries, raw	1	Tr	6	30	126
Grapefruit (whole fruit weighed)	Tr	Tr	3	11	46
Oranges (weighed with peel and pips)	1	Tr	6	27	113
Peaches, canned in syrup	Tr	Tr	17	66	277
Plums, Victoria dessert (weighed with stones)	1	Tr	9	36	151

Food	g per 100 g Protein	Fat	Carbo-hydrate	kilo-calories per 100 g	kilo-Joules per 100 g
Prunes, stewed without sugar	1	Tr	20	81	340
Rhubarb, stewed without sugar	Tr	Tr	1	5	21
Strawberries	1	Tr	6	26	109
Nuts					
Peanuts, kernels	28	49	9	600	2 520
Vegetables					
Beans, canned, baked	6	Tr	17	93	390
Beans, boiled, runner	1	Tr	1	7	29
Brussels sprouts, boiled	2	Tr	2	16	67
Cabbage, boiled, Savoy	1	Tr	1	9	38
Carrots, boiled	1	Tr	4	19	80
Cauliflower, boiled	2	Tr	1	11	46
Lettuce, raw	1	Tr	2	11	46
Mushrooms, fried	2	22	Tr	220	924
Onions, boiled	1	Tr	3	13	54
Peas, boiled, fresh	5	Tr	8	49	206
Peas, canned	6	Tr	17	86	361
Potatoes, boiled, old	1	Tr	20	80	336
Potatoes, chips	4	9	37	240	1 008
Potato crisps	6	38	49	560	2 352
Tomatoes, raw	1	Tr	3	14	59
Sugar, preserves, sweets					
Boiled sweets	Tr	Tr	87	330	1 386
Chocolate, milk	9	38	53	590	2 478
Chocolate, plain	6	35	53	540	2 268
Chocolates, fancy	4	19	73	470	1 974
Honey	Tr	Tr	76	290	1 218
Ice cream	4	11	20	200	840
Jam	1	Tr	69	260	1 092
Liquorice allsorts	4	2	74	320	1 344
Marmalade	Tr	Tr	70	260	1 092
Mars bar	5	19	67	450	1 890
Pastilles	5	Tr	62	250	1 050
Peppermints	1	1	98	390	1 638
Beverages					
Bournvita, powder	11	8	68	370	1 554
Bovril (in jar)	18	1	Tr	80	336
Cocoa, powder	20	26	35	450	1 890
Fruit squash	Tr	Tr	36	140	588
Horlick's	14	8	71	400	1 680
Lemonade	Tr	Tr	6	21	88
Lucozade	Tr	Tr	18	67	281

Food	g per 100 g Protein	Fat	Carbo-hydrate	kilo-calories per 100 g	kilo-Joules per 100 g
Nescafé, powder	12	Tr	11	90	378
Ovaltine	13	6	72	380	1 596
Oxo cubes	10	3	12	120	504
Cakes, etc.					
Cherry cake	5	24	57	450	1 890
Chocolate cake	8	25	61	500	2 100
Currant buns	7	8	55	310	1 302
Currant cake	6	18	60	420	1 764
Ginger biscuits	6	17	71	450	1 890
Jam tarts	4	15	63	390	1 638
Lemon tarts	6	25	50	445	1 848
Mince pies	5	22	44	390	1 638
Plain fruit cake	6	16	54	380	1 596
Rock cake	6	16	66	420	1 764
Scones	8	13	57	370	1 554
Sponge cake	9	7	55	310	1 302
Puddings					
Apple pie	2	8	30	190	798
Bread and butter pudding	2	8	30	190	798
Bread and butter pudding	6	8	17	160	672
Custard tart	6	17	30	290	1 218
Jam roll	4	19	55	400	1 680
Jelly	2	Tr	19	82	344
Pancakes	5	15	37	300	1 260
Rice pudding	4	8	16	140	588
Syrup sponge pudding	4	15	55	370	1 554
Treacle tart	4	14	63	380	1 596
Trifle	3	6	22	150	630
Yorkshire pudding	7	9	27	220	924
Meat and fish dishes					
Beef stew	11	9	4	140	588
Fish cakes	12	14	10	220	924
Hot pot	10	5	11	130	546
Sausage roll	7	36	36	500	2 100
Shepherds pie	10	4	9	110	462
Steak and kidney pie	15	19	17	300	1 260
Toad-in-the-hole	8	20	19	290	1 218
Sugar, white	Tr	Tr	100	390	1 638
Syrup, golden	Tr	Tr	79	300	1 260
Toffees, mixed	2	17	71	440	1 848
Egg and cheese dishes					
Scrambled egg	10	25	1	280	1 176

Food	g per 100 g Protein	Fat	Carbo- hydrate	kilo- calories per 100 g	kilo- Joules per 100 g
Welsh rarebit	14	22	26	360	1 512
Soups, sauces, etc.					
Soup, mixed	2	1	4	37	155
Spaghetti, canned in tomato sauce	2	1	12	60	252
Tomato soup, canned	1	3	9	69	290
Vegetable soup, canned	2	Tr	8	43	180

Table freely adapted from: Medical Research Council Special Report no. 297. *The composition of foods*, R. A. McCance and E. M. Widdowson. HMSO, 1960.

Table 2

The calcium, iron and vitamin composition of some foods

1 international unit (i.u.) Vitamin A = 0.000 6 mg
1 international unit (i.u.) Vitamin D = 0.000 025 mg

All values per 100 g of edible portion, raw unless otherwise stated.

Foodstuff	Calcium mg	Iron mg	Vitamin A i.u.	Vitamin B Thiamine mg	Riboflavin mg	Nicotinic acid mg	Vitamin C mg	Vitamin D i.u.
Cereals								
Barley, dry, pearl	10.58	0.71	0	0.11	0	2.47	0	0
Biscuits, plain	126.98	1.76	0	0.14	0.04	1.41	0	0
Biscuits, sweet	84.66	1.06	0	0.11	0.04	1.06	0	0
Bread, white	91.71	1.76	0	0.18	0.04	1.76	0	0
brown	95.24	2.47	0	0.21	0.07	2.47	0	0
wholemeal	24.69	2.82	0	0.21	0.11	3.53	0	0
Flour, white	116.40	1.76	0	0.28	0.04	1.76	0	0
wholemeal	35.26	3.88	0	0.39	0.18	4.94	0	0
Oatmeal	56.44	4.23	0	0.49	0.11	1.06	0	0
Rice	3.53	0.35	0	0.07	0.04	1.41	0	0
Cornflakes	7.05	2.82	0	0.04	0.11	1.76	0	0
Dairy Products								
Butter	14.10	0	3 492	0	0	0	0	38.80
Cheese, Cheddar	811.29	0.71	1 410	0.04	0.49	0	0	14.10
Cream, single	77.60	0.35	705	0.04	0.11	0	0	7.05
Eggs, fresh	56.44	2.47	988	0.11	0.04	0	0	169.31

| Foodstuff | Calcium | Iron | Vitamin A | Vitamin B | | | Vitamin C | Vitamin D |
| | | | | Thiamine | Riboflavin | Nicotinic acid | | |
	mg	mg	i.u.	mg	mg	mg	mg	i.u.
Eggs, dried	190.48	7.76	5 008	0.35	1.20	0.35	0	239.86
Milk, whole	119.90	0	141	0.04	0.14	0	2.12	1.41
Milk, evaporated	289.24	0.35	353	0.07	0.35	0.35	1.41	3.53
Milk, condensed, whole	345.68	0.35	353	0.11	0.39	0.35	2.82	3.53
Milk, condensed, skimmed, sweetened	384.48	0.35	0	0.14	0.42	0.35	3.17	0
Milk, dried, whole	959.44	0.71	1 199	0.28	1.21	0.71	10.58	10.58
Milk, dried, skimmed	1 266.30	0.71	0	0.35	1.59	0.71	10.58	0
Fats								
Cooking fat, lard, etc.	0	0	0	0	0	0	0	0
Margarine	3.53	0.35	2 998	0	0	0	0	317.40
Fish								
Kipper	119.93	2.12	141	0	0.32	3.53	0	917.10
White fish, haddock	31.74	1.06	0	0.07	0.11	2.82	0	0
Fried fish, white	81.13	0.35	0	0.07	0.11	2.82	0	0
Herring	102.29	0.14	141	0.04	0.32	3.53	0	917.10
Salmon, tinned	67.02	0.14	317	0.04	0.11	7.05	0	493.80
Sardine, tinned	409.17	3.90	106	0	0.21	4.93	0	317.40
Meat								
Bacon	14.10	1.41	0	0.39	0.14	1.41	0	0
Ham, cooked	14.10	2.47	0	0.49	0.21	3.53	0	0
Beef, corned	14.10	9.88	0	0	0.21	3.53	0	0
Beef, fresh (average good quality)	10.58	3.88	0	0.07	0.21	4.93	0	0
Beef, stewing	10.58	3.88	0	0.07	0.21	4.93	0	0
Chicken	10.58	3.53	0	1.06	0.18	7.41	0	0
Kidney, sheep	14.10	11.64	987	0.32	2.01	8.11	10.58	—
Liver, ox	7.05	14.10	20 000	0.32	3.00	13.05	31.74	45.86
Tripe	70.50	0.71	35	0.28	0.11	3.53	0	0
Mutton	10.58	0.21	0	14.10	0.25	4.94	0	0
Luncheon meat, tinned	17.60	1.41	0	0.39	0.21	3.53	0	0
Pork	3.53	0.35	0	0.99	0.21	4.94	0	0
Sausage, pork	14.10	2.47	0	0.35	0.07	1.41	0	0
Vegetables								
Beans, baked	59.96	2.12	494	0.07	0.04	0.71	3.53	0
Beans, tinned								
Beans, haricot	179.89	6.70	0	0.46	0.14	2.50	0	0
Beans, runner	35.25	0.71	494	0.04	0.11	1.06	21.20	0

Foodstuff	Calcium	Iron	Vitamin A	Vitamin B			Vitamin C	Vitamin D
				Thiamine	Riboflavin	Nicotinic acid		
	mg	mg	i.u.	mg	mg	mg	mg	i.u.
Beetroot, boiled	28.25	0.71	0	0.04	0.04	0	3.53	0
Brussels Sprouts	28.25	0.71	670	0.11	—	0.71	98.76	0
Cabbage	74.08	1.41	494	0.07	0.04	0.35	59.96	0
Carrot	49.38	0.71	20 000	0.07	0.04	0.71	7.05	0
Cauliflower	17.60	0.71	35	0.11	0.11	0.71	70.25	0
Lentil	38.90	7.76	0	0.49	0.25	2.47	0	0
Lettuce	24.70	0.71	1 658	0.07	0.07	0.35	14.10	0
Onions	31.74	0.35	0	0.04	0.04	0.35	10.58	0
Peas, tinned	14.10	1.76	494	0.32	0.14	2.47	24.70	0
processed, green	24.70	1.76	494	0.11	0.71	1.06	0	0
Potato	7.05	0.71	0	0.11	0.04	1.06	32–7	0
chips	14.10	1.41	0	0.11	0.04	1.06	21–7	0
Spinach	70.50	3.17	10 018	0.11	0.21	0.71	59.96	0
Tomato	14.10	0.35	1 164	0.07	0.04	0.71	21.16	0
Turnip	59.96	0.35	0	0.04	0.04	0.71	24.69	0
Watercress	222.22	1.76	5 009	0.11	—	0.71	59.96	0
Fruit								
Apple, fresh	3.53	0.35	35	0.04	0.04	0	3.53	0
Apricot, tinned	10.58	0.71	1 658	0.04	0	0.35	3.53	0
Apricot, dried	91.71	4.23	5 996	0	0.21	2.82	0	0
Banana	7.05	0.35	317	0.04	0.07	0.71	10.58	0
Blackcurrants	59.96	1.41	317	0.04	0.07	0.35	201.00	0
Dates	67.02	1.76	705	0.07	0.04	2.12	0	0
Figs, dried	282.10	4.23	705	0.11	—	1.76	0	0
Gooseberries, cooking	28.21	0.35	317	—	0.04	0.35	38.80	0
Grapefruit	17.63	0.35	0	0.04	0.04	0.35	38.80	0
Lemon	7.05	0	0	0.04	0	0	49.38	0
Melon	17.63	0.71	3 316	0.04	—	0.35	24.69	0
Orange	42.32	0.35	71	0.11	0.04	0.35	49.38	0
Peach, fresh	3.53	0.35	847	0.04	0.04	1.06	7.05	0
Peach, tinned	3.53	2.12	423	0	0.04	0.71	3.53	0
Pear	7.05	0.35	0	0.04	0.04	0.35	3.53	0
Pineapple, tinned	14.10	1.76	71	0.04	0.04	0.35	7.05	0
Plum	14.10	0.35	353	0.04	0.04	0.35	3.53	0
Prunes	38.80	2.82	1 658	0.11	0.21	1.41	0	0
Raisins	59.96	1.41	0	0.11	—	0.35	0	0
Strawberries	21.20	3.53	0	0.04	0.04	0.35	0	0
Nuts								
Coconuts, desiccated	21.20	3.53	0	0.04	0.04	0.35	0	0

| Foodstuff | Calcium | Iron | Vitamin A | Vitamin B | | | Vitamin C | Vitamin D |
| | | | | Thiamine | Riboflavin | Nicotinic acid | | |
	mg	mg	i.u.	mg	mg	mg	mg	i.u.
Almonds	246.91	4.23	0	—	—	2.12	0	0
Peanuts, roasted	59.96	2.12	0	0.21	0.11	15.87	0	0
Soya flour	208.11	7.05	0	0.74	—	2.12	0	0
Preserves, etc.								
Chocolate, plain	24.69	31.74	71	0.04	0.35	1.06	0	0
Jam	17.63	1.41	0	0	0	0	10.58	0
Marmalade	35.30	0.71	71	0	0	0	10.58	0
Sugar	0	0	0	0	0	0	0	0
Syrup	28.21	1.41	0	0	0	0	0	0
Honey	7.05	0.35	0	0	0.04	0.35	0	0
Beverages								
Beer	10.58	0	0	0	0.04	0.71	0	0
Cocoa powder	52.91	14.46	71	0.07	0.28	1.76	0	0
Coffee, ground	0	0	0	0	0.21	9.88	0	0
Tea, dry	0	0	0	0	0.92	6.00	0	0
Cakes								
Cake, Dundee	77.60	2.12	212	0.07	0.11	0.35	0	14.10
Buns	91.70	2.47	0	0.18	0.04	1.41	0	0
Custard sauce	213.46	0	106	0.04	0.11	0	0	0

Investigation 4.3 Non-fuel energy sources
Part a
The Shuman-Boys solar power plant constructed in 1913 consisted of five parabolic mirrors 4.3 m wide and 63 m long. These were rotated around horizontal axes to follow the Sun's apparent motion. The solar energy was used to generate steam, which drove an engine designed to produce 37 kW for pumping purposes.

Surprisingly the harnessing of solar radiation by technological means has a history of over 100 years. The following extracts are from 'An appraisal of the use of solar energy', a paper by Dr. H. Heywood published in 1966.

In order to appreciate the attitude underlying these developments one must realise that in the period between one hundred to fifty years ago, continuation of energy supplies for mankind in general was a subject of considerable anxiety. Coal reserves were known to be dwindling, oil was relatively new and the potential supply insufficiently explored, nuclear power was undreamed of, except by Jules Verne. Consequently, direct solar radiation was regarded as the one unbounded source of energy that could in certain locations and in spite of obvious limitations, be used in perpetuity to supply a large proportion of the essential energy requirements of mankind. As an example of this attitude one can quote from the writings in 1876 of the famous inventor John Ericsson, who envisaged a chain of solar power stations across North Africa, the Middle East, India, Australia and Central America which would supply continuous electrical energy.

Needless to say, the position has changed greatly since these early days. Not only do the potential supplies of oil and natural gas exceed by many fold the rather gloomy earlier prophesies, but nuclear power, both by fission and by fusion, ensures an adequate energy supply for all industrial purposes, which have now reached a magnitude that could not by any stretch of imagination be satisfied by direct solar radiation. This does not imply, however, that solar energy utilisation cannot at present and for many years to come, perform an essential function under certain circumstances and in appropriate localities. The great body of research in progress at many universities and other organisations is evidence that many scientists and engineers have faith in the immediate possibilities . . .

Devices were constructed for utilising solar energy by the following inventors at the dates shown below:

1854–1873	C. Guntner (Austrian)	Solar boiler with mirrors
1860–1880	A. Mouchot (French)	Solar boiler, steam engine and pump; solar operated refrigerator (ammonia)
1878	A. Pifre (French)	Solar boiler and steam engine
1868	H. Bessemer (English)	Solar furnace
1864–1888	J. Ericsson (American)	Solar boilers and radiation measurements Hot air engine
1876	W. Adams (English)	Solar cooker in India
1883	J. Harding (English)	Solar water distillation in Chile
1900	A. G. Eneas (American)	Solar power plants
1902	H. E. Willsie and J. Boyle (American)	Solar power plant with non-aqueous volatile working fluids

1906–1914	F. Shuman (American) with Sir Charles Boys and A. S. E. Ackermann (English)	Solar boilers and power plants for water pumping in USA and Egypt

Thus almost the whole scope of solar energy utilisation, apart from the complex photo-electric devices of recent development, had been investigated to some extent before 1900. Many of the constructions involved heavy capital expenditure, particularly the solar water still constructed in Chile by Harding, which had a surface area of $4\,600\,\text{m}^2$ and the solar boiler and steam driver pump devised by Shuman with Sir Charles Boys and A. S. E. Ackermann as consultants . . .

During the period between the two world wars progress lapsed in the development of solar energy utilisation but in 1940 there was a definite stimulus by the Godfrey L. Cabot bequest to the Massachusetts Institute of Technology to promote research in this subject. From the renaissance, work on the subject has spread to research teams in many universities both in USA and other major countries in the world, as well as to national research laboratories in Australia, France, Israel, India, Japan and Russia, to mention only the main countries that have taken an interest in the subject. International organisations such as the United Nations Organisation and the Association of Mediterranean Countries (COMPLES) are studying the problems, and conferences in USA and other countries are held at frequent intervals. The Solar Energy Society, Arizona, USA, publishes a journal which disseminates scientific and practical information on various aspects of solar energy utilisation. Yet in spite of all this activity, the scope of research remains substantially the same as was envisaged by the pioneers of nearly a century ago, except of course, for the fields of photo- and thermo-electricity promoted by the developments in space travel. The field of simple water heating, which includes the greatest number of actual applications at present, was apparently ignored by the early pioneers; possibly they thought such a mundane project was beneath their dignity.

Obviously scientific knowledge has increased vastly since the second world war, and new materials and technological processes have been developed, but the courage to build large scale installations has, with a few exceptions, been lacking. Even in the field of water heating, there are few examples of size exceeding $10\,\text{m}^2$ area, though possibly something of the order of $200\,000$ small scale heaters of $5\,\text{m}^2$ area and below are in operation in various parts of the world . . .

Water distillation
Many areas in the tropics lacking drinking water could make
use of solar energy to purify salt or brackish water. The simple
form of water-still now in use is basically the same as originally
designed by Harding in 1868, namely, a shallow tray filled with
salt or brackish water covered by a sloping glass roof. Radiation
evaporates the water from the tray and the vapour condenses
on the glass roof, the condensate running down the inside
surface to a collecting trough at the lower edge. Such
stills have an output of distilled water of up to $5\,\mathrm{kg\,m}^{-2}$
daily in suitable localities, though this is about the upper limit
of performance . . .

Solar ponds
Another development which originated at the National
Physical Laboratory of Israel concerns collectors of large
areas. The cost of artificially constructed flat plate collectors in
terms of acres would be prohibitive, but a shallow pond would
be feasible as a collector were it not for the excessive heat losses
in the normal circumstances. If, however, the pond consists of
a layer of salt water at the bottom covered by a layer of pure
water above, then the radiation absorbed by the base of the
pond heats the salt water and although there is a decrease in
density by expansion, the salt water layer is still dense enough
to remain at the bottom of the pond, insulated from the
atmosphere by the top layer of pure water. Experiments have
shown that the bottom layer of salt water can attain a
temperature of 90 °C without mixing with the pure water, and
very large quantities of heat could thereby be stored and
subsequently extracted. No really large ponds have yet been
constructed, but there is no doubt of the working possibilities
of such a system . . .

Notes on the construction of solar water heaters
The essential features of a solar water heater consist of:

(i) The collector plate – usually of metal and preferably
copper, with some system of piping or channels through which
water can flow and collect the radiant energy absorbed by the
plate.

(ii) Heat insulation at the back of the plate.

(iii) Glass or mylar plastic in front of the collector plate to
reduce wind loss and trap the re-radiation away from the
surface of the plate.

(iv) A casing to enclose and support the above items.

(v) A hot water storage tank connected to the collector plate
by piping. If natural circulation of the water is adopted this
tank must be higher than the absorber plate, but if forced

circulation by pump is used the tank may be below the collector.

The principle of operation is as follows.

Solar radiation impinges on the front of the glass plates, a small amount is absorbed by the plates and some is reflected from the surfaces, the proportion increasing rapidly as the angle of the rays approaches a direction parallel with the surface of the plates. When the Sun approximately faces the surface, about 90 per cent of the radiation should reach the collector plate and be converted to heat. There will be cooling losses due to wind and re-radiation from the absorber, but a maximum efficiency of heat recovery of 70 per cent may be attained in the middle of the day under the most favourable conditions. All day efficiencies of 50 to 60 per cent are commonly attained, but the efficiency will decrease as the water temperature is raised due to the greater heat losses . . .

Research and development work is continuing in the fields of water heating, house heating and water distillation (to obtain drinking water from salt or brackish water).

Part b

The tidal motions of the oceans are the result of the gravitational forces of both Sun and Moon. The details are complex, but since such dissipative forces as viscous drag are continually being overcome it is clear that an energy transfer is involved. Any tidal basin with a large rise and fall is in principle suitable for harnessing tidal power, but there are considerable difficulties, chief among which are the high capital cost of such schemes, the awkward tidal cycle, and the variation between neap and spring tides. A tidal barrage used for several years in France for driving electric generators has been stated to have been consistently uneconomic.

Part c

Geysers and hot springs occur in areas of the Earth's surface subject to volcanic action (see *Patterns 4* Section 5 'Changes in the Earth', and the topic book *Earth patterns*). In these areas particularly it is clear that there is an energy flow out from the interior of the Earth. The cause for this is examined later: in principle it could be either the cooling down of an originally hot Earth, or an energy source inside the Earth. (See Investigation 4.19.)

Part d

The energy transfer effected by a windmill clearly comes from the kinetic energy of the air. This in turn is one aspect of the atmospheric circulation which is maintained against dissipative

forces by solar radiation (see the topic book *Weather patterns*).
Part e
Cruachan, in Argyll is a pumped storage power station. At times
of high demand it operates as a normal hydroelectric power
station, but at times of low demand energy is drawn from the
National Grid and used to pump water to the reservoir at high
level. This in effect gives a convenient way of storing energy
until it is needed, obviating the construction of additional coal-
fired, oil-fired or nuclear power stations.

Further notes on energy sources are included in Investigation
4.19.

Investigation 4.4 Food is more than a fuel
The food-test work can be considerably shortened, or even
omitted, depending on individual circumstances.

Pupils could collect packets and advertisements of food claim-
ing to contain vitamins and particular elements. Vitamins are
essential in the diet because the body cannot synthesise them
(except vitamin D in small amounts). They probably play a role
in enzyme systems. Deficiency of a vitamin reduces the efficiency
of the metabolic processes in which it is involved with consequent
widespread effects (symptoms of deficiency disease). Vitamin D
can be made in the body if exposed to sunlight, which converts a
precursor substance present in the skin to the vitamin. Vitamin D
is not therefore absolutely essential in the diet. The table below
gives further information about vitamins.

Table 3
Vitamins

Vitamin	Principal sources	Daily needs (from food)	Function	Effect of lack
A	Halibut-(or cod-) liver oil, ox liver, milk and derivatives, spinach, watercress	1.5 mg	Regulates skin growth; aids night vision	Skin dry, cornea dry; poor night vision
B group Thiamine (B_1)	Wheat or rice 'germ', wholemeal flour; yeast extract	1.3 mg	Helps chemical changes in respiration; in heart especially	Heart disorders; 'beri-beri' when polished rice is main food
Riboflavin	Yeast extract, liver, eggs, cheese, milk	1.8 mg	As thiamine (but different reactions)	Children's growth checked; sores at mouth corners

Vitamin	Principal sources	Daily needs (from food)	Function	Effect of lack
Nicotinic acid (niacin)	Meat, wholemeal bread, yeast extract	16 mg	Still further respiratory changes	Pellagra (skin troubles, diarrhoea) especially when maize is main food
Many other B vitamins	Liver		Various; some still unknown	—
C, Ascorbic acid	Fresh fruits: rose hips, blackcurrants, oranges, lemons, tomatoes, green vegetables (especially in spring), potatoes	30 mg	Concerned with making strong skin and other tough parts of the body	Scurvy, in which the skin of the gums becomes pulpy and bleeds
D	Halibut-(or cod-) liver oil, egg-yolk, margarine (also made by action of sunlight on the skin surface)	None, unless lacking sunlight	Not known exactly, but concerned with bone formation	Rickets
E	Wheat germ, brown flour, liver, green vegetables	Probably none in man	In rats, affects muscles and reproductive system; found in man, but functions unknown	
K	Spinach, cabbage, Brussels sprouts	Probably none, since it is made by bacteria in the gut	Necessary for clotting of blood	Clotting time increased

Most deficiency diseases can be cured by repairing the deficiency. In some cases, however, permanent physical damage may result (such as in rickets). Rickets is a malformation of bone and can still be found in Britain. Lack of certain atom building blocks also cause deficiency diseases. The Derbyshire neck story is worth telling and hence the necessity to add iodine to table-salt. (Ask pupils to look at the information on contents on salt packets in the local supermarkets.) Iodine is essential for the pro-duction of thyroxin, the hormone produced by the thyroid gland situated in the neck. The hormone controls metabolic rate. Over production of this hormone thus leads to excitability, inability to relax and the 'pop-eyed' condition. Deficiency results in lethargy. Lack of iodine leads to deficiency of the hormone and compen-satory enlargement of the thyroid gland which is situated in the neck. Other important elements are calcium and phosphorous for bone and teeth, the solid parts of which are largely calcium carbonate and phosphate; iron is an essential element in haemo-globin, the red pigment in blood cells. Deficiency leads to anaemia. The reference in the 'Sample scheme' gives details of practical work possible in examining foods for these elements.

Whilst half the world suffers from bad health because they do not get enough food, the other half often suffers because they get too much of the wrong sort! Yudkin has suggested a causal relationship between sugar intake and coronary heart disease. This is controversial and pupils should realise that it cannot be accepted as the full story. Figure 4.20 (*Patterns 3*) shows, for instance, that the Dutch and the French have a relatively high sugar consumption but a low incidence of mortality from heart disease and so are exceptions to the apparent pattern. Other factors involved in heart disease probably include: smoking, nervous tension, high fat intake (increasing the cholesterol levels of the blood), high blood pressure, etc.

Investigation 4.5 Are you eating a balanced diet?

Much of this work needs to be done outside normal school hours.

The tables on pages 170–7 and 182–3 will be needed for this investigation.

A similar problem concerning the estimation of the amounts of food eaten applies here as in ▷ Investigation 4.1 and a similar solution could be employed. If any pupils have performed the food project their information on measured amounts will be useful for the rest of the class at this point. Those who may have estimated the energy content of food during project work obviously need not repeat this part of the investigation. If the practical difficulties in this investigation prove insurmountable the 'perfect' meal could be analysed as suggested and then compared with a pupil's typical meal. The short news extract about rickets can also be used. Reference to the tables will show that milk contains no iron and very little Vitamin D.

If pupils fall below the figures quoted for a balanced diet they should not worry. Remind them of the conditions of the measurements and of variation patterns!

▷ *Investigation 4.6* Feeding the world

This is an open-ended discussion. Co-operation with other departments is clearly possible.

A great deal of material is available and individual selections can be made. The following has proved of value (charges are usually fairly reasonable and some material is free).

From VCOAD, Education Unit, 69 Victoria Street, London SW1

a *The development puzzle*: a source book for teachers containing collated information about materials available on the rich world/poor world division – a 'must'. This lists all the material below and much more.

b *Development despatches*: duplicated fact sheets, e.g. 'Protein malnutrition', 'Science transforms agriculture'.
c *Research sheets*: duplicated fact sheets, e.g. 'Population explosion'.
d *Background statistics*: duplicated fact sheets, e.g. 'World food', 'Who gives aid?'.
Most of the above are free from VCOAD but a small charge may be necessary if a quantity is required.
From OXFAM, Education Department, 274 Banbury Road, Oxford
a *Charting poverty*: four wall charts. Diagrams, graphs, maps of (1) malnutrition; (2) disease; (3) illiteracy; (4) population increase. Teachers' notes.
b *Hunger: causes and solutions*: set of 12 photographs, 25 cm × 20 cm.
c Free information sheets: send for the list.
From UNICEF, New Gallery Centre, 123 Regent Street, London W1
Photographs of diets, 30 cm × 25 cm
a African child, 2–7 years
b Caribbean child, 4 years
c South East Asian child, 7–10 years
d British child, 10 years.

The photographs in *Patterns 3* used to illustrate methods of improving food production provide a basis of discussion, perhaps along the following lines. The problem of world hunger is no easy one to solve and requires a knowledge of many patterns. Amongst the approaches being adopted to improve food production are the following.

1 *Improving crop yields*

Involves knowledge of patterns of: inherited variation (to improve strains), cycles of materials (to improve nutrient supply), life cycles (to control pests and diseases), photosynthesis (to improve efficiency with which we use crop plants as 'fixers' of solar energy), energy transfers in food chains (to channel energy efficiency once it has been 'fixed').

2 *Improving farming patterns*
Involves a knowledge of local social, economic, cultural, and geographical patterns as well as improvements in technology. Improving traditional agriculture is one of the most important practical fronts on which the war with hunger is being fought.

3 *Novel approaches to food production*
Such as irrigation of deserts (e.g. with sea water which in-involves a knowledge of osmosis); farming the sea, which involves

185

increasing its productivity by understanding the patterns involved in food chains. Pupils will be familiar with some of the patterns mentioned, others come later. The list is formidable and illustrates the efforts being made.

▷ *Investigation 4.7* Deciding priorities for aid

This is based on the OXFAM *Aids committee game*, a simulation game designed to give pupils practice in decision-making. By taking on the role of an aid committee having to discuss a number of possible projects in developing countries, pupils have the opportunity to consider how and on what basis decisions on spending for development are made. The possible projects are drawn from actual proposals to OXFAM who have available the following for each country:

a fact sheet on country concerned
b cyclostyled map of country concerned
c descriptions of possible projects
d slides and commentary
e instructions for use.

Investigation 4.8 Energy transfer in communities

A good deal of time could be spent on examining the mini-pond communities for feeding relationships and hence it needs limiting. It is far better to encourage pupils to make continual observations and gradually build up a picture of the food web. Alternative situations could easily be used instead of the mini-ponds. The food web centred around a rose-bush, as described in *Patterns 3*, could be studied.

Investigation 4.9 What happens to organisms when they die?

A more strictly correct control than that suggested would be to 'cook' both sets of clippings and leave one set open to the air for a while afterwards. Alternatively, the latter could be set up as a third flask. Grass cuttings should be left in the flasks until a clear temperature rise has been recorded in the unsterilised set.

It will be necessary to demonstrate microbiological techniques if these are not familiar. (See *Teachers' guide 1*, Section 4.) Mixing a few clippings from each flask with a little sterilised distilled water in sterilised containers (e.g. Petri dishes) will provide the two extracts suitable for inoculating the agar plates. To ensure comparability between the two sets of clippings it will be noted that this treatment is exactly the same for both. To preserve sterile conditions keep extracts covered. After 48 hours or more of incubation a good growth of decomposers (moulds and bacteria) should be observed on the plate inoculated with the extract prepared from the unsterile clippings. Some (much less) may also be observed on the sterile 'control' plate. This is largely due to the difficulty of maintaining perfectly sterile conditions at all stages in the investigation.

Investigation 4.12 Plants and the source of carbon

To avoid a possible difficulty when testing for carbohydrate use destarched plants for this investigation. This can be done by leaving plants in the dark for 48 hours before required. Light has not yet been established as a factor in the carbohydrate synthesis picture and so it will be pointless to tell pupils to leave their experiments in a 'well-lit position'. Questions arising from this instruction could be embarrassing at this stage. An alternative arrangement for this experiment is shown in the figure. (Ignore those parts relevant to the following investigation.)

As far as possible a wide variety of plants should be used for for this investigation.

Sugars are the initial product of photosynthesis but are usually rapidly converted to starch except in many monocotyledons (e.g. iris, sugar cane). Even here monosaccharides are usually quickly converted into sucrose and so extracts must be hydrolysed before testing. (The sugar test will probably be negative on most potted plants.) The reference given in the 'Sample scheme' describes an investigation into the conversion of sugar to starch. Proper precautions are necessary when using ethanol (or alternative) near a flame.

Investigation 4.13 Testing a hypothesis

Destarch plants for 48 hours in the dark. The alternative approach illustrated in figure 4.3 on page 188 can also be used here. Once again a wide variety of plants should be used in order that patterns can be drawn which have some validity.

▷ *Investigation 4.14* The structure and function of leaves

This investigation is a simple one designed to introduce the leaf as a photosynthetic organ. The relationship of structure to function is considered. From an examination of leaf surfaces pupils will see stomata as holes through which gases can diffuse. Privet, *Tradescantia sp.*, mother of thousands (*Saxifraga sarmentosa*), busy Lizzie (*Impatiens sp.*) and iris could all be used. The underside of the leaf usually has a greater number of stomata per unit area than the upperside and this can be linked with the numerous air spaces in the lower half of the leaf. Iris, being a 'vertical' leaf, tends to have equal numbers of stomata on both sides. The nail-varnish technique for obtaining an impression of the leaf surface is not particularly appropriate here because it will not show the stomata as holes. A question is designed to draw the pupils' attention to the transparent nature of the outer layer of cells (the epidermis) which allows light to pass through into the cells which photosynthesise.

Figure 4.3 Two possible ways of depriving leaves of carbon dioxide (ii) and light (iii). In b the three conical flasks are shown attached to one plant for convenience. Separate plants could be used instead.

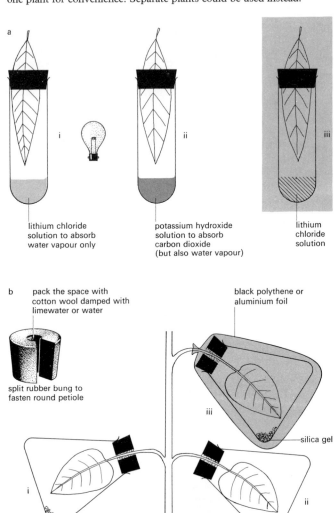

a

i

ii

iii

lithium chloride
solution to absorb
water vapour only

potassium hydroxide
solution to absorb
carbon dioxide
(but also water vapour)

lithium
chloride
solution

b   pack the space with
cotton wool damped with
limewater or water

black polythene or
aluminium foil

split rubber bung to
fasten round petiole

iii

silica gel

i

ii

silica gel to
absorb water
vapour only

sodalime to absorb
carbon dioxide
(but also
water vapour)

This provides a link with the next investigation, which uses second-hand evidence although prepared slides of leaf sections could be examined. The air spaces between cells allow gases to diffuse to individual cells and in one of the photographs a stomatal pore can be seen opening into this space. The chloroplasts are not clear but can be made out. They are more concentrated in the palisade cells in the upper part of the leaf. (Which part receives most sunshine?) This explains why many leaves are a darker green on top than underneath. The palisade cells are placed vertically (rather than horizontally) and close to each other, an arrangement which allows carbon dioxide to reach each cell more easily and at the same time ensures maximum exposure of the chloroplasts to light. The veins serve two functions, firstly to 'service' the leaves by supplying water and carrying away the products of photosynthesis, and secondly to provide support for the leaf. The thinness and large surface area of leaves (surface area to volume pattern) should be pointed out as structural features which ensure minimum time for gaseous exchange between cells and the atmosphere and maximum utilisation of light.

Investigation 4.15 What is the significance of chlorophyll?

This is a well known experiment which should present no difficulties. A variety of variegated (yellow-white and green) leaves should be tested by different members of the class. Possible examples include variegated privet (*Ligustrum sp.*). *Pelargonium zonale*, various decorative maples (*Acer sp.*) are also useful. Yellow leaves will possibly give positive results so avoid these. The yellow-white part of the leaf should give negative results whereas the green parts will give positive results on testing for starch.

Figure 4.4

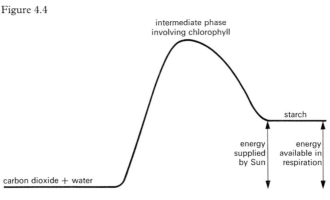

189

Chlorophyll is acting as a 'catalyst' in the reaction:

carbon dioxide + water → starch.

A summary of the interactions is shown in figure 4.4 on page 189.

A useful model to demonstrate the action of light on chlorophyll can be demonstrated by the teacher. $20\,cm^3$ of 0.1 per cent thionine solution is poured into a large test-tube and acidified with a few drops of concentrated hydrochloric acid. Three large spatula-fulls of solid iron(II) sulphate crystals are dissolved in the mixture.

The solution is divided into two halves: one half is kept as a control. When the other half is held in bright light (e.g. a slide projector beam) it is bleached; when it is removed from the beam it reverts to its original blue colour. This can be repeated. The light energy causes a particle interaction to occur, which in this case is reversible.

▷ *Investigation 4.16* Can plants with red-brown leaves photosynthesise?

It is essential to use young leaves without detectable tinges of green.

This investigation must be flexible: it is possible that greenness will be apparent when the pigments are extracted prior to testing the leaf for carbohydrate (starch). Alternatively this may not happen but the result of the starch test will be positive. Pupils must observe carefully and be honest about what they find. It may be necessary to run a simple chromatogram of an extract from some of these leaves in order to detect chlorophyll after a positive starch test.

Figure 4.5

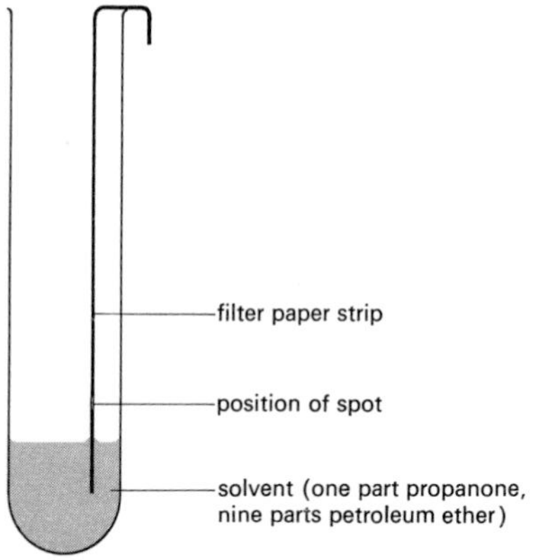

filter paper strip

position of spot

solvent (one part propanone, nine parts petroleum ether)

Crush some leaves in a mortar containing a little sharp sand and a small volume of solvent (ethanol or 80 per cent propanone). Using a small rod, dab some of the resulting extract on a spot one centimetre from the base of a strip of filter paper. Allow it to dry and then apply another dab. Repeat until a concentrated spot has built up (figure 4.5). Repeat with an extract from green leaves. Run the chromatograms and compare the results.

▷ *Investigation 4.17* Why are green leaves green?

A flat-sided container is most suitable for holding the chlorophyll extract. (Be careful of the effect of the organic solvents on some types of plastic container.) A reasonable volume of extract, from plant material rich in chlorophyll such as nettle or spinach leaves (or frozen chopped spinach), should be prepared. (See *Technicians' manual 3* for full details.) A chromatogram run at some time during this investigation will show green and yellow pigments present in chlorophyll and this can be related to the absorption spectrum observed.

Investigation 4.18 Fossil fuels

For this experiment coal must be treated as follows, prior to the lesson. Use dull coal. Crush about 5 g of coal into fragments (about 3–5 mm) and place in a clean glass flask. In a fume cupboard *cautiously* and with great care add sufficient cold concentrated nitric acid to cover the fragments. This must now be left for a period which may vary, according to the type of coal and size of fragments, from one or two hours to several days. Only experimentation will indicate the appropriate period. At the end of the selected period decant the nitric acid into a large volume of water, taking care not to lose any of the sample. Add distilled water to the remaining sample and decant again. Repeat.

Add sufficient 2M potassium hydroxide solution to cover the sample and leave for a few hours. Pour the sample into a fine-meshed sieve (taking great care when collecting the liquid) and work through thoroughly with water. Transfer the residue to a beaker. Pupils should take a little of this, place in a watch glass containing a little water and examine for recognisable plant debris under the microscope. The spores of spore-producing plants (common in the Carboniferous era) can often be seen. Figure 4.6 on next page shows some examples.

Investigation 4.19 Other energy sources

New deposits of fossil fuel are being located faster than fuel is being used, so that it is true that the 'reserve' is increasing. But the rate of using the fuels is increasing rapidly, so the period for which the reserve will last is actually decreasing. As fuels become more expensive to extract, it may be expected that other

Figure 4.6 Spores from coals of Carboniferous age: a polar compression, b lateral compression

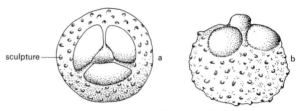

Setosisporites sp. size $2 \times 10^{-4} - 3 \times 10^{-3}$ m

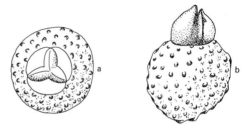

Lagenicula sp. size $5 \times 10^{-4} - 2 \times 10^{-3}$ m

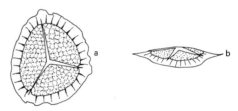

Triangulatisporites sp. size: $3 \times 10^{-4} - 1 \times 10^{-3}$ m

energy sources will gradually replace them, so it is an over-simplification to talk in terms of a single rate of use: this is variable depending on several factors in an unpredictable way. The cost of alternative energy sources (e.g. from nuclear power stations), people's attitudes to pollution of the atmosphere, developments in extraction technology and the rate at which energy use increases are all important in this context. However it is obvious that supplies are not unlimited and in the long term other energy sources must be used, because fossil fuels such as peat are being produced at a slow rate. The following extracts and graph illustrate the difficulties of prediction, and the possibility of the discovery of new types of deposit.

No substitute for oil – and known reserves are increasing

World energy consumption, expressed in tons of oil equivalent, rose from 2 338 million in 1955 to 4 964 million in 1970, and is expected to reach 11 388 million in 1985.

These are only estimates which, like all forecasts, have a margin of uncertainty. To some extent, therefore, they are dangerous for businessmen and governments who want to use them as a basis for their plans. But they are essential to give some idea of what the demand for energy is likely to be in the short, medium and long term.

The actual and estimated consumption figures are particularly significant for oil. World consumption of crude oil (including bunkers and non-energy uses, especially in the chemical industry) amounted to 2 275 million tons in 1970, or almost as much as total consumption of energy from all primary sources 15 years earlier. By 1985, when the figure is expected to be 5 960 million tons, consumption of energy produced from oil should exceed overall world consumption by 1 000 million tons in 1970 . . .

In 1970 western Europe used 27.5 per cent of all the energy produced from crude oil in the world, almost matching the United States which consumed 30.8 per cent. Only 15 years previously, in 1955, the corresponding figures were 15.1 per cent for western Europe and 53.6 per cent for the United States.

It is expected that by 1985 western Europe will be the biggest world consumer of crude oil, both relatively and absolutely, with 1 450 million tons or 24.3 per cent of the total . . .

We have been discussing how the pattern of energy consumption changed from 1955 to 1970 and how it is expected to develop up to 1985. But are the sources of energy capable of satisfying the demand? In particular, are there sufficient reserves of crude oil to cover a rising rate of increase in future? All studies give an affirmative reply.

Taking a middle value between the maximum and minimum estimates and assuming a compound annual increase of 7.5 per cent to 8 per cent between 1950 and 1970, the world's proved oil reserves should last until AD 2006. At the end of 1970 the world's proved reserves of crude oil stood at 118 000 million tons, of which 36 000 million, or about 30 per cent, had already been extracted. But there is a wide difference between proved and potential resources, which are much bigger. The most recent estimates put the quantity of oil trapped in the Earth and under the sea bed at a minimum of 193 000 million tons and a maximum of 300 000 million. Taking an intermediate figure of 234 000 million tons, the amount of oil extracted up to the end of 1970 amounted to barely 14 per cent of the total.

These are conservative figures; nothing changes more rapidly than the geological map for oil. By oil exploration Libya was transformed only yesterday from a box of sand into a strong box of black gold, which on the basis of proved finds to date, should last for at least 25 years. Today, a similar transformation is taking place under the North Sea from which the United Kingdom hopes to become self-sufficient in oil supplies.

The overall picture is therefore reassuring both physically and statistically. It is a particular source of comfort because today, and for many decades to come, there can be no alternative to oil . . .

from *The Times*, 5 July 1972.

Gases
'Solid' fuel found in Soviet Union

Overall resources amounting to some 10 billion cubic metres of gas may be present in the areas of permafrost which cover half the Soviet Union. So far, more than 30 deposits of this "solid" gas have been found.

Natural gas combines with water to form a hydrate. This has been known for a long time, but it is only recently that discoveries have shown that at great depths, under conditions of extreme pressure and very low temperature, 50 times as much gas combines with each litre of water, giving a concentration of 200 cubic metres of gas equivalent a litre. Conditions suitable for the formation of this concentrated gas/water compound are found underneath areas of permafrost, and here it will naturally be in its solid state. But if the pressure on the hydrate is reduced, or some catalyst, having a similar effect to that of salt on ice, can be added, the gas can be liberated and piped to industrial centres in the usual way.

The first of the hydrate deposits to yield commercial quantities of gas is in operation near Norilsk.

By **Nature-Times News Service**
© **Nature-Times News Service, 1971.**
The Times, 25.3.71.

World's reserves of oil

From Mr Gerald Foley

Sir, Mario Salvatorelli's article "No substitute for oil—and known reserves are increasing" could give rise to a number of important misconceptions.

Known reserves are indeed increasing but they are not increasing nearly fast enough. The all-important figure in this context is the ratio between reserves and production. This has been in steady decline since the mid-fifties. Last year it fell again and now stands at about 35. That means present known reserves would last 35 years at present rates of production.

It is presumably this which your correspondent has in mind when he gives a date of 2006 for the depletion of present reserves. At the $7\frac{1}{2}$ per cent growth in consumption which he quotes these reserves would last about 15 years—until 1987!

The ultimate total of oil ever likely to be recovered is quoted as 234 billion tons. This is in the middle of the range of estimates now being quoted by informed and responsible opinion. It can scarcely be regarded as unduly conservative or cause for painting a picture which is "reassuring both physically and statistically".

Using Salvatorelli's own growth figures all these reserves would be completely exhausted by about 1995. Even if we go no further than he does and take the figure of 5,960 million tons a year in 1985 as the highest consumption we are ever likely to reach there would only be 29 years' consumption left before the last recoverable drop was used—hardly a reassuring "many decades to come".

But of course this pattern of high growth or high consumption until all the oil is used is not possible. Consumption declines as scarcity grows. The theoretical depletion pattern shows a levelling off of consumption midway through the depletion.

Beyond this point consumption declines. For a 234 billion ton ultimate reserve total this absolute decline would begin in about 1988 with a slackening in the growth of consumption commencing within the next decade. Such curves have been drawn by Warman of BP and by King Hubbert in the United States (v *Scientific American*, September, 1971) and deserve to be more widely known because of their importance.

The theoretical model is however optimistic. It postulates an ideal situation of global cooperation to extract oil from all sources difficult and easy alike with capital resources flowing freely as required. Political reality is different as was pointed out by your Diplomatic Correspondent, A. M. Randel, last month (June 24) and can only act to make the situation worse than the theoretical.

Far from giving any cause for confidence the situation as described by Salvatorelli—and there are many who would paint it blacker—is very disturbing. The time-scale before pressures of scarcity, that is demand outstripping supply, albeit at higher levels of consumption than now, is extraordinarily short. Quite possibly it is within the present decade.

This clearly has immense implications for all areas of our social and industrial activity. Transport and urban planning come immediately to mind. The current estimates of trebled road traffic by the end of the century on which so much planning is based can no longer be regarded as realistic. Indeed the position of the motor industry itself must begin to come into question.

These are issues which need full and urgent debate.

Yours faithfully,
GERALD FOLEY,
12 Whitehall Gardens,
London W4 3LT.
July 5.

Figure 4.7

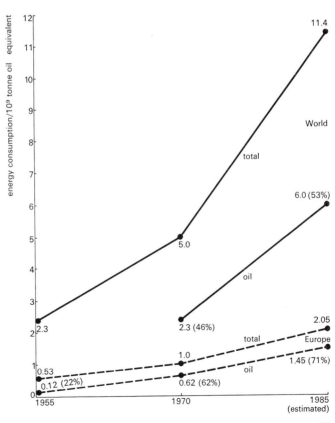

195

Sources of energy

The sources available are winds, tides, geothermal energy, and solar radiation.

The table below shows (on a logarithmic scale) the values of various energy transfers and energy stores. (Condensed from a table compiled by John Harpum in *The elements rage* by F. W. Lane. The original scale was in ergs and has been converted to joules – 10^7 ergs = 1 joule.)

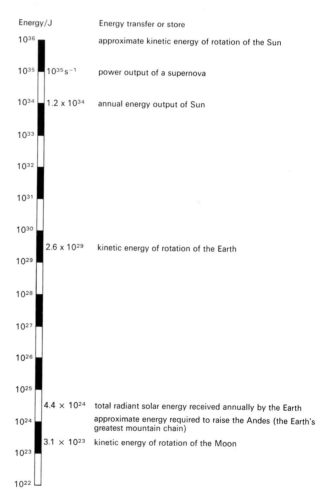

Energy/J		Energy transfer or store
10^{36}		approximate kinetic energy of rotation of the Sun
10^{35}	$10^{35}\,\text{s}^{-1}$	power output of a supernova
10^{34}	1.2×10^{34}	annual energy output of Sun
10^{33}		
10^{32}		
10^{31}		
10^{30}		
	2.6×10^{29}	kinetic energy of rotation of the Earth
10^{29}		
10^{28}		
10^{27}		
10^{26}		
10^{25}		
	4.4×10^{24}	total radiant solar energy received annually by the Earth
10^{24}		approximate energy required to raise the Andes (the Earth's greatest mountain chain)
	3.1×10^{23}	kinetic energy of rotation of the Moon
10^{23}		
10^{22}		

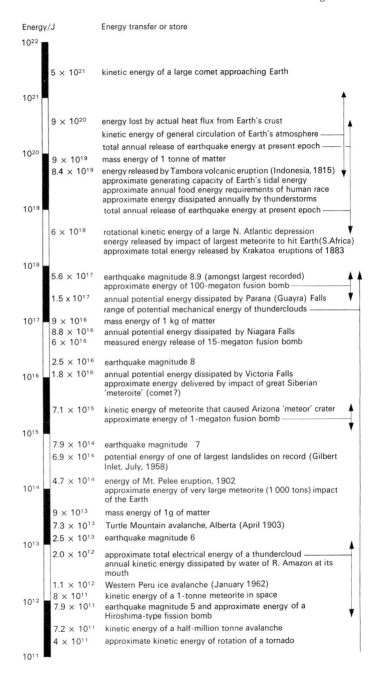

Energy/J   Energy transfer or store

10^{22}

5×10^{21} kinetic energy of a large comet approaching Earth

10^{21}

9×10^{20} energy lost by actual heat flux from Earth's crust
                 kinetic energy of general circulation of Earth's atmosphere ———
                 total annual release of earthquake energy at present epoch ———
10^{20}
9×10^{19} mass energy of 1 tonne of matter
8.4×10^{19} energy released by Tambora volcanic eruption (Indonesia, 1815)
                 approximate generating capacity of Earth's tidal energy
                 approximate annual food energy requirements of human race
                 approximate energy dissipated annually by thunderstorms
10^{19} total annual release of earthquake energy at present epoch ———

6×10^{18} rotational kinetic energy of a large N. Atlantic depression
                 energy released by impact of largest meteorite to hit Earth(S.Africa)
                 approximate total energy released by Krakatoa eruptions of 1883

10^{18}
5.6×10^{17} earthquake magnitude 8.9 (amongst largest recorded)
                 approximate energy of 100-megaton fusion bomb ———

1.5×10^{17} annual potential energy dissipated by Parana (Guayra) Falls
                 range of potential mechanical energy of thunderclouds ———
10^{17} 9×10^{16} mass energy of 1 kg of matter
8.8×10^{16} annual potential energy dissipated by Niagara Falls
6×10^{16} measured energy release of 15-megaton fusion bomb

2.5×10^{16} earthquake magnitude 8
10^{16} 1.8×10^{16} annual potential energy dissipated by Victoria Falls
                 approximate energy delivered by impact of great Siberian
                 'meteorite' (comet?)

7.1×10^{15} kinetic energy of meteorite that caused Arizona 'meteor' crater
                 approximate energy of 1-megaton fusion bomb ———

10^{15}
7.9×10^{14} earthquake magnitude 7
6.9×10^{14} potential energy of one of largest landslides on record (Gilbert
                 Inlet, July, 1958)

4.7×10^{14} energy of Mt. Pelee eruption, 1902
10^{14} approximate energy of very large meteorite (1 000 tons) impact
                 of the Earth

9×10^{13} mass energy of 1g of matter
7.3×10^{13} Turtle Mountain avalanche, Alberta (April 1903)
2.5×10^{13} earthquake magnitude 6
10^{13}
2.0×10^{12} approximate total electrical energy of a thundercloud ———
                 annual kinetic energy dissipated by water of R. Amazon at its
                 mouth
1.1×10^{12} Western Peru ice avalanche (January 1962)
8×10^{11} kinetic energy of a 1-tonne meteorite in space
10^{12} 7.9×10^{11} earthquake magnitude 5 and approximate energy of a
                 Hiroshima-type fission bomb

7.2×10^{11} kinetic energy of a half-million tonne avalanche
4×10^{11} approximate kinetic energy of rotation of a tornado

10^{11}

197

Sources of energy

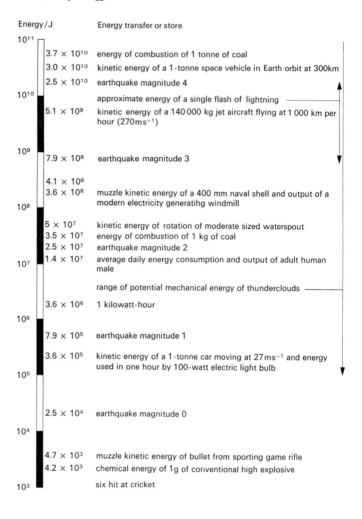

Energy/J   Energy transfer or store

10^{11}

3.7×10^{10} energy of combustion of 1 tonne of coal

3.0×10^{10} kinetic energy of a 1-tonne space vehicle in Earth orbit at 300km

2.5×10^{10} earthquake magnitude 4

10^{10} approximate energy of a single flash of lightning ———

5.1×10^{9} kinetic energy of a 140 000 kg jet aircraft flying at 1 000 km per hour (270ms⁻¹)

10^{9}

7.9×10^{8} earthquake magnitude 3

4.1×10^{8}

3.6×10^{8} muzzle kinetic energy of a 400 mm naval shell and output of a modern electricity generatihg windmill

10^{8}

5×10^{7} kinetic energy of rotation of moderate sized waterspout

3.5×10^{7} energy of combustion of 1 kg of coal

2.5×10^{7} earthquake magnitude 2

1.4×10^{7} average daily energy consumption and output of adult human male

10^{7} range of potential mechanical energy of thunderclouds ———

3.6×10^{6} 1 kilowatt-hour

10^{6}

7.9×10^{5} earthquake magnitude 1

3.6×10^{5} kinetic energy of a 1-tonne car moving at 27ms⁻¹ and energy used in one hour by 100-watt electric light bulb

10^{5}

2.5×10^{4} earthquake magnitude 0

10^{4}

4.7×10^{3} muzzle kinetic energy of bullet from sporting game rifle

4.2×10^{3} chemical energy of 1g of conventional high explosive

10^{3} six hit at cricket

The table shows present and estimated future total use of energy from geothermal sources in the main countries concerned.

Country	Present use/MW	Possible future use/MW
Italy	330	330
New Zealand	150	280
Iceland	80	500
United States	10	100
El Salvador	0	100

(Source: Science Journal, based on 1961 UN survey)

The total power in principle available from winds and tides would be much greater. Wind power is very suitable for remote areas as the following extract shows.

Communication
Windmill drives telephones

The Swedish Telecommunications Administration has reverted to windmills to provide telephones in villages without access to main electricity supplies. In Sweden's rugged environment many remote hamlets have no electric current. One of these, Ruokto, now has a wind-driven electric plant which serves an automatic telephone exchange for 10 subscribers.

The windmill itself differs considerably from the old style grinding mills. Its six-bladed propeller, two and a half metres in diameter, starts revolving when the wind speed is about 5 metres a second, and stops when the wind drops below 3.5 metres a second.

With a maximum output of 300 watts, for wind speeds above 15 metres a second, this installation north of the Arctic Circle should be well able to accommodate the needs of its exchange.

By **Nature-Times News Service**
© **Nature-Times News Service, 1971**
The Times: date not known.

The following data relating to solar radiation may be found useful.

Effective wavelength range: 0.4 to 3.0 μm.
Half radiation in visible range: 0.4 to 0.7 μm.
(For comparison the range emitted by black object at 100 °C is from 5.0 to 30 μm with a peak at about 8 μm.)

If the Jodrell Bank radio telescope dish (diameter 75 m) were used to collect solar energy the maximum power transfer would be 300 kW. It has been calculated that the capital cost of such a project would be about ten times that of an equivalent conventional power station.

The diagram (figure 4.8) shows, in simplified schematic form, the energy transfers for the whole Earth system, and the various 'banks' or stores of energy.

Pupils should not be allowed to ignore the fact that growing vegetation is one way of harnessing solar radiation, which can be of very low capital cost and quite low labour cost. Present-day photosynthesis is in a quite different category from that in the past as far as energy resources are concerned.

The temperature increases with depth below the Earth's surface at a rate of $0.01-0.04 \, Km^{-1}$, and this can only mean an energy flow out of the interior.

Investigation 4.20 Why is it hot in the tropics?

This investigation provides a lead into the topic book *Weather patterns* in which the questions asked are more fully answered. Temperature differences between the tropics and the poles can be treated qualitatively in a simple way. Temperatures at the tropics are higher because the Sun is directly overhead (the angle of incidence of radiation is more nearly $90°$ – in simple qualitative terms the radiation is more 'concentrated'), for longer periods and also has less atmosphere through which to travel.

Temperature differences between the tropics and the poles are less marked as a result of the redistribution of energy by large scale movements of air. These in turn are the result of the temperature differences themselves. Apart from objective 2e other patterns, which one might expect to be in the everyday experience of the pupil, are obviously used.

Figure 4.8 The rate at which various energy transfers take place within the Earth-Sun system

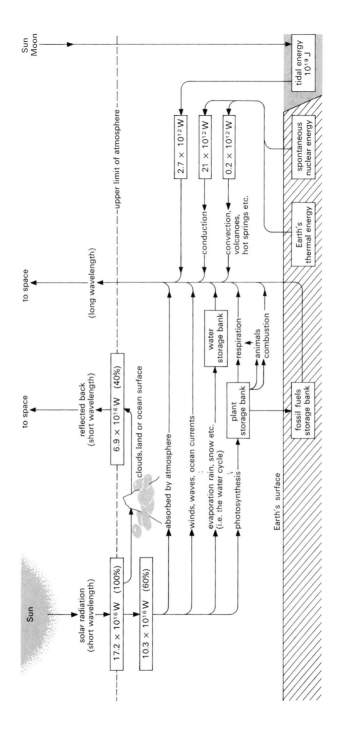

Sources of energy

Sample questions

1 The following graphs illustrate the daily diets of four different children over several years. All of the children had an adequate supply of vitamins and the elements essential for growth.

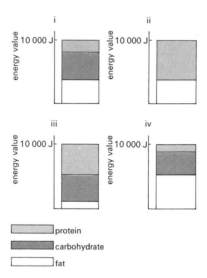

protein

carbohydrate

fat

Which one of the children is likely to be the least healthy?

A i

B ii

C iii

D iv (correct)

Study the food web below and answer questions 2 and 3 which follow.

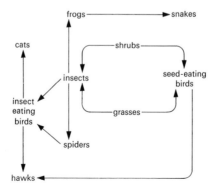

2 Which one of the following pairs would be best described as herbivores?

   A seed-eating birds and insects (correct)

   B spiders and frogs

   C shrubs and grasses

   D hawks and cats

3 Snakes and hawks are best described as:

   A producers

   B consumers

   C predators (correct)

   D decomposers

   Questions 4 to 6 refer to the following paragraph.

   An oak tree grows in a forest, but is blown down in a gale. It begins to decay. Mosses, green algae, and micro-organisms (moulds and bacteria) can be found living in and on the decaying tree. Wood-boring beetle grubs, worms, spiders, and some young frogs are also found on, in or under the tree.

4 Which one of the following is a decomposer?

   A moulds (correct)

   B green algae

   C mosses

   D wood-boring beetle grubs

5 Which one of the following is a consumer?

   A mosses

   B frogs

   C bacteria

   D wood-boring beetle grubs (correct)

6 Draw a food web to represent the above system.

7 There are two major parts to the production of carbohydrates by green plants. In one, light is involved: in the other, enzymes are involved. Which one of the following would provide evidence for this?

   A photosynthesis will be influenced by a change in light intensity

   B photosynthesis will be influenced by a change in concentration of carbon dioxide

   C photosynthesis will be influenced by a change in temperature at very high light intensities (correct)

   D photosynthesis will be influenced by a change in carbon dioxide concentration at very high light intensities

8 A suggestion has been made that the most efficient and convenient form of agriculture for less-developed countries would be to replace existing crops by a single crop, part of which could be used as the sole source of food for people, and the remainder as fuel for driving engines as well as for warming dwellings. Write a few sentences indicating what qualities would be essential in a

crop which could be used for this purpose. Assuming that a suitable crop could be found, give reasons why you think such a crop might not be used.

9 It is assumed that height and mass can be used to measure the

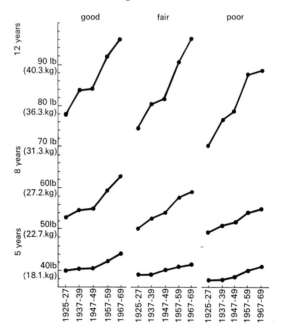

comparative average masses of girls in five 3-year periods

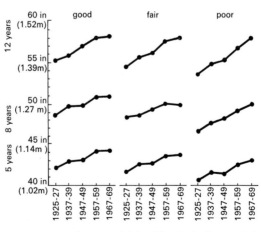

comparative average heights of boys in five 3-year periods

adequacy of a diet (greater mass and height suggesting a better diet). If this is a reasonable assumption what patterns are shown by the data in the two figures on page 204? ('Good', 'Fair' and 'Poor' indicate the type of district in which the children live.)

10

Substance	Latent heat/ kJ mole^{-1}	Boiling point/K	Transfer of energy on burning/kJ mole^{-1}
1	0.3	82	283
2	0.5	112	890
3	1.3	240	—
4	0.01	4	—

(273 K = 0°C)

a From the data, which one of the substances would make the best fuel (assuming costs are equal)?

A 1

B 2 (correct)

C 3

D 4

b Which of the substances would make a good refrigerant?

A 1

B 2

C 3 (correct)

D 4

11 Which of the following are *not* fuels?

 i hot springs

 ii electricity

iii manufactured gas

A i and iii

B i only

C ii only

D i and ii (correct)

12 An inventor claims to have designed a new engine in which water and carbon dioxide are caused to interact to produce food, at the same time releasing useful energy. Why should you be highly sceptical about this?

A food must be grown naturally

B carbon dioxide is difficult to obtain in quantity

C food made from water and carbon dioxide would not represent a balanced diet

D food releases energy when it interacts forming water and carbon dioxide, so the reverse would not release energy. (correct)

▷13 An oil leak was reported. Which is the most likely place for the leak to have occurred?

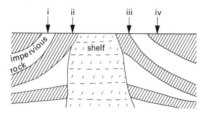

A i
B ii (correct)
C iii
D iv

14 Some people suggest there could be a danger of an energy shortage throughout the world in the future, because the use of energy is increasing, but fuel supplies are limited. A journalist writes an article pointing out that this must be nonsense, since there is a well-known principle in science that energy is conserved. Which of the following is the best reply to the journalist?
A scientific principles are always liable to be proved incorrect
B one can always find new supplies of fuel
C the principle is accepted by scientists, but does not apply in this case
D the principle is accepted by scientists, but utilising fuels and other energy sources spreads the energy out so that it is less useful (correct)

15 Imagine that a decision has to be made about which way energy should be supplied to a factory in a remote area where a large-scale chemical process is performed requiring a considerable amount of energy. The choice is between oil, coal and gas. Which one of the following is not directly relevant to this decision?
A possibility of supplies being cut off
B availability of cooling water (correct)
C the possible need to purify waste gases before releasing them to the atmosphere
D the possible need to dispose of solid wastes

16 Coal output for the UK is shown in millions of tonnes.

Year	Output	Export
1800	11	0.2
1850	49	3
1900	227	44
1950	204	20
1955	210	16
1960	194	5
1965	187	4

Which one of the following can best be deduced from the information in the table?

A there is no future for the coal industry in the UK

B the coal industry continues to expand rapidly

C we are heading for large redundancies in the coal industry

D the coal industry is important to the UK, though not so important as it was once. (correct)

17 A man wishes to put a central heating system into his house, and has to decide between four systems: gas, solid fuel, off-peak electricity and oil. The cost of putting the systems in (installation), the price of the energy supplied, and the efficiency are shown in the table.

a What is the annual cost of running each system? Draw a graph to show how the total cost (installation plus running cost) varies for the four systems during the first eight years. Which system is cheapest during the first eight years? Which system is cheapest over the first two years? over the first five years? Assume that 10^5 MJ of useful energy are needed each year, and ignore any price changes that may occur.

Fuel	Installation	Price of energy/ $p\,MJ^{-1}$	Efficiency/ per cent
Gas	£400	0.077	70
Solid fuel	£350	0.070	70
Electricity	£200	0.120	100
Oil	£350	0.060	75

b In fact the man decides to put in a gas system. Which of the following are sensible reasons for his choice?

i the distribution method means the supply is unlikely to be cut off

ii the discovery of Natural Gas under the North Sea makes it likely
that gas will become cheaper relative to the other systems

iii over a long period it is bound to be cheaper than the other systems

    A i and ii (correct)
    B i and iii
    C ii and iii
    D iii only

18 The table gives information about four elements.

Element	Energy required to vaporise/ $kJ\,mol^{-1}$	Nature of oxide produced on burning in air	Energy transformed when one mole is burnt in air/kJ	Volume of 1 mole at room temp./cm^{-3}
A	0.42	neutral	146	1 200
B	12.6	strongly acidic	393	15.5
C	136.0	strongly basic	598	14
D	719.6	slightly acidic	393	5.3

On this evidence alone, answer the following questions:

a which two of the four elements listed would you choose as
domestic fuels? Explain why you made this choice and also why
you rejected the other two elements.

b how could both of the elements chosen be stored in the home?

c what other factors in addition to storage need to be taken into
consideration in using these two elements as domestic fuels?

5 Using energy efficiently

Introduction

One of the most important technical problems for man is how to harness energy. The main principles governing this process are the first law of thermodynamics (i.e. the conservation of energy, roughly speaking) and the second law of thermodynamics (concerned with the efficiency of energy transfer, and how this is related to temperature). In *Patterns*, the conservation of energy is one of the listed patterns, but a full treatment of the second law is not attempted. However, it is expected that pupils will become familiar with the tendency of energy to 'spread', i.e. to be shared among the particles of a system, and with the fact that energy which has become shared in this way is difficult to harness. The section starts with work to reinforce and extend the concepts of potential and kinetic energy as a preparation for consideration of the efficiency of mechanical transfers. Then the efficiency of chemical transfer of energy is dealt with, followed by the efficiency of its electrical transfer, which leads to quantitative work on transmission lines and high voltages. Finally, the efficiency of energy transfer in a food chain/web is considered.

In all of these instances it is found that a good way to increase efficiency is to minimise or eliminate steps in which energy is shared among the particles of a system in a random manner (recognised as a temperature rise). This work draws heavily on concepts and patterns developed in earlier sections of *Patterns 3: Energy*, and emphasises the importance for people of the different energy transfers being performed efficiently.

Lastly the control of energy transfer (including automatic control) is examined leading to the concept of homeostasis, which is applied to both biological and physical systems, and extends beyond energy control.

Objectives

Skills

1 To recall and understand the following concepts: system, energy transfer, energy spread, energy conservation, position, motion, distribution, efficiency, temperature, resistance, current, power,

chemical bond, food chain/web, pyramid of number/biomass/ productivity, control, equilibrium, feedback, homeostasis.

2 To recall and to understand the following patterns.

a A system can possess energy (i) because the whole system or parts of it are in motion (kinetic energy) and (ii) because of the position of its parts in relation to other parts with which they interact (potential energy).

b The efficiency of many energy transfers can be increased by minimising processes which lead to energy being spread (i.e. shared) among the particles of a system.

c Energy is required to break a chemical bond: energy is released when a chemical bond is formed.

d General models of food chains/webs can be expressed in quantitative forms as pyramids of number, biomass, energy, or energy transferred per unit area per unit time (productivity). As energy passes through a food chain/web the amount available for future use by organisms decreases.

e Homeostasis (equilibrium involving control through feedback, i.e. automatic control) is a property of many systems but particularly of those involving living building blocks.

(These patterns are linked to patterns in the *Teachers' handbook* as follows: 2a with 30; 2b with 37; 2c with 22; 2d with 29, 37 and 48; 2e with 47. Patterns 34 and 36 are implicit throughout this section.)

3 To solve problems using the above (and other) patterns (4).

▷4 To be aware that predictions of electrical demand rely on a critical appraisal of information about past demand to establish patterns of trend and statistical variation, and that consequently these predictions may on occasions be considerably in error (3, 4).

5 To design and perform experiments to investigate electrical transmission of power quantitatively in the laboratory (8).

6 To understand that the problem of transmitting large amounts of power electrically is solved by using high voltages (despite the inherent difficulties), and by using alternating currents because these can be transformed easily and efficiently to higher or lower voltages (6).

7 To have some awareness of the technical, social and economic problems associated with transmitting power across the country electrically (6).

8 To understand the significance of patterns of energy transfer for agricultural methods (6).

▷9 To design an investigation into the control of body water content by the kidney (8).

▷10 To understand that a transistor is a semiconductor device with many applications in the fields of control and amplification of electric signals (6).

Attitudes

11 To be concerned about the impact of electrical transmission of power on the visual environment (11).

12 To be sceptical about some quantitative models of the food chain/web and to be willing to search for more precise expressions (10).

13 To be concerned about certain methods of agriculture practised in relation to objective 8 (11).

Flow diagram

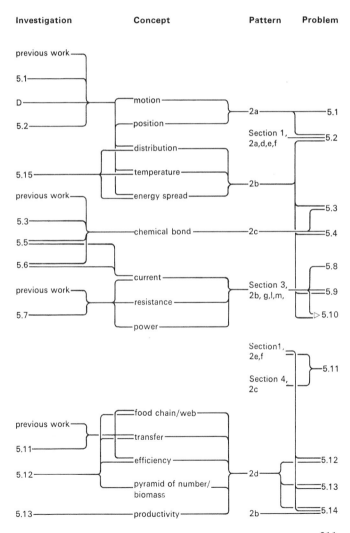

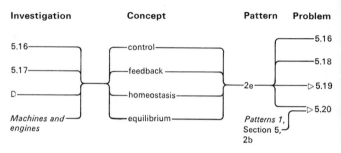

Patterns 34 and 36 (see *Teachers' handbook*) are implicit through-out and the concept of system is useful.

Sample scheme

Time allocation for this section: $4\frac{1}{2}$ weeks.

	Description	Reference	Notes
►5.1	Storing energy and using energy		Kinetic energy and various forms of potential energy
►5.2	Increasing mechanical efficiency		
D	Causes of inefficiency		
▷B	*Friction*	*Patterns* topic book	
►5.3	Using the energy from chemical interactions mechanically		Demonstration
►5.4	Increasing the efficiency of the link between the chemical interaction and the machine		
5.5	Using the energy from chemical reactions electrically		

	Description	Reference	Notes
5.6	Increasing the efficiency of the link between chemical reactions and electricity		
5.7	Transferring energy electrically	NP Year IV, expt 154 a, b, c	Experiment and/or demonstration
▶ 5.8	Increasing the efficiency of electrical transfer of energy	NP Year IV expt 154d	Theoretical problem and demonstration
▶ 5.9	Why use overhead cables?		Relates the human problems to the scientific patterns
D	Electricity and the environment		
▷ ▶ 5.10	Electricity generation and distribution		Deals with planning and prediction of demand
▷ T	*Titans of tomorrow*	Films from CEGB Film Library, 15 Newgate St. London EC1	Power station construction
▷ T	*Anywhere but here*		Problems of electricity distribution
▷ R	*Electricity and the environment*	Booklets published by CEGB	
▷ R	*Power controlled*		Also suitable for pupils
▷ R	*How electricity is made and transmitted*		Also suitable for pupils
▷ R	*Overhead or underground : the facts*	Estates and Wayleaves Bulletin no. 8 (Nov 1969), CEGB	For teachers

		Description	Reference	Notes
▷	R	*Ecological energetics*	Philipson, J., Edward Arnold for Institute of Biology 1966	Useful background concisely presented
▶	5.11	What is the fate of energy as it is transferred through a food chain/web?		
▶	5.12	Constructing a quantitative model of a food chain		
▶	5.13	Limitations of the food web model		
▶	5.14	Efficiency and food production	NSS Field 3.17	Factory farming considered
	5.15	Throwing away energy		
▶	5.16	Controlling energy transfer	NSS Field 5.42	Substitute the section 'Control' in topic book *Machines and engines* if time is short
	5.17	Automatic control		Automatic control of constant state involving feedback, application to both physical and biological systems
D		Homeostasis		
D		Automation		
▶	5.18	Do changes in environmental temperature affect body temperature?		
▷ ▶	5.19	How does the body respond to a variable intake of water?	NSS Field 3.18	Mainly an exercise in controlled investigation

214

Description	Reference	Notes
▷ ▶ 5.20 The kidney: an organ of control	NB Year IV, Ch 14	
▷ T *The kidney*	Film loop, Macmillan	
B *Machines and engines*	*Patterns* topic book	Section on 'Control'

Teaching progression

Potential energy and kinetic energy (the labels do not have to be remembered) are elaborated by way of many examples in Investigation 5.1, achieving objective 2a and raising economic questions also. The hints about efficiency in this investigation are taken further in respect of mechanical transfer of energy in Investigation 5.2, introducing the first aspect of objective 2b. It consists entirely of problems using patterns from earlier sections, and the same is true of many of the investigations in this section. Objective 2b is further achieved by 'chemical system efficiency' in Investigations 5.3–5.6. Objective 2c is also achieved here.

The efficiency considerations of transferring energy by electrical means (objective 2b) are dealt with in Investigations 5.7 to 5.10. The qualitative observations of the advantage of high-voltage transmission lead to the mathematical and experimental analysis of the situation (objectives 5 and 6) which in turn leads to economic, technological and social (environmental) questions in connexion with overhead transmission (objectives 7 and 11).

The human implications of prediction in situations subject to both random and systematic variation are dealt with in ▷ Investigation 5.10, achieving ▷ objective 4, and this investigation also compares electrical transfer of energy with other possible methods of transfer on a large scale.

Investigations 5.11–5.13 gradually build up the achievement of objective 2d. This objective has a strong relationship with objective 2f, Section 1 (linked to pattern 37 in the *Teachers' handbook*) and will also contribute to the overall achievement of pattern 48 (see *Teachers' handbook* and *Patterns 4*). Investigation 5.11 uses the efficiency pattern to help pupils understand how little solar energy is eventually useful in terms of food. It must be pointed out that this pattern is used in a somewhat novel way: 'Joules consumed' as 'total energy transferred'. Pattern 2f, Section 1, also helps to explain why food chains are relatively short. Because energy is dissipated through respiration and consequent loss to the surroundings (see Section 1, objective 2f) at each

215

stage in a food chain, it is relatively easy to predict and construct quantitative models of food chains. Thus Investigations 5.12 and 5.13 achieve objective 2d and objective 12. Because of the inefficiency of food chains, agricultural methods are designed to reduce the energy loss to the surroundings (see also objective 2b). These methods are considered in Investigation 5.14 (and in Investigation 5.11 to some extent) in which objective 8 is achieved. However, some modern agricultural practices, designed to minimise energy dissipation, are the cause of much concern (objective 13).

Investigation 5.15 raises some of the 'second-law' questions which cannot be covered fully, bringing out the fact that while reducing the energy shared among the particles of a system is desirable (objective 2b) it is not completely possible.

The remainder of this section is concerned with the control of energy transfers, a topic of increasing importance leading to such applications as automatic devices, robots and automation, and applying also to biological systems. The ideas of feedback and homeostasis are introduced. (Objective 2e.)

Objective 2e is used in Investigation 5.18 and ▷Investigation 5.19, although in the latter the problem component is largely associated with the experimental design. Investigation 5.18 will relate closely to work done in Investigation 5.17 and in Section 2. ▷Investigation 5.20 examines the kidney as an organ of control. Its structural and functional relationships are considered.

Teaching notes

Investigation 5.1 Storing energy and using energy

Not all the systems would be used on any given occasion, but enough would be used to develop the ideas of potential and kinetic energy and to show that they apply to widely diverse situations.

To a large extent the questions posed near the beginning of the investigation have similar answers for all systems.

i The storage of energy is recognised by the fact that it can be transferred to do a job which is known to require energy (many examples might be chosen). The capacity to transfer energy really is the significant attribute of an 'energy store' because if, for a system which had not hitherto been regarded as one, a new transfer-mechanism was developed, it would then become an energy store. An example of this sort would be the hydrogen in sea water. If, and when, a controlled nuclear fusion process becomes available this hydrogen will represent an almost unlimited energy store. A more prosaic example is a mass at a certain level, which represents an energy store only if there is a mechanism for lowering it and utilising the energy thus transferred. (Strictly it is the mass/Earth system from which energy is transferred.)

ii In some cases a force can be observed at the macroscopic level, and forces are used in all explanations of potential energy at the particle level. Forces are not essentially involved in the case of kinetic energy. The question of kinetic energy and relative motion is avoided here.

iii In every potential energy example forces between particle building blocks can be envisaged, and where macroscopic forces can be observed the larger objects involved are obvious.

iv Although the forces commonly vary with distance, in each case the idea that the energy transfer is measured by the work (force × distance) can be applied.

v Any moving parts have kinetic energy.

vi The answers to this question are clearly specific to the system considered. Some suggestions follow.

Part a

Repelling magnets close together, or attracting magnets at a distance, store energy. Almost any uses of magnets can be considered in energy terms.

Part b

This system is similar to a hydro-electric scheme in essentials.

Part c

Repulsion between similarly charged particle building blocks is an essential part of chemical theory.

Part d

For details of this experiment see Nuffield Physics *Guide to experiments IV*, experiment 119, a, b, c, d. A high capacitance, 12-V capacitor will drive a small motor for a brief time. Very high capacitance capacitors are now available. Electrolytic capacitors should be connected to the battery with care in order to obtain the correct polarity. All capacitors should be discharged after use to avoid accidental shocks.

The general explanation is as follows. Charged particles (normally electrons) flow round the circuit until the potential difference between the plates is the same as that provided by the battery. A deficit of electrons on one plate and a surplus on the other lead to unbalanced (long range) forces of attraction between the particles of the plates (this is balanced by mechanical forces holding the plates apart, i.e. 'contact' forces between other particles (atoms and/or molecules)). When the plates are connected through a load, the potential difference through the circuit (corresponding to a force-gradient through the circuit on any charged particle) causes a flow of charged particles and consequent energy transfer.

Capacitors are useful energy stores only for short periods, because of leakage problems.

Part e

As always the pressure force (macroscopic) can be identified with innumerable particle-impact forces. Compressed air systems are used industrially and on many heavy vehicles as energy stores.

Part f

Used for simple model aeroplanes, catapults.

Part g

Many applications, e.g. retractable ball-point pen.

Part h

Details can be kept to a minimum. In many ways a cell can be likened to a capacitor.

Part i

The interaction of hydrogen ions and hydroxyl ions is based on the supposition of electrostatic forces. The main effect is temperature rise.

Part j

In this case some energy is transferred on account of the volume change ('pushing back the atmosphere'). A similar effect is used in soda/acid fire extinguishers.

Part k

As in any chemical interaction, the forces involved are those leading to bonding. The parallel with respiration should be well-known by now.

Part l

Kinetic energy only (unless such matters as height above the floor are considered).

Part m

Rotational kinetic energy can be considered in terms of the particles of the object, which at any instant have each a certain speed. The direction of motion continually changes, but this does not affect the energy available for transfer if the speed of each particle is unaltered.

Flywheels are important for car engines, many industrial machines, and in a tape recorder (to minimise speed fluctuations).

Part n

A continual interchange takes place between kinetic energy (maximum at the mid-point, i.e. the equilibrium position) and potential energy (gravitational and strain). The variation with distance is illustrated in the sketch graph, in which the curves are parabolas (assuming the spring obeys Hooke's law).

Figure 5.1

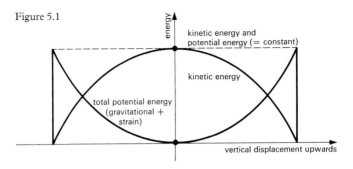

Part o
This system is formally similar to the previous one. In this case, only gravitational potential energy is involved, and in place of the parabola the graph would be a circle. (For small displacements the two would be indistinguishable.)
▷ Part p
This is again a similar oscillatory system, this time with rotational kinetic energy.
▷ Part q
In the absence of resistance this would be an undamped oscillatory system. In practice it is significantly damped in normal instance, but is otherwise similar to parts o and p, although instead of kinetic energy the energy associated with the magnetic field of the current is involved. The kinetic energy of the electrons is very small.
▷ Part r
By now pupils should be thoroughly familiar with the fact that food supplies the energy for all the body's activities.
Part s
Food stores and reserves in the human body act as an energy store (indeed the whole body ultimately) and we are usually in constant motion.

In the latter part of the question the values in the table are very approximate (one significant figure). They do illustrate rather effectively, however, that the economic aspect is important for large-scale transfers of energy, but less so for small-scale ones. Discussion would bring out the fact that in detail the relative and absolute costs are continually changing.

Since energy transfer by a man costs about 2 500 times as much as that from a cheap fuel, the former would be used in preference to the latter only when other factors are important. Typically the important factor has been control, since man is almost totally adaptable to changes in a situation. This means that machines driven by fuel have been used since the early days of the first industrial revolution to do routine and repetitive tasks needing little control, but that human beings have been used where precise control is necessary, either controlling the energy-transfers from fuel or those from food in their bodies.

The trend to much more sophisticated systems for automatic control has led to the situation where, in the foreseeable future, human control may be needed only for the most subtle aspects of work, and the completely automatic factory is at present a practical (if not yet an economic or political) proposition.

The relationship between capital cost and running cost is relevant to fuel cells and solar cells where capital cost is all-important. In less developed countries fuel-based energy transfers tend to cost much more, for obvious reasons, and consequently animal and human labour is still an important means of energy transfer.

The cost of energy transfer in hydro-electric stations would be very variable, depending on the geographical circumstances. The running costs are very small, but the capital costs large.

Capacitors, as stated above, are not practical energy sources over long periods, and in many cases have to be charged using energy from some other source. They might be compared to the pumped storage system used by the CEGB.

Investigation 5.2 Increasing mechanical efficiency
Part a
While it is not difficult to see that there is very little friction involved in the 'good' (i.e. highly efficient) machines like the lever pivoted at its centre of gravity, and the well-pivoted pulley, more thought is required to discern how much friction there is in the others. Very inefficient machines have very obvious frictional forces, dissipating energy among the particles of the system.

Part b
Lubrication, and redesign of bearings are obvious ways to improve efficiency, as is the reduction of unproductive load, e.g. the weight of a pulley block.

▷Part c
The friction of a mechanical jack is sufficient to prevent it slipping back, i.e. it is greater than the corresponding force derived from the weight of the vehicle. When raising the car this friction must be overcome as well as the central load, so the efficiency is below 50 per cent. If it were more than 50 per cent, the friction would be inadequate to keep the car up, but in the normal version a force is needed to help the car down. Friction

is small and viscous drag can be very small in a hydraulic machine. A valve is used to allow the fluid to pass in only one direction. To lower the vehicle this is released, or a by-pass opened.

Part d

The flow to the machine must be inadequate. An obvious reason would be the viscous and surface drag in the pipe. This could be reduced by using a shorter and/or wider pipe.

▷Part e

A higher pressure would overcome the pipe losses and also deliver adequate power to the drill. As in part d, a shorter or wider pipe would improve the efficiency.

In all cases, low efficiency means energy is spread out among the particles of a system, whereas high efficiency means this is prevented.

Investigation 5.3 Using the energy from chemical interactions mechanically

The magnesium and sulphuric acid interact. Fast-moving hydrogen gas molecules are evolved which cause mechanical work to be done when the plunger of the syringe moves. The mechanical work can be calculated by knowing the force on the piston (atmospheric pressure is $103\,000\,\mathrm{N\,m^{-2}}$, so the force on the piston will be about $100\,\mathrm{N}$) and the distance (in metres) which the piston has moved.

Much of the energy made available from the chemical interaction was not used in doing mechanical work. The increase in temperature of the flask and contents shows this.

Investigation 5.4 Increasing the efficiency of the link between chemical interaction and the machine

An extract from *Science* which explains how the engine works is now quoted. (Naturally, no details should be learnt by pupils!)

Mechanochemical Turbine: A New Power Cycle

Abstract. *A basic thermodynamic cycle for the production of mechanical power from materials that may be made to contract forcibly and reversibly is described. The cycle differs from existing mechanical power cycles which generally employ expanding fluid as working substances. A "contraction turbine" operating on this cycle has been devised, which has collagen fiber as its working substance and salt solution as fuel and produces mechanical work directly from chemical free energy. Direct conversion of chemical to mechanical energy is routinely effected in muscle but not in usual man-made engines.*

The direct conversion of chemical free energy into mechanical motion is routinely effected in muscle but does not occur in usual man-made engines. In this laboratory mechanochemical engines have been built which do effect the

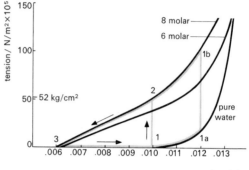

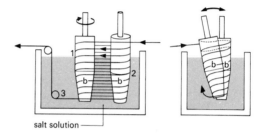

Fig. 1 (top). Tension-length dependence of collagen fiber in LiBr (*2*). Fig. 2 (above). Contractile fiber-actuated turbine. Front and side views. Fiber tension builds up on cylindrical spindle sections between (1) and (2) at constant specific length. Stepwise contraction occurs between (2) and (3) as the fiber helix descends the conical portions of the spindles (*b*).

direct conversion (*1*). We now describe a basic thermodynamic cycle for effecting direct conversion of chemical to mechanical energy. The cycle provides a general method for the production of mechanical power from any material which may be made to contract forcefully and reversibly. We have devised a new engine operating on this cycle whose features are basic for efficient production of mechanical work from contractile (rather than "expansile") working substances. (In mechanical power cycles expanding fluids are normally used as working substances.)

In the new engine, which we call a "contraction turbine," regenerated collagen fiber (*2*) cross-linked by formaldehyde is used as working substance, with the reversible contraction that the fiber demonstrates when immersed in concentrated aqueous salt solution, such as LiBr, $CaCl_2$, $MgCl_2$, and KSCN, producing mechanical shaft work.

Figure 1 shows the variation of force (per unit of dry cross-sectional area) with length of collagen fiber in contact with aqueous solutions of LiBr at various concentrations (*3*). At zero tension the specific length of this particular collagen fiber in $8M$ aqueous LiBr solution (L_0) is 60 percent of its specific length in water (L_w). A tension of 52 kg/cm^2 cross-sectional area is required to maintain the salt-treated fiber at its salt-free length (L_w). The fiber can be repeatedly moved between states on Fig. 1, by subjecting it to the indicated salt concentration and tension, although some degeneration of fiber properties occurs after 100 or more cycles.

These characteristics of collagen in LiBr (and in similar aqueous salt solutions) are exploited to produce mechanical work continuously by subjecting the collagen to the ideal cyclical process 1-2-3-1 (hatched marks in Fig. 1). At 1, water-washed collagen fiber, having

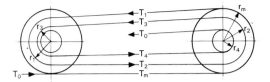

Fig. 3. Contraction turbine. End view showing a four-stage contraction process.

specific length L_w and substantially zero tension, is constrained so that it cannot shrink, and brought into equilibrium with a concentrated LiBr solution. There it absorbs salt and experiences an isometric tension increase (path 1 to 2). The tensed fiber then releases its elastic energy as work by shrinking reversibly along the $8M$ tension length line (path 2 to 3), from maximum tension (at 2) to near zero tension (at 3). (For shrinkage to occur reversibly, the fiber must act against a force which decreases at the same rate as the fiber tension; or the fiber must contract in many small discrete steps, opposed at each step by a force corresponding to the tension at that step.) The cycle is closed by equilibrating the contracted salt-laden fiber with fresh water, and during this process it loses salt and expands to the initial state (path 3 to 1). The cycle may now be repeated.

A practical cycle based on the above ideal cycle was realized by devising means for isometrically tensioning and reversibly contracting the working fiber in a continuous and repetitive fashion. Isometric tensioning of a moving fiber was achieved by using a pair of canted (slightly tilted axes) cylindrical spindles (Fig. 2). Fiber wrapped about a pair of such spindles spontaneously follows a helical path as the spindles rotate. (The helix pitch depends on the axis angle and the spindle diameter.) The spindles run partially submerged in concentrated LiBr. Washed collagen fiber at a tension and specific length corresponding to state 1 (Fig. 1) contacts the spindles above the LiBr solution. After two full turns about both spindles, the specific length of the fiber is fixed at L_w because (i) both spindles have identical surface speeds and (ii) friction between fiber and spindle prevents fiber slippage. So constrained, the collagen spirals down the spindle surface into the LiBr solution where it absorbs salt and experiences a sharp tension rise (path 1 to 2, Fig. 1).

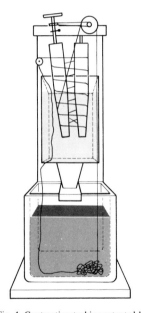

Fig. 4. Contraction turbine actuated by collagen-LiBr. Upper tank contains turbine spindles immersed in LiBr solution. Lower tank is the regenerating (water) bath. Endless collagen fiber loop moves through the cycle in a clockwise direction. Power takeoff is horizontal pulley on upper left.

223

A nearly reversible contraction work process is achieved when conical extensions are placed on each tensioning spindle (*b*; Fig. 2) which function as a multiple-stage contraction turbine. The contractile fiber, in passing helically from one conical spindle to the next, moves repeatedly from a larger to a smaller radius surface, contracting at each pass by a fraction equal to the ratio of the radii. The fiber therefore follows a process resembling the dotted steps in Fig. 1.

Since each complete turn of the fiber helix encompasses two contraction stages, a five-turn helix comes within 90 percent of reversible contraction (*Tx*).

Operation is made continuous by forming the fiber into a closed loop and disposing the spindles and water bath so that the fiber loop passes from one bath to the other.

The maximum mechanical work that can be obtained from collagen fiber moving through the 1-2-3-1 cycle is the area enclosed by the ideal cycle on the tension-length plane (Fig. 1). For fibers having a specific length (dry of 270 cm/g and a density of 1.3 g/cm^3, this area (maximum or reversible work) is 7.85×10^6 erg per gram of fiber. Consequently a turbine, such as that shown in the Fig. 4 photograph, which has a collagen throughput of 0.09 g/sec, has a maximum or ideal power output of 70 mw. Our actual turbine has delivered about 30 mw, corresponding to a mechanical efficiency of 40 percent.

Free energy conversion efficiency (ratio of work output to free energy of dilution of the salt solutions consumed) is at present considerably smaller (>1 percent) than the mechanical efficiency, because relatively large quantities of salt solution and wash water cling to the fiber surface and are mechanically carried from one bath into the other, mixing without contributing to the engine output. This deficiency can probably be reduced by incorporating fiber-wiping devices in the cycle.

The work output per cycle can be augmented if the water-washed fiber is slightly elongated (pretensioned) before immersion in salt solution, as shown by the cycle 1-1a-1b-2-3-1 (Fig. 1). Pretensioning is achieved by placing short inverted conical sections immediately above the cylindrical portions of the turbine spindles. Collagen working fiber can also be fueled with $CaCl_2$, $MgCl_2$, KSCN, and other aqueous solutions. We have in fact operated the turbine in brine taken directly from the Dead Sea.

The turbine and power cycles described here may be employed with any linearly disposed contractile material which undergoes an appreciable reversible shrinkage or tension increase (or both) when subjected to a change in its environmental potential. The environmental change may be other than chemical. For example, a thermally powered contraction turbine can be operated with linear crystalline polyethylene or rubber working fibers, provided that a heat bath replaces the water regenerating bath.

It is thermodynamically possible to operate all of these cycles backward as pumps so that the foregoing thermal engine would function as a refrigerator or air conditioner which uses an elastomeric refrigerant.

M. V. SUSSMAN*
A. KATCHALSKY

Polymer Department, Weizmann Institute of Science, Rehovot, Israel

References and Notes

1. A. Katchalsky, I. Steinberg, A. Oplatka, A. Kam, U.S. Patent No. 3,321,908, 30 May 1967; 1 Steinberg, A. Oplatka, A. Katchalsky. Nature 210, 568 (1966).
2. The collagen fiber, manufactured by Ethicon Corp., Somerville, N.J. is cross-linked by treatment with 0.5 percent formaldehyde before it is used.
3. M. Levy, unpublished data on the force-length dependence of collagen fiber after repeated contractions and expansions.
4. Supported by NIH special research fellowship IF3-GM-36,897-01 (to M.V.S.)

*On leave from the Department of Chemical Engineering, Tufts University, Medford, Mass.

3 June 1969; revised 22 August 1969

Investigation 5.5 Using the energy from chemical interactions electrically
The type of thermometer used will determine whether the poly-ethylene bottle can be used upright or inverted.

Pupils should draw an energy level diagram for the interaction:

$$Zn(s) + Cu^{2+}(aq) \rightarrow Zn^{2+}(aq) + Cu(s)$$

Clearly, it would be foolish to try to make steam by this method, and so perhaps the intermediate step (i.e. the formation of fast-moving steam particles) can be eliminated. (Pupils might like to calculate the mass of zinc needed to boil 1 kg of water, and to estimate the total cost of the operation!)

Investigation 5.6 Increasing the efficiency of the link between chemical interaction and electricity
Part a
The same overall reaction is taking place as that in the previous investigation. The 'half reactions' are:

i $Zn(s) \rightarrow Zn^{2+}(aq) + 2e^-$
ii $Cu^{2+}(aq) + 2e^- \rightarrow Cu(s)$

Reaction i occurs at the zinc rod and reaction ii takes place at the copper rod. The electrons are transferred from the zinc rod to the copper rod via the external circuit. (In time, all Cu^{2+} ions are used up and so the blue solution becomes colourless.) The important point of contrast with the previous investigation is that in the Daniell cell a means has been found for the zinc to react with copper ions without actually being in direct contact with them.

Part b
The two 'half reactions' are

$$Mg(s) \rightarrow Mg^{2+}(aq) + 2e^-$$
$$2H^+ + 2e^- \rightarrow H_2(g)$$

Much of the hydrogen is not evolved at the graphite but at the magnesium and so these electrons are not transferred from graphite to magnesium via the external circuit. The temperature of the acid increases considerably.

Investigation 5.7 Transferring energy electrically
The parallel which is most obvious between electrical transfer and the transfers considered in Investigation 5.2 is that dissipative components are concerned in the opposition to flow in each case. Resistance has similarities to both friction and viscosity, although there are differences of detail.

Part a
The lamp at the distant end of the transmission lines is dimmer, indicating less energy per unit charge is available, i.e. the

225

potential difference across it is less. A voltmeter gives a simple check.

As a.c. is used in part b, there is an argument for using it also in parts a and c. On the other hand a.c. voltmeters are less commonly available.

Part b

Care is needed, in demonstrating with mains voltage. Attention should be given to insulation, and pupils should not be near the transmission lines. Adjustments should be made only with the current switched off at the socket, and preferably with the plug removed also. The two lamps are almost the same in appearance. Pupils may insist on the two lamps being interchanged to make sure they are identical. The fraction of the energy lost in the lines is much less.

Part c

Measuring current and potential difference at both ends will probably be suggested. This can be done, but the current measurement is unnecessary, since it is clearly the same in both cases (assuming ideal voltmeters). If the input potential difference is V_1, and the output potential difference V_2, the efficiency is $V_2 I / V_1 I$, i.e. V_2/V_1.

The efficiency is much greater at the higher voltage, and the reason can be understood as the smaller fraction of the input energy which is dissipated on account of the resistance of the lines.

Investigation 5.8 Increasing the efficiency of electrical transfer of energy

Part a

i 2.0 A, ii 0.10 A are the currents, so that the potential differences in each case needed to drive these currents through the 5 Ω transmission line are 10 V and 0.5 V respectively. In fact 2.0 A does not flow in the first case, because the total resistance is too great.

Part b

A step-up and a step-down transformer, preferably identical, will achieve the desired result. Of course, a.c. is needed. For details see the reference.

Part c

Input power	$= (30\,000 \times 16)\,\text{W} = 480\,\text{kW}$
∴ output power	$= 95\% \times 480\,\text{kW} = 456\,\text{kW}$
∴ output current	$= 456\,000/240 = 1\,900\,\text{A}$
power dissipated	$= 24\,\text{kW}.$

This is equivalent to 24 one-bar electric fires, and if special arrangements to dissipate this to the surroundings are not made the windings could burn out. Oil is commonly used (it also solves insulation problems), and this may circulate by pump or by natural convection.

Part d

The high voltages lead to less power loss for a given power transmitted. The overall efficiency is greater with two transformers than without, except for very short distances. Lower power requirements, and insulation and safety considerations lead to the lower voltages for local distribution.

Investigation 5.9 Why use overhead cables?

This work shows how environmental and aesthetic questions cannot be answered without reference to scientific, technological and economic details. Precise analysis of the situation in scientific terms is needed before the most desirable courses of action can profitably be discussed. Parallels can be drawn with many other instances. Teachers will no doubt refer to topical or local examples.

The case against pylons is sometimes overstated. Very little ground is occupied, and the CEGB is justly proud of its pylon designs.

Part a

Clearly underground cable would be very much more costly.

Part b

The current in the cable $= (4 \times 10^9/4 \times 10^5)\,\text{A} = 10^4\,\text{A}$
The power dissipated per metre $= (10^4 \times 10^4 \times 2.5 \times 10^{-6})\,\text{W}$
$= 250\,\text{W}$

This can readily be lost to the air, but not so readily to soil, particularly when electrical insulation is also present. The cable temperature will be higher, assuming equal area of conductors, and the insulation must stand this temperature. Thicker conductors could be used, and/or special insulation.

Part c

Access is much harder to underground cables, and fault-finding more difficult also.

Parts d and e

While people may disagree on where the balance between economy and appearance should be, it is important for pupils to realise that the question is one of balancing two desirable factors, and that there is no right, or even easy, answer in many cases. Further information is available in the CEGB publication *Overhead or underground? The facts*. The Board does take considerable trouble on occasions to route power lines where they will obtrude least. A relevant fact is that new insulators are being introduced of greater mechanical strength, so that single instead of double supports can be used, with consequent improvement in appearance of the pylons.

▷ *Investigation 5.10* Electricity generation and distribution

The initial questions bring out the point that electricity must be generated when needed. Batteries and capacitors can store only comparatively small quantities of energy (although pumping water to a high reservoir is a method that is occasionally used). Anticipation of demand is thus essential, and the engineers concerned are highly experienced in this. They also need to minimise cost by using the nuclear stations at full load, using thermal stations selectively in order of cost, and using gas turbines and pumped storage for 'topping up' at relatively high cost.

Most of the time people behave fairly predictably, at least on average, and short term weather forecasting is now quite good. However the Meteorological Office does go wrong on occasions, and one can never be sure when a vital football match is going to go on to extra time, or a new series on television becomes unexpectedly popular. The effect of television is indirect, as the power needed for the sets is not very great. The sudden increase comes at a break or at the end of a programme when lights, kettles and cookers go on. It is necessary to have surplus output capacity because breakdowns do occur, and some capacity must be available for unexpected increases in demand. Before 1969, there was a shortage of surplus capacity, and power cuts were more frequent in cold weather. Now the main cause of power cuts is industrial disputes.

The extracts are included to encourage pupils not to consider the present technological practice in any field as the only possible one. The fact that something is done one way can inhibit the introduction of a better way, because of high capital investment in the old way, and uncertainty about problems connected with the new way.

Investigation 5.11 What is the fate of energy as it is transferred along a food chain?

The efficiency of the energy transfer from grass to bullock works out between 3 and 4 per cent. This is rather on the low side due to rounding off of the figures given. The actual 'gross growth efficiency' (joules of growth/joules consumed) for beef cattle raised on grassland is about 4.1 per cent. The remaining energy is lost to the surroundings through respiration and in the non-assimilated grass as faeces. This low efficiency explains why food chains are generally very short usually of no more than four or five links. Most of the 'grass energy' not consumed by the bullock passes to the decomposers and some to the other consumers. To maximise the solar energy 'fixed' by photosynthesis (and this itself is a very small portion of the total) it would clearly be advantageous to be mainly herbivorous, but there are, of course, balanced diet considerations. By reducing the amount of potential food passing to decomposers and to consumers, other than to beef, a greater proportion can be channelled in the desired direction.

Techniques to achieve this include careful regulation of grazing, and cropping and processing grass. Figures 5.2 and 5.3 may be useful at this point. The similarity of figure 5.3 with figure 4.1 can be seen.

Figure 5.2
Building block and
energy transfer in the
individual consumer

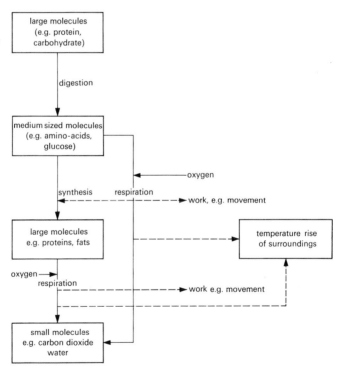

229

Figure 5.3
Building block and
energy transfer in the
community system.
In *Patterns 1* it was
established that
producers obtain
essential building
blocks such as
nitrates for protein
synthesis from the
environment.
However the
availability of such
building blocks has
not yet been overtly
linked with
decomposers (the
nitrogen cycle). Nor
has the production of
oxygen in the
photosynthetic
process been
investigated. Both of
these important links
in the 'web of life'
are dealt with in
Patterns 4. Otherwise
pupils should now be
familiar with the
entire pattern shown

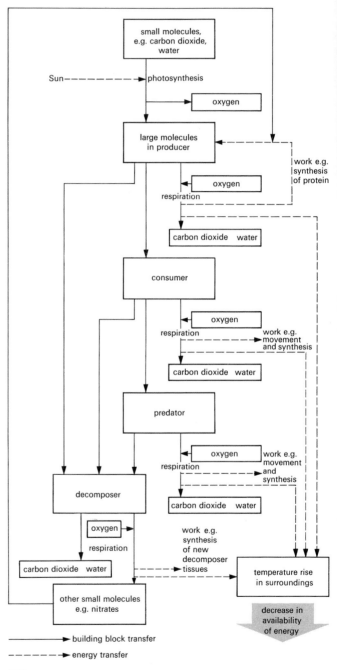

230

Investigation 5.12 Constructing a quantitative model of a food chain

The food chain needs to be set up several weeks beforehand so that it is well established and balanced for this investigation. *Technicians' manual 3* gives full details.

The most 'correct' relationship which pupils are likely to predict can be illustrated as shown in figure 5.4. However, a

Figure 5.4

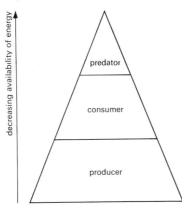

number or biomass relationship may be predicted. The limitations of all these models are discussed below. It is the number relationship which is tested in this investigation. The producers (e.g. algae) can be expected to be most numerous. There will be fewer consumers (e.g. Crustacea such as *Daphnia sp.*) and merely one or two predators (e.g. fish).

The methods used for counting the populations in the three tanks are those used for the mini-pond communities (for a full description see *Patterns 1*, Section 3). If time is pressing a qualitative impression of numbers can be obtained.

Daphnia has a gross growth efficiency of 4–13 per cent. If the main aim were to make the maximum conversion of solar energy into animal protein then clearly *Daphnia* would be a better food animal than beef cattle. However, 'harvesting' problems and food preferences must also be taken into account.

Investigation 5.13 Limitations of food web models

The limitation of the number model can be clearly illustrated by considering an example such as a tree community. Here only one producer supports large numbers of consumers and mass would give a closer approximation to this situation. This can be refined to mass per unit area. Nevertheless the example of the phytoplankton and zooplankton illustrates an apparent anomaly. It

Figure 5.5 A sample taken at a particular time of the year could well show more consumers (zooplankton) than producers (phytoplankton) due to the expected interaction between these two components of the food web

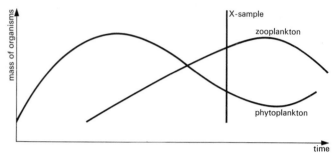

can be explained by reference to figure 5.5. This shows that time is a factor to be considered and that the model should be expressed in terms of mass (or better still, energy per unit area per unit time (i.e. productivity). Figure 5.20 in the *Patterns 3* compares the productivity of various communities.

The productivity of cultivated plant communities can be improved by intensive all-year-round agriculture (hence reducing the time when land is totally unproductive) and by the cultivation of highly efficient 'fixers' of solar energy. Sugarbeet has been shown to fix about 9 per cent of available solar energy during the middle part of its growing season.

Investigation 5.14 Efficiency and food production

The data suggested for use in this experiment stem from an investigation suggested at the end of *Patterns 1*, Section 4. The graph may be expected to flatten as the mouse reaches maturity. The efficiency of the young in converting food to flesh is obviously higher than in older animals. Gross growth efficiency of young beef cattle and chickens is about 35 per cent. (Compare this with the 4–5 per cent over their whole lives – see Investigation 5.11.) To raise livestock beyond the age of maximum growth efficiency is wasteful in terms of food production for man. It is therefore important to determine the optimum moment of sale for slaughter for meat, and pupils should do this for their mouse example.

The figures supplied on pig production show that, for the same amount of pig growth (1 kg) less food is now needed than in the past. (3.8 kg compared with 4.9 kg.) Despite rising costs, the price of bacon has thus been kept down. This increase in efficiency has been achieved in a variety of ways: better pig-food and modern agricultural methods. The latter are considered critically and should prompt much discussion. Factory farming aims to maximise the efficiency of food production by reducing energy 'wastage'. Keeping intensive rearing units warm and restricting movement reduce the energy dissipated to the surroundings. In addition the amount of available plant material reaching the animals is maximised by harvesting and processing so reducing losses to decomposers and other consumers.

Investigation 5.15   Throwing away energy

All the devices illustrated are mechanisms for dissipating energy to the atmosphere. This is another aspect of the second law of thermodynamics which cannot be dealt with thoroughly. It is hoped that the investigation will at least help pupils to realise that improving the efficiency is not altogether a practical suggestion in many instances, as at present operated. All the engines referred to deal at some stage with energy shared among the particles of some system (i.e. thermal energy if a term is needed), and only a relatively small fraction of this can be used in practice for doing useful jobs. Strictly these statements should be phrased in terms of a system performing a complete cycle, so that the net effect is the abstraction of energy from a hot object. When this is done, only a certain fraction is available as work, the rest inevitably going to a cooler object (the surroundings, usually). For more details refer to any text book of thermodynamics, e.g. Bent, H., *Second law: an introduction to classical and statistical thermodynamics*, 1967, Oxford University Press, or Angrist, S. W. and Hepler, L. G., *Order and chaos*, Basic Books, 1967.

Since, when energy is shared among the particles of a system, it is in one sense 'muddled' or randomly distributed, then there is a correspondence between this and more obviously statistical events like mixing coloured balls. Obtaining 'ordered energy' from 'random energy' is what is difficult.

Investigation 5.16   Controlling energy transfer

If time is short Investigations 5.16 and 5.17 could be substituted by the section on 'Control' in the topic book *Machines and engines*.

The various control techniques used in the separate parts of the investigation will help to build up an overall picture of the diversity of ways to achieve similar ends. This is a necessary background to the ideas developed in the next investigation, dealing with automatic control, a topic of increasing importance in many fields.

Part a

Water- and gas-taps have a progressive action, increasing the resistance to flow gradually by decreasing the size of an aperture. The designs can be virtually identical, a simple cock, but both the higher pressure and the need to obtain very small rates of

233

flow lead to the more complex type of water tap usually used. In contrast a light switch is a two-state (bistable) device: the resistance effectively changes from an almost infinite value to one near zero in a very short time.

In the circuit shown a series rheostat which can be gradually cut in would be effective. These are made with a built-in on/off

Figure 5.6

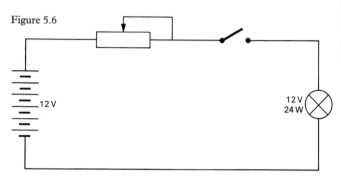

switch for such purposes as volume controls on amplifiers. The maximum value of the resistor is that to cut the current to 250 mA. The total circuit resistance would be $(12/0.25)\,\Omega = 24\,\Omega$, so the rheostat would need to be at least $46\,\Omega$. In practice a $50\,\Omega$ or a $47\,\Omega$ (preferred value) would be used. Faster pupils could calculate the power dissipated when the slider is in a different position, and derive a power rating which would be safe.

▷Part b

Relays represent a very common and very simple application of electromagnetism. Designs and ratings vary considerably but a low operating current is usually desirable since this reduces the power needed for a given magnetic effect. However, it tends to imply a high resistance and high voltage device. One common type of relay is the starting solenoid on a car. The experiment can easily be done with battery, ammeter, rheostat and relay. Valves will need to be found by trial.

▷Part c

Cheap n-p-n silicon transistors are suitable (for sources see radio and electronics magazines). If p-n-p (germanium) transistors are used, all batteries will need to be reversed from the polarity shown in the diagram. A simple way of considering a transistor is as a switch controlled by the potential difference between emitter and base: the emitter-collector resistance is high for low values of this potential difference (a small fraction of a volt) and becomes low above a certain value of this potential difference (less than 0.5 V, usually). The base current is often so small (microampère region) that it is difficult to measure. It is always considerably less than the maximum collector current.

If the lamp and a suitable battery are included in the collector circuit, a small voltage applied to the base will switch on the lamp. The transistor must be capable of handling the necessary current.

Figure 5.7

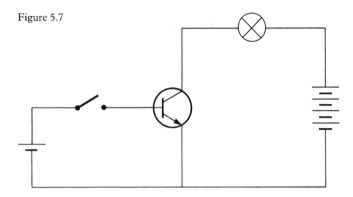

Remote control is easily achieved with a low voltage, low power circuit.

A discussion on the possible uses of bugging devices might arise from consideration of miniaturisation of semiconductor devices.

The valve market was nearly saturated by 1965, and the transistor market by 1969. Actual numbers sold may soon start to fall as integrated circuits are more widely used. The drop in price has been dramatic, an integrated circuit unit (e.g. a pair of logic gates, or an amplifier) now costing no more than an individual transistor a few years ago. The only limitation for many applications is the power dissipation: the devices can be highly efficient, controlling hundreds of times the power they dissipate, but if significant power has to be dissipated a substantial metal heat sink must be attached, to prevent undue temperature rise.

Part d

Liquid expansion is a method which has been widely used to operate automatic sprinkler systems, but other techniques are also employed. Pupils will probably suggest bimetallic strips, and possibly electrical resistance change. Another possibility is the use of a low melting-point alloy.

Part e

The response of maggots to light can be shown easily by placing them in a corked test tube. Point the end containing the maggots at a source of light. A relatively small amount of light stimulates the transfer of a much larger amount of energy in terms of maggot movement (and the respiration this implies).

▷ Part f

Regarding man as a mechanism, the signals controlling the muscles are transmitted by the nerves from the brain. Regarding the brain as a 'signal processor' is a possible approach, but is not very useful for two reasons: the relationship between input information (or signals) and the output is an excessively complex one, requiring, in effect, a description of at least the outward aspects of what we call thinking; also we are aware of the dimension of consciousness, so any attempt at 'purely objective' description of man as a mechanism tends to seem exceedingly artificial.

In certain limited and specified contexts the 'systems' approach to people can be useful, but the broader the context (i.e. the more like real life and the less like an artificially devised experiment), then the less useful it tends to be. The unpredictability of people, singly or in groups, is proverbial.

▷ Part g

Amplifiers are used in analogue computers, in instruments to record small signals (e.g. from a radiotelescope or a Geiger-Muller tube), in oscilloscopes, and in many control devices. Sound amplifiers (and various others) need fidelity, so that all audible frequencies are amplified nearly equally.

Some pupils may like to pursue the theme of electronic amplifiers. Several systems for constructing simple electronic circuits, with or without soldering, are marketed, and can save a good deal of time.

The block diagram of the amplifier would be as shown (several versions are possible).

Figure 5.8

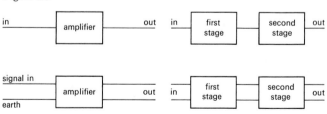

Useful graphs would be: output (a.c.) voltage against input voltage under various conditions (different frequency supply voltage), output voltage against frequency for fixed input voltage, output power against load resistance. Experiments would involve

236

applying a signal from a signal generator to the input, and measuring the output (with an oscilloscope).

Part h

The Bunsen burner provides the activation energy required to burn magnesium in air. When catalysts are employed in chemical reactions it can be assumed that their function is to lower the activation energy.

Figure 5.9a

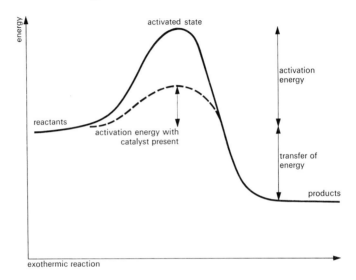

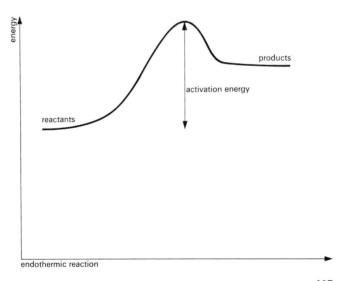

Investigation 5.17 Automatic control

This investigation is written in such a manner that the feedback of information is emphasised. Automatic control can only be achieved by some form of indication to the input that the situation differs from that intended, i.e. the feedback of information. There are various parts of such a system which can be distinguished, although on occasions two or more functions are performed by a single component. A *sensor* is needed to detect the value of the controlled variable. A *comparator* registers any difference between this and the desired value, using this difference to operate an actuator, which effects a change in the system. This changes the value of the controlled variable, and feedback occurs from sensor to comparator, leading to a (fairly) stable state achieved through equilibrium. Oscillation can occur if there is insufficient damping in the system, because of inevitable time-lags.

Part a

The water level is maintained because any drop is detected by the floating ball (sensor, comparator) which lowers the lever opening the inlet valve (actuator), which allows water to enter the tank. As the tank fills the valve is progressively shut by the rise of the ball.

Part b

The thermostat is an on/off device in most cases. Bimetallic strip versions are probably commonest in domestic situations, although differential expansion is used in some oven thermostats.

▷ Part c

The Watt governor, a remarkable invention at the time, maintains the speed of rotation, because decrease in speed leads the balls to drop, opening the steam valve to allow more power to be transmitted.

Part d

The visual feedback of information about position (and velocity) is prompt and accurate, because of familiarity. One is easily able to maintain a straight course in a desired direction. In the absence of any feedback, progressively increasing deviation from the intended course usually occurs. With indirect feedback both the small amount of information and the time delay become significant, leading to oscillation.

Part e

The iris controls the size of the pupil and hence the amount of light entering the eye. The retina registers the amount of light and the signals they send via the optic nerve are used to control the size of the pupil. The system is a reflex one which cannot be consciously controlled. Note that both irises respond even though light may be shone into only one eye.

238

▷Part f

Temperature is maintained nearly constant by a thermostat which feeds information back to an energy distribution system. Normally in this country energy has to be added to a room or building to maintain a comfortable temperature, and it is lost to the cooler atmosphere by conduction and other means. In hot countries more complex systems are needed to remove energy at certain times. In addition to temperature, humidity needs to be automatically controlled for a room to be consistently comfortable. Increasingly buildings in this country are being designed with full air conditioning, and a recent development has been to apply the concept of thermal balance to the design of buildings. A combination of low thermal losses (insulated walls and relatively small windows), high levels of illumination (around 1 000 lux), and the use of the energy dissipated by people in the building leads to designs which require no additional energy input to maintain a comfortable environment so long as the outside temperature is above 5 °C or so. Energy can be stored over periods of about a day by means of hot water vessels, and the same exchangers are used for warming or for cooling the air as necessary. Any lack of energy can be made good at night using off-peak electrical transmission. This can be illustrated diagrammatically as shown. Integrated design, as the electricity boards

Figure 5.10
Diagram to illustrate
thermal balance

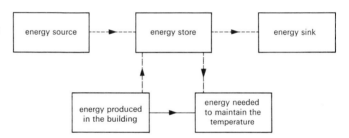

and Electricity Council call this idea, has been used in a number of prestige buildings throughout the country. The running costs are comparably lower than conventionally centrally heated buildings; capital costs are somewhat higher, but can be significantly less than a conventional building with full air conditioning.

It may be of interest to list some typical values for the power per square metre from different sources in a typical office building. These represent in total an adequate input of energy in most conditions, if thermal insulation is considered in the design of the building.

Energy source	$W\,m^{-2}$
Lighting (600–1 000 lux)	35
People	10
Office machines	5
Fans etc.	20
Cafeteria/kitchen (peak)	45
Total (peak)	115
Total (mean)	80

Part g

See Investigation 2.24 part aii. The similarities between maintaining a constant environment inside a building and maintaining a constant environment inside the body are striking. Temperature and water are both controlled, and energy loss is adjusted according to energy dissipation. There is an area in the hypothalamus region of the brain responsible for temperature control. This might be compared to a thermostat. In terms of the questions posed at the beginning of the investigations the following would be acceptable.

1 Normal body temperature.
2 Sense organs in skin detect changes in environmental temperature. Sense organs in carotid arteries detect changes in blood (body) temperature (sensors). Feedback information via nerves to the hypothalamus (comparator).
3 Information via nerves to muscles of blood vessels supplying skin causing dilation or constriction so increasing or decreasing blood supply (actuator).
4 Normal body temperature restored by conserving or dissipating energy.
5 As 2.

▷Part h

Acceptable answers to the questions posed at the beginning of the investigation:

1 population number
2 more consumers, therefore more food for predators (feedback)
3 greater numbers of predators
4 reduction in number of consumers
5 fewer consumers, therefore less food for predators (feedback)
6 fewer predators therefore 2 etc.

This is a good example of oscillation in a control system.

▷Part i

Any buffer solution could be used, although the one in the *Pupils' manual* is an ammonia/ammonium chloride solution.

0.1 M solutions used in the proportions of 1 part ammonia : 4 parts ammonium chloride give a pH of 9.5. A control solution of ammonia, again of pH 9.5, should be available.

Pupils should count the number of drops of 1.0 M hydrochloric acid needed to neutralise the buffer solution and an equal volume of ammonia solution. (Universal indicator solution should be used to show the pH of solutions.)

The following details of the buffer action need not concern pupils. The ammonium chloride is highly ionised. The ammonia is mainly present as neutral molecules.

The equilibria which exist are:

$$NH_4^+(aq) \rightarrow NH_3(aq) + H^+(aq)$$
and $H^+(aq) + OH^-(aq) \rightarrow H_2O(l)$.

Addition of $H^+(aq)$ ions results in the formation of more $NH_4^+(aq)$ ions. The pH remains nearly constant.

Pupils could repeat the experiment, but instead of adding hydrochloric acid, they could add sodium hydroxide solution. (Brilliant cresyl blue indicator must be used.) Addition of $OH^-(aq)$ ions causes the following changes:

$$H^+(aq) + OH^-(aq) \rightarrow H_2O(l)$$
$$NH_4^+(aq) \rightarrow NH_3(aq) + H^+(aq).$$

Once again, the pH remains nearly constant.

Figure 5.11
Generalised automatic control diagram showing the role of feedback

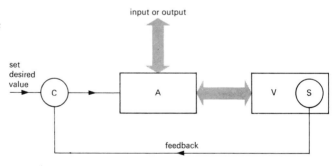

V	system for which a variable is controlled
S	Sensor
C	Comparator
A	Actuator

———→ flow of information

⬌ flow of energy or matter

241

The term 'homeostasis', meaning literally 'maintaining the same (conditions)' need not be confined, as it has been traditionally, to the biological contexts, since to do so tends to obscure the very real similarities between the diverse situations in which automatic control occurs in biology, engineering, economics and sociology. The two latter types of systems are in real- as opposed to theoretical-situations, so much more complex making full analysis impossible (at least at present). However, progress is being made in simulating such situations and developing computer models of their behaviour. In such models feedback is a key concept.

One form of generalised feedback diagram is as shown in figure 5.11 on page 241. Other versions are possible, depending on the degree of complexity desired. The way in which specific systems 'fit' this general pattern is shown in the final section of the topic book *Machines and engines*.

Investigation 5.18 Do changes in environmental temperature affect body temperature?

The obvious predictions are: no change of body temperature, and a drop of skin temperature. The apparatus and method used is that described for Investigation 2.24 part aii. Tape one thermocouple to an arm and use the other for the mouth. Record the galvanometer readings. Plunge the other arm into a bucket of ice cold water. There should be little deviation of mouth temperature but a marked drop in skin temperature caused by constriction of the blood vessels supplying the skin of the arm. The reaction would be more pronounced if both lower legs were subjected to lower temperature. The overall net effect is to maintain body temperature by reducing energy 'loss' through the skin.

▷ *Investigation 5.19* How does the body respond to a variable intake of water?

This investigation gives a very good opportunity to practise an important piece of experimental design: the 'matched control'. One problem of all investigations in biology is the variability of biological material. Sometimes this is controlled by taking large samples so that, although individuals vary, these variations tend to be cancelled out in a large number. When it is impracticable to use large samples the technique of the 'matched control' is sometimes used. In this technique, a conscious attempt is made to identify as many as possible of the variable factors and then to pair each experimental subject with a control subject which matches the experimental subject in all variables except the one under test.

Pupils are paired off as evenly as possible, each pair being matched for such characteristics as mass or preferably surface area, and the expected degree of physical activity during the day.

Each pupil undertakes to measure accurately the whole of the urine output in a day and is provided with a measuring cylinder or a plastic wide-mouthed 2-litre kitchen measure for the purpose; these must be rinsed with diluted domestic bleach after use. The urine produced during the night and expelled first thing in the morning is not counted. Each pair keeps together for as much of the day as possible, undertaking the same activities and consuming as far as possible the same quantities of fluid. One member of the pair, however, takes an extra pint of fluid during the morning and another pint during the afternoon. They must reach prior agreement about the quantity to be taken after school. If a number of pairs are involved, the amount of extra fluid taken could be varied and the results plotted on a graph to show the extra fluid intake against the amount of extra urine produced.

Other methods of controlling the experiment might be used, for example:

i dividing the class at random into a control group and an experimental group and pooling the results from each;

ii taking measurements over two days, the whole class being the experimental group one day and the control group the next day.

▷ *Investigation 5.20* The kidney: an organ of control

This investigation closely follows Nuffield Biology Year IV, Chapter 14. The blood supply of the kidneys is brought to the attention of pupils because it is in this medium in which wastes and excesses are transported to the kidneys. Urine is voided via the urethra upon relaxation of a sphincter muscle at the base of the bladder. In bisecting a kidney (groups of four or more pupils to economise) a sharp scalpel should be used. The kidney should be cut in a vertical plane down its widest axis. *Patterns 3*, figure 5.32 shows the appearance of the bisected kidney) and the Bowman's capsules in the cortex. Microslides or transparencies made from injected specimens clearly show the glomerulus situated in the Bowman's capsule (*Patterns 3*, figures 5.34 and 5.35).

Figure 5.36 in *Patterns 3* illustrates a single nephron and associated blood vessels. The nephrons provide a formidable 'filtration' plant. Wastes and excesses, such as water, are carried in the blood to the glomerulus. Blood pressure (note that the capillary leaving the glomerulus is slightly smaller than that entering) forces all material, except blood cells and very large molecules such as protein, through the capillary and capsule walls which are only one cell thick. The glomerulus and capsule act as a dialyser (see *Patterns 1*, Section 6). The capillary leaving the glomerulus then extends to the rest of the nephron. Here, useful materials (e.g. necessary water and glucose) are

243

progressively reabsorbed into the blood leaving wastes and any excess materials to pass to the collecting duct and hence to the ureter for eventual storage in the bladder as urine. From the details given, pupils may be able to suggest something of this simplified account at least in respect to water. The further details, shown in the table, may help.

Sample of fluid from	Blood plasma	Bowman's capsule	End of first convolution	Collecting duct
Flow rate	500	100	20	1
Protein concentration	a	nil	nil	nil
Glucose concentration	b	b	nil	nil
Urea concentration	c	c	$3c$	$60c$
Na^+ concentration	d	d	d	$2d$
NH_4^+ concentration	e	e	e	$150e$

Figures are quoted as an arbitrary index taking the blood plasma level as the base level.

Flow rate is an indication of the quantity of water and its drop is the direct cause of changes in the solute indices.

The above account necessarily avoids many complexities. For further details see any general biology text.

Patterns 3, figure 5.37 shows that the kidney does respond to increased protein nitrogen in the diet by a higher level of excretion. However, the level of nitrogen in the blood also rises. The kidney is not therefore very precise in its control: rather it keeps the level of nitrogen in the body within tolerable limits.

Sample questions

1 The transfer of energy for the interaction

$$C + O_2 \rightarrow CO_2$$
(coke) (air)

is 22.5 kJ mole^{-1} if one mole of carbon is burned. If the stove burning the coke is 25 per cent efficient, what would be the corresponding increase in energy for a pan of water placed on top of the fire?

2 About how many $\frac{1}{4}$-litre cups of tea could be made from ice cold water (0 °C) when 1 litre of paraffin is burnt, assuming the stove is 50 per cent efficient? (Transfer of energy when paraffin is burnt is $3\,\text{kJ}\,\text{g}^{-1}$; density of paraffin is $800\,\text{kg}\,\text{m}^{-3}$.)

A 2
B 20
C 200 (correct)
D 2 000

3 A boy scout is trying to light a fire by twirling a hard pointed stick so that the point rubs in a hollow in a wooden block, using a bow to rotate the stick (see diagram):

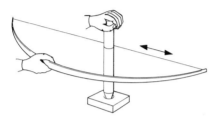

a If the 'machine' has an efficiency of 60 per cent, and he exerts a force of 15 N through 0.60 m each time he pushes the bow forward or pulls it back, how much energy is transferred from his muscles to the point and hollow in each double stroke (forward and backward)?

A 10.8 J (correct)
B 12.0 J
C 18.0 J
D 30.0 J

b Assuming that the intention is to warm 0.1 g of wood from normal temperature (300 K) to red heat (900 K) and ignoring any energy lost or gained through burning, how much energy is required to heat up the wood? The specific thermal capacity of wood is $1\,200\,\text{J}\,\text{kg}^{-1}\,\text{K}^{-1}$.

A 20 J
B 50 J
C 72 J (correct)
D 200 J

c If the required energy is supplied after 200 double strokes of the bow, roughly what percentage of the available energy is retained in the 0.1 g of wood?

A 9 per cent
B 4 per cent
C 3 per cent (correct)
D 1 per cent

4 Waves of many sorts are used to transfer information. In each of the following cases indicate whether the statement 'Transfer of information is more important than transfer of energy' is true or false.

a a solar cooker (F)   d a room light (F)
b a telephone (T)   e a lighthouse light (T)
c an echo sounder (T)   f a baby crying (T)

5 Energy transfer from a system can always be equated with energy transferred to other systems, i.e. energy is conserved. During an experiment a battery is used to drive a motor which lifts a load and it is noted that during the process, the temperature of the motor rises. In a second experiment an identical battery is used to drive an identical motor, but the load is not lifted. Assume that the energy transfer from the two batteries is the same and that no energy is lost from the motors to the surroundings (they are well insulated).

Which one of the following statements about the temperature rise of the two motors can be made?

A the temperature of the first motor will rise more
B the temperature of the second motor will rise more (correct)
C the temperature rise will be the same
D it is impossible to use this pattern to predict anything about the temperature rise of the motors

6 The following devices are used to raise a load through 2 m. Assume that all the devices are 100 per cent efficient.

Device	Effort needed to raise load/N	Distance effort moves/m	Load/N
2-pulley system	40	1.0	20
lever	80	0.5	40
capstan and pulley	10	8.0	40
6-pulley system	50	12.0	300
hydraulic jack	200	50.0	500

Using this data, which one of the following patterns explains the observations?

A the devices are force multipliers
B devices involving pulleys are distance multipliers
C the distance moved by the effort is proportional to the distance moved by the load (correct)
D the devices are either force multipliers or distance multipliers but they all do the same amount of work (measured as force × distance)

7 The effects of temperature rises on the viscosity ('thickness') of five oils are shown in the sketched graphs (which are taken from an oil manufacturer's publication).

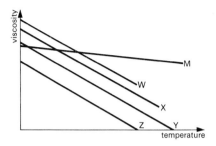

Graphs W, X, Y and Z refer to single grade oils; graph M refers to a multigrade oil.

Which one of the following statements is the best pattern which can be deduced from these graphs?

A viscosity measurements show that multigrade oil is a mixture of four single grade oils

B the viscosity of single grade oil does not decrease to the same extent as multigrade oil for the same temperature rise

C the viscosity of single grade oil decreases as the temperature increases, whereas the viscosity of multigrade oil increases with increase in temperature

D the viscosity of all four single grade oils and of the multigrade oil regularly decreases as the temperature increases (correct)

8 In steel making the ore has to be raised to a considerable height in order to put it into the furnace.

a In calculating how much fuel would be needed in a week to do this job, which of the following patterns must be used? You can assume that the quantity of ore to be used is known.

i work = force × distance

ii power = rate of transfer of energy

iii efficiency $= \dfrac{\text{energy transferred as desired}}{\text{total energy transferred}}$

    A only i and ii

    B only ii and iii

    C only i and iii (correct)

    D i, ii and iii

    You will need to use some or all of the following information to answer 9b and c.

Mass of ore used in one week 5×10^6 kg

Density of ore	$5 \times 10^3 \, \text{kg m}^{-3}$
Height raised	$25 \, \text{m}$
Pull of gravity on 1 kg	$10 \, \text{N}$
One week equals	$6 \times 10^5 \, \text{s}$
Efficiency of engine	25 per cent
Efficiency of rest of machine	50 per cent
Energy of combustion of 1 kg of coal	$2 \times 10^7 \, \text{J}$

b In one week how much energy would be transferred to the iron ore in lifting it?

A $2.5 \times 10^7 \, \text{J}$

B $1.25 \times 10^8 \, \text{J}$

C $2.5 \times 10^8 \, \text{J}$

D $1.25 \times 10^9 \, \text{J}$ (correct)

c How much coal would be needed in a week to do this?

A 23.4 kg

B 117 kg

C 125 kg

D 500 kg (correct)

9 Coal fires are known to be extremely inefficient. What, therefore, are the advantages of a coal fire in the home? Are there disadvantages in addition to the inefficiancy?

10 At present, man's main source of protein food is meat but there is a progressive shortage of protein throughout the world. Two kinds of experiment are in progress to ease this situation:

i those designed to increase the yield from animals by selective breeding, etc. and

ii those designed to investigate methods of obtaining protein foods directly from plant material.

Write an essay, indicating why you would favour one of these lines of enquiry rather than the other.

11 The graph shows the food intake of United States soldiers in different climatic conditions. In terms of energy value, the soldiers could eat as much as they liked. (Each measurement is an average for groups of 50 or more men.)

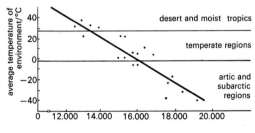

Which of the following would not be a contributing factor to the pattern shown?

A the men in the colder climate are given a more balanced diet (correct)

B energy is being spread to the surroundings

C the effects of much heavier clothing in colder climates

D the necessity to maintain constant body temperature

12 Which one of the following agricultural practices would be least likely to improve efficiency of energy transfer between links in food chains important to man?

A feeding livestock with processed foods from available plant sources

B production of eggs by battery hens

C raising livestock on grassland (correct)

D raising livestock in specially constructed warm, surroundings

13 Several laboratory based food chains were set up in aquaria to investigate the variation in size of a population of *Daphnia* (water flea) subjected to different levels of feeding and predation. The food supplied to the *Daphnia* was the green algae *Chlamydamonas* which was added at three different levels. Level 1 was one ration per day; level 2, two rations per day; and level 3, three rations per day. The *Daphnia* were 'predated' by man who took out from 5 per cent to 80 per cent of the young every four days. A sensitive method for determining the mass of *Daphnia* removed every four days was available. The results of one set of experiments are shown graphically below.

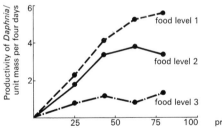

The most efficient use of the food occurred at:

A the maximum predation level (80 per cent) and the maximum food supply (level 3)

B the minimum predation level (5 per cent) and the minimum food supply (level 1)

C the maximum predation level (80 per cent) and the minimum food supply (level 1) (correct)

D the minimum predation level (5 per cent) and the maximum food supply (level 3)

14 The growth of hens declines markedly 3–4 months after hatching. Hens begin to lay eggs at 5–6 months old. Which would be the best course of action to follow if attempting to improve food production (assume that the amount of food needed by hens is constant throughout life and that a supply of young chicks is available).

A kill the hens for meat when 5–6 months old

B kill the hens for meat when 3–4 months old (correct)

C allow the hens to live to produce eggs as long as they are able

D allow the hens to produce eggs for a short period and then kill for meat

15 Give reasons for selecting your answer to question 14.

16 Study the food web shown below and answer the question which follows

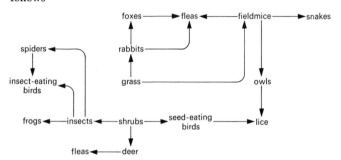

Which one of the following groups of organisms would probably have the greatest total mass:

A foxes, owls, frogs, insect-eating birds, spiders, snakes

B field mice, seed-eating birds, insects, rabbits, deer

C grass and shrubs (correct)

D lice and fleas

17 Which of the following represents homeostasis?

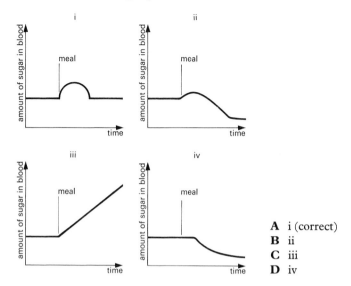

A i (correct)
B ii
C iii
D iv

18 Animals which live in deserts (such as the familiar gerbils) rarely drink water but the amount of water present in their body varies little between wet and dry seasons. Some animals were kept in two sets of controlled laboratory conditions in which dry food but no water was supplied. The following results were obtained.

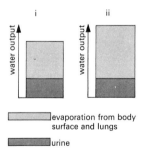

☐ evaporation from body
surface and lungs

▨ urine

The temperature was kept the same in both cases, but the moisture content of the air in ii was kept lower than i.

Which one of the following will be most likely to happen to the animals in i?

A respire more (correct)
B respire less
C spend a great deal of time curled up in a ball
D breathe more slowly

Index

Bold figures indicate diagrams.